Call Her a Citizen

NUMBER 114
Centennial Series of the Association of Former Students
TEXAS A&M UNIVERSITY

KELLEY M. KING

Call Her a Citizen

PROGRESSIVE-ERA ACTIVIST AND EDUCATOR ANNA PENNYBACKER

TEXAS A&M UNIVERSITY PRESS
College Station

First edition

This paper meets the requirements of ANSI/NISO Z39.48–1992 (Permanence of Paper).
Binding materials have been chosen for durability.

ON THE COVER: Anna Pennybacker (r) and Eleanor Roosevelt (l) at the Chautauqua Women's Club. Photograph by Harold Wagner, the Chautauqua Institution.

LIBRARY OF CONGRESS CATALOGING-IN-PUBLICATION DATA
King, Kelley M. (Kelley Marie), 1964–
Call her a citizen : progressive-era activist and educator Anna Pennybacker / Kelley M. King.—1st ed.
p. : ill. ; cm.—(Centennial series of the Association of Former Students, Texas A&M University ; no. 114)
Includes bibliographical references and index.
ISBN-13: 978–1-60344–185–8 (hardcover : alk. paper)
ISBN-10: 1–60344–185–9 (hardcover : alk. paper) 1. Pennybacker, Percy V., Mrs., 1861–1938. 2. Educators—Texas—Biography. 3. Women educators—Texas—Biography. 4. Social reformers—Texas—Biography. 5. Women social reformers—Texas—Biography. 6. Texas Federation of Women's Clubs—History. 7. General Federation of Women's Clubs—History. 8. United States—History—1913–1921. 9. Texas—History—1846–1950. I. Title. II. Series: Centennial series of the Association of Former Students, Texas A&M University ; no. 114.
CT275.P56K45 2010
303.48′4092—dc22
[B]

2009035817

CONTENTS

LIST OF ILLUSTRATIONS

(see gallery following page xviii)

ACKNOWLEDGMENTS

MANY PEOPLE AND ORGANIZATIONS contributed to the completion of this work. I thank especially O. L. Davis Jr. for introducing me to Anna Pennybacker and suggesting her life and work were worthy of in-depth study. His careful comments and editing have shaped every part of this work. Don Carleton, director of the Center for American History at the University of Texas, provided invaluable insight into the wealth of resources available there. Dr. Carleton, Sherry Field, Mary Lee Webeck, and Chara Bohan provided unfailing encouragement and insightful feedback, and David Alexander provided wise guidance in difficult times. The librarians, archivists, and other staff at the Center for American History, the University of Texas, the University of North Texas, Texas Women's University, and the General Federation of Women's Clubs provided such knowledgeable and pleasant support that I enjoyed my many hours of research in these collections. Thank you especially to Ann Barton of the Blagg-Huey Library Women's Collection at Texas Women's University. Her precise knowledge of the Texas Federation of Women's Clubs provided essential clues to deciphering sometimes cryptic letters. I have greatly appreciated the time and efforts of Dawn Letson at Texas Woman's University and Jonathan Schmitz and Jason Rodriguez at the Chautauqua Institution who were invaluable in helping me locate images of Anna Pennybacker to include here. Thank you as well to my reviewers and editors at Texas A&M University Press for their careful reading and detailed, insightful comments.

Institutional support for this project took many forms. The University of North Texas has supported my work for the last three years and has funded my travel to numerous conferences to discuss Anna Pennybacker's life and work. Research travel and other expenses were covered in part by the Ellen Clarke Temple Award in the Study of Women and by a travel grant from the General Federation of Women's Clubs. My biggest debt is to my parents, Hugh and Diane King, who cared more for my children than any grandparents should be called on to do. Without them, none of this would have been possible. Finally, I thank my children, Vashti and Elijah—Eli for completing homework at a dining table littered with drafts and books, and Vashti for delaying flute practice each night until Mom was done writing.

INTRODUCTION

MRS. PERCIVAL V. PENNYBACKER, born Anna McLaughlin Hardwicke, was a Texas educator, clubwoman, writer, lecturer, and social and political activist whose influence in the early twentieth century extended nationwide. As an educator and social activist, Pennybacker was influential in promoting public education, women's suffrage, social reform, and the League of Nations. Born in the American South in 1861, she was certainly influenced by nineteenth century ideals of southern womanhood, which demanded that a southern lady be a moral force exercising indirect influence over southern culture by her actions within a subordinate, domestic sphere. However, the Reconstruction years brought about changes for women in the South that increased their educational and career opportunities and allowed some women the leisure to participate in voluntary associations.[1] Even as a young woman in the waning years of the Victorian Era, Pennybacker's ideas and activities leaned toward the progressive, as she took full advantage of the opportunities becoming available for southern women. Pennybacker would reach her most productive middle years at the peak of the Progressive Era, and she would become one of the leading progressive women of her time. The Progressive Era, roughly 1895 to 1920, brought a wave of social, political, and economic reforms, as Americans struggled to understand and adapt to the immense changes wrought by industrialization and urbanization. Gilded Age laissez-faire policies had brought about growing disparities among the wealthy and the working people, and the Progressive Era brought to the fore questions about the role of government in regulating industry and protecting citizens. Americans of the era rethought the meanings of democracy and citizenship.[2] Anna Pennybacker both shaped and was shaped by the many ideas and movements of the era, and these themes shaped her life and work.

Anna spent the early years of her life in Virginia, North Carolina, West Virginia, and Kansas. Having graduated from high school in Leavenworth, Kansas, in 1878, she moved to Texas with her family that same year. In 1879 she won a scholarship to attend the first Normal School for Teachers in Huntsville, Texas, where she met Percival V. Pennybacker, her future husband. Together they worked to develop fledgling public school systems in Bryan, Tyler, and Palestine, Texas.[3] In 1888, as a young teacher, Pennybacker wrote *A New History of Texas,* which was to become the state-adopted textbook for Texas history for many years. Pennybacker's husband published and marketed the book until his death in 1899. That year, Pennybacker took over the family's financial affairs, including those related to the textbook. In 1900, she and her three young children moved to Austin as she and Percy had earlier planned. Prior to this move, Pennybacker had become involved in the growing women's club movement. Subsequently, in the early 1900s, she held several elected positions, including the presidency, in the Texas Federation of Women's Clubs. Her role in the Texas federation led her to national prominence as the president of the largest women's organization in the country, the General Federation of Women's Clubs. Women's clubs wielded surprising political power in their day as they pushed for social reforms, education, and cultural improvement. The Texas Federation of Women's Clubs, for example, claims credit for establishing more than 70 percent of the libraries in Texas, building a women's dormitory at the University of Texas, and founding Texas Women's University.[4]

During World War I, she worked with the War Camp Community Service to better conditions for the nation's military personnel. In the teens and twenties, she supported the woman's suffrage movement in Texas and nationwide. She served as a trustee of Carrie Chapman Catt's Leslie Woman Suffrage Commission and worked with the Texas Equal Suffrage Association and the National American Woman Suffrage Association to gain for American women the right to vote, although her dedication to this cause was sometimes questioned. In 1919, prior to and in preparation for women's suffrage, she attended the Democratic National Committee as an associate member. She supported the founding of the World Court and League of Nations and regularly attended meetings of the latter organization in Geneva. She also supported a wide range of progressive causes, including increasing government support for women and children through programs such as the federal Children's

Bureau, the Sheppard-Towner Maternity and Infancy Act, and vocational education, including home economics, for women. Pennybacker sustained a fourteen-year friendship with Eleanor Roosevelt, which began when the Roosevelts lived in New York, and continued into FDR's presidency. She traveled throughout Europe and the United States, lecturing on the many issues that were important to her, and her articles were published popular national magazines. For a short time, she wrote a regular column for the *Ladies' Home Journal.*

Educated as a teacher, Pennybacker continued her involvement in education throughout her life. In 1925 and 1926, she took part in a historic Texas state survey of education, and for most of her life she vacationed at New York's Chautauqua Institute, a resort dedicated to education and cultural edification. In her later years, she applied much of her energy to continuing the Institute by garnering the social and financial support of prominent citizens, including the Roosevelts. Pennybacker, an ardent supporter of public schools, understood the educational possibilities of institutions other than schools and worked with a wide range of organizations and institutions to promote education and learning opportunities for the general public and for women in particular. She understood her civic participation to be an extension of her role as teacher.

In her history of female teachers, Nancy Hoffman argues that early biographies of nineteenth- and early-twentieth-century American teachers could be characterized as hagiographies.[5] The women are portrayed as saints, rather than being examined in their complexity. The same can be said of existing accounts of Anna Pennybacker's life. Pennybacker is the subject of two biographical books: Helen Knox's *Mrs. Percy V. Pennybacker, an Appreciation* (1916) and Rebecca Richmond's *A Woman of Texas: Mrs. Percy V. Pennybacker* (1941). These accounts are uncritically adulatory of Pennybacker and thus do not provide a comprehensive picture of her politics or her life. Arguably Pennybacker can be understood as taking part in what has been called the "first wave of American feminism" which arose in the nineteenth century and continued into the early twentieth century. This wave of feminism focused on social reform and women's suffrage and waned in the 1920s after achieving suffrage. The use of the term "feminism," however, is not without complication. Certainly Pennybacker was active in many of the social movements of the time that we now consider related to early feminism in the United States. However, having made its way from Europe, the term was just coming into use in the United States in the 1910s, and its meaning was and remains imprecise. The early uses of the term in the

United States were often derogatory and meant to diminish the women it described. Those women who adopted it early on tended to be less conciliatory toward existing structures of gender, race, economics, and power. Anna Pennybacker preferred to cast herself as a southern lady in many respects, and she remained concerned always to maintain proper public decorum and to manage her public image. She most likely would not have used the term for herself, nor would those who called themselves feminists have included her when using the term. However, Pennybacker clearly saw herself as part of a women's movement which at the time was broader in terms of participation and which helped to lay the groundwork for activists who would adopt the term "feminist."[6]

The twentieth-century U.S. women's movements have often been criticized for overlooking how upper- or upper-middle-class white values have shaped goals for women.[7] This critique appears to be true of Pennybacker as well. Although an ardent reformer, Pennybacker appears to have accepted and promoted many of the dominant values of her time. The General Federation of Women's Clubs, for example, excluded African American women,[8] and women's suffrage was linked to issues of race and ethnicity, with some southern suffragists arguing that middle-class white women's votes would serve to counter those of black men and resident aliens.[9] Additionally, although struggles between labor and capital were a key feature of her times, Pennybacker had little interaction with the labor movement.

My exploration of Pennybacker's life and work relies on existing histories of progressivism, women's suffrage, and the early-twentieth-century women's movement. In this work I have addressed the following broad questions: Who was Anna Pennybacker? What did she accomplish? What were her beliefs about politics, education, and the role of women in society? How did these beliefs shape her accomplishments? What were the ideological, economic, political, and cultural imperatives and constraints that affected her life? How did she operate within these imperatives and constraints to effect social change? Why was she important in her time and why does she merit attention now?

My work seeks to portray Pennybacker's life in greater complexity than has been done heretofore, as well as to offer insight into the personal and political choices she made, and the impact these choices had in her life and the culture at large. As I do so, I recognize that the depiction I present is my interpretation of Pennybacker's life. Still, I have sought to present both my understanding of who Pennybacker was as well as my understanding of how she understood both herself and her life. Pennybacker had a rich personal life that cannot be entirely separated from her professional life. Although I touch on her personal life here, I primarily focus on her public work. I focus on her work for a number of reasons. First, given the wealth of materials documenting Pennybacker's life (Pennybacker's manuscript files at the University of Texas Center for American History span fifty-two linear feet), I necessarily had to frame this work. Second, existing archival materials document her work more so than her personal life, and my research at other institutions leads me to believe that Pennybacker's work is fairly well represented in these documents. This is less the case with Pennybacker's personal life. Discretion regarding personal matters seems to have been the custom for Pennybacker. Thus existing letters regarding important personal events frequently gloss over details of her personal life. Tracing these details would have been difficult, if not impossible.

In her history of the women's club movement in the U.S. Northwest, Sandra Harsanger argues that American clubwomen failed to get credit for their many accomplishments "because the women in these clubs did not possess the formal political power to enact measures or the financial means to sustain their designs."[10] Municipalities and legislatures (and the men who ran them) took credit, and the women's clubs, pleased to have accomplished their social goals, encouraged this. Harsanger's argument that clubwomen have not received credit for their achievements because they did not possess the "formal" political power reserved for males rings true for Anna Pennybacker's life as well. In writing a Pennybacker biography, I will engage in the discovering of what Barbara Ryan calls a "hidden history."[11] Ryan notes the importance of activist women's lives for "historical and present knowledge bases." In reading about the lives of women activists, Ryan notes, we learn about their "beliefs, joys, sorrows, and life choices" as well as their social world and the way they interact with and change it.[12] Pennybacker, like many female activists, has been left out of conventional, male-centered histories. Despite her centrality to some of the major social movements of her time, she has been omitted from almost all women's histories as well. "Well behaved women seldom make history," wrote Laurel Ulrich Thatcher and the now ubiquitous maxim rings true in Pennybacker's case, at least in the sense that making history means being remembered by history.[13] The Progressive Era women remembered by history are often those who flouted social conventions much more than did Pennybacker. Her life includes no stories of arrests and force feedings and no overtly revolutionary speeches. Still, if making history is understood to mean actively participating in the culture and events of one's time and of having an impact in the world, Pennybacker did make history and her work deserves examination. Pennybacker's work should be of interest to scholars of American history, Texas history, the Progressive Era, and twentieth-century women's movements. It might, as well, be of interest to a current generation of activists, especially female activists, who seek to understand how those who have come before them worked through and around social expectations for female behavior in order to take on roles of influence and power.

Call Her a Citizen

FIG. 1. Anna Pennybacker as president of the Texas Federation of Women's Clubs, 1901–1903. Courtesy of the Women's Collection, Blagg-Huey Library, Texas Women's University.

FIG. 2. Anna Pennybacker in middle age. Photograph from the Chautauqua Institution, Smith Memorial Library.

FIG. 3. Anna Pennybacker at Chautauqua's 1928 week on foreign relations. *From left to right*: James T. Shotwell, attendee of the Paris Peace Conference under President Wilson; two unidentified women; Bettie Manroe Sippell, president of the General Federation of Women's Clubs, 1928–1932; Pennybacker; Carrie Chapman Catt; and Chautauqua's Arthur Bestor. Photograph by Harold Wagner, the Chautauqua Institution.

FIG. 4. Anna Pennybacker with prominent women at the Chautauqua Women's Club. *From left to right*: Mrs. Thomas Edison, Mrs. Henry Ford, Mrs. Pennybacker (standing), Mary Miller Nichols, Anne Studebaker Carlisle, and Mrs. Robert A. Miller. Photograph by Harold Wagner, the Chautauqua Institution.

FIG. 5. Sketch of Anna Pennybacker by well-known illustrator Violet Oakley, Geneva, 1927.

FIG. 6. Anna Pennybacker (r) and Eleanor Roosevelt (l) at the Chautauqua Women's Club. Photograph by Harold Wagner, the Chautauqua Institution.

Chapter One

1861–1880

Early Life and Career

RESIDENTS OF PETERSBURG, VIRGINIA, who numbered about eighteen thousand in 1860, realized that the election of Abraham Lincoln in November of that year threatened the economic and social systems on which the city, state, and region were based.[1] In Petersburg, as in much of the South, the tension consumed the minds and emotions of the residents. The first half of 1861 saw southern states respond with a flurry of secessions in response to Lincoln's election. South Carolina seceded in December 1860, followed by Mississippi, Florida, Alabama, Georgia, Louisiana, and Texas in the weeks between January 10 and February 9, 1861. February brought the birth of the Confederate States of America and the inauguration of Jefferson Davis as its president. In April, with the attack on Fort Sumter, the Civil War began. May 6 made it official: Tennessee and Arkansas joined the secession, and the Confederacy recognized a state of war with the United States.[2]

Against this backdrop, Anna Hardwicke was born on May 7, 1861. A girl's birth in Petersburg, Virginia, to native Virginians Martha and John Benjamin Hardwicke a day after the Confederacy declared war against the United States hardly seems of historic consequence. However, the historical circumstances surrounding her birth, that she was born a southerner in a state that would soon join the Confederacy, would be of consequence to newborn Anna for the rest of her life.

Anna's parents were of old Virginian stock, descended from established families. John Benjamin Hardwick, or J. B. as he was called, was born in Buckingham County, Virginia, on August 9, 1830, to Samuel P. Hardwicke and Lucy Hudson Flood, the daughter of Capt. John Flood and granddaughter of the Reverend Noah Flood. J. B., named for his grandfather Hardwicke, a Baptist preacher, was the eldest of fifteen children, two of whom died in infancy. Perhaps unsurprisingly, given clergy on both his paternal and maternal sides, J. B. was religiously active as a youth. In 1842, at the age of twelve, he made a profession of faith and united with the Enon Baptist Church. Ten years later, in 1852, he became an ordained minister serving two Baptist churches in Campbell County, Virginia, before moving to Greenfield, Virginia. A "ponderous" man, J. B. stood six feet tall and was possessed of stern, square features, dark eyes, a full mustache and beard, and mass of thick, dark hair.[3] Despite his imposing features, J. B. would be remembered by family members as "empathetically a peacemaker though of impulsive nature." A gifted speaker and writer, he swiftly became "prominent among the young preachers of the country."[4] In Greenfield, he worked to rescue churches from the "growing influence of anti-mission teachers."[5] He remained in Greenfield until 1860, when he moved with his young family to Petersburg, Virginia.[6]

J. B. married Anna's mother, Martha Jane Dews, on November 6, 1855, when both were twenty-five years old. Martha was the daughter of native Virginians, William Dews and Nancy Ellington Dews. Her parents had the financial means to "give her every opportunity," and she has been described as lovely, "possessing the usual accomplishments of the Virginia belle of the day."[7] She was, in addition, "far in advance in mental qualifications," with a gift for figures and a love of study, despite an unremarkable education that, as was the custom for Virginia belles of the time, ended when she was sixteen. The education available for women of South during her youth in the 1850s was "light, physically and mentally." Girls at boarding schools and seminaries studied toward " 'a superficial knowledge of twenty branches of learning' without a true comprehension of any."[8] Despite the early end to her formal education, Martha would continue attempts to enrich herself through study throughout her life.[9] Martha's beauty, accomplishments, and social standing made her highly sought after as a wife. Despite this relatively comfortable beginning, however, Martha already had experienced enormous loss in the short years of her adult life. She was a widow when she married J. B. Hardwicke, having previously been married to Dr. William Holland. While married to Holland, she bore three children, all of whom died in infancy. A picture of her as a young woman portrays a slight, serious-looking woman with dark hair and eyes. Although she appears timid in her picture, she is reported to have had a sparkling personality. In later years, she enjoyed socializing with Anna and her friends.[10]

J. B. and Martha moved to Petersburg, Virginia, in 1860, when he accepted a position at its Second Baptist Church. Anna was born there less than a year later. Anna was thirty-year-old J. B.'s third child, the sixth borne by her mother, and the seventh child in the household. Anna's large family included two older full brothers: four-year-old Andrew Fuller Hardwicke, born in Pittsylvania County, Virginia, in August 1856, and Samuel Poindexter Hardwicke, born in near Riceville, Virginia, in October 1858, making him two years old at the time of Anna's birth. In addition, although Martha's three children by her first husband died, she continued to care for four stepchildren from Holland's previous marriage, and these children lived in the Hardwicke household. In the twelve years following Anna's birth, the family would see the births of five more children: Leola in December 1863, John Benjamin Jr. in September 1865; and Martha Dews, who was born in 1867, but who died ten months later. Sallie Hardwicke, born in September 1870, would be Anna's only surviving sister. Her youngest brother, Abel Sinnat, known as Sinnette, was born in 1873. In addition to Martha and J.B.'s many children, around the time of Anna's first birthday, her paternal uncle, seven-year-old Richard Edward Hardwicke, joined the household upon the death of his and John Benjamin's mother, Anna's paternal grandmother, Lucy Hudson Flood Hardwicke. Richard's father and Anna's paternal grandfather, Samuel P. Hardwicke, had died little more than a year earlier, the month before Anna was born. Richard's arrival would have made Anna the eighth youngest of the household's thirteen children, not all of whom lived past childhood.

THE CIVIL WAR YEARS

War came swiftly to Petersburg. Just two weeks after Anna's birth, Virginia officially joined the Confederacy. The war years likely were years of privation for the Hardwicke family, as they were for many others. Accounts of daily life in the South during the war tell of families used to a comfortable lifestyle adapting to greatly reduced conditions. One woman reminisced that "corn bread formed the sole bill of fare at meals in families accustomed to comfort and even luxury. Imitation coffee often became a luxury out of reach of many unless taken without sugar or cream, especially during the last two years of the war." She continued, "If a family could afford a slice of meat around for dinner, and home-made molasses at other meals, they considered themselves fortunate, and pitied the poor. . . . New clothes couldn't be thought of by the majority."[11] Petersburg, situated on the James River, was a seaport as well as a railroad center through which ran supply lines into the Confederate capital, Richmond. For these reasons the city was important militarily.[12] The city filled rapidly with soldiers and supplies. Rebecca Richmond speculates that Martha, "lying with her new baby beside her," would have heard from beyond her windows "the measured tread of men, the clap-clap of the hoofs of cavalry horses, and the rumble of wagons loaded with the household goods of families goaded into flight by apprehension of the approach of war."[13] Despite the tensions, the Hardwicke family remained in Petersburg for some time. J. B. joined the Confederate Army as a chaplain, and split his time between his church and the military hospitals established in Petersburg during the war.[14] Anna's earliest memories of him are of a "big man in Confederate gray."[15]

In June 1864, Petersburg came under siege as Union general Ulysses Grant attacked Confederate general Robert E. Lee's armies in an attempt to seize transportation arteries and isolate Richmond. Petersburg would be the locus of fighting for the next six months.[16] With much of Virginia a battlefield, Martha and the children, including three-year-old Anna, fled the state, seeking refuge in Fayetteville, North Carolina. Many others from Petersburg joined this quiet exodus. The influx of people to Fayetteville during the war brought additional hardships as food became scarce. One resident recalled, "The town was never a very good market for fresh meats, butter, etc., but when it became crowded with refugees from down the river and the increase attendant on the many new operatives and officials employed in the new and comparatively extensive works carried on at the Arsenal, these articles became luxuries reserved for those whose wealth still continued available, and they were by no means a large class."[17] Although farther south than Petersburg, Fayetteville soon felt the incursion of Union troops. A family story from Anna's childhood tells of the Hardwicke's home being raided by federal troops seeking supplies. When the Hardwickes' home was searched, the raiders discovered a small supply of flour that Martha had concealed in a barrel she had disguised as a dressing table. Also discovered was J. B.'s Masonic apron. Upon that discovery and the understanding that the house belonged to a fellow Mason, the Union soldiers left the home and later offered a guard for the Hardwicke family, as Martha was alone with the children. The family found itself under the protection of a young Yankee lieutenant whom Anna quickly befriended. An intelligent little girl with engaging dimples, Anna charmed the lieutenant, and he entertained her with stories. One day, however, eyeing the buttons on the young man's uniform, Anna recognized that he wasn't a Confederate soldier and began wailing, convinced that her friend's Yankee affiliation meant that he would be barred from heaven upon his death. Earlier biographers make clear that Anna's beliefs regarding God's opinion of the Yankees came from playmates and acquaintances, and were not imbued by her family.[18]

Presumably Martha and the Hardwicke children would have been in Fayetteville when news of General Lee's surrender reached the town. One Fayetteville resident described how, in April 1865, a battalion of Confederate cavalry passed through town with the news. The girls from town had lined the main road to offer flowers and "encouraging smiles" to the soldiers, as rations were so low they had no meat or other supplies to offer. When riders approached with news of Lee's surrender, the women "begged the soldiers not to give up" as they could not believe it "possible that the South was really subdued." In the wake of defeat, citizens of the South were traumatized to realize that, as one woman expressed, "All the privations, self-denials, losses, had been in vain. All the precious lives had been sacrificed, and for what? Defeat at last. . . . The earth seemed turned upside down, and chaos seemed to reign."[19] The Hardwickes could hardly have been immune to the troubles of the time. However, the reaction in the Hardwicke home to news of the defeat is unknown, as are many of the details of the family's postwar years. If these years were particularly difficult for the Hardwickes, the family left no documentation. Family lore is silent with regard to postwar hardships. However, the family reputedly harbored no animosity toward the Union states, and J. B. and Martha "impressed upon their children that it was the hangers-on of the armies who were responsible for the outrages."[20]

A BLUESTOCKING MIND

For young Anna, the war's end reunited her family. Her father's return provided great pleasure to her, as she was, or became, particularly close to him. After the war, J. B. held pastorates in Goldborough, North Carolina, and Parkersburg, West Virginia, before moving the family to Kansas, and then to Texas. Each new position required uprooting an ever-expanding family. Anna's parents fervently believed in education, and, despite the many relocations, the family library remained the center of the household. In a family in which "books were taken as much for granted as daily food" and the children were allowed to read without restriction, Anna learned to read by age four. A precocious child and an avid student, she spent hours with her father in his study reading. Her love of study was so great that long after others in the household had retired for the night, Anna remained her father's study reading "until the wee hours of the morning."[21] She did not, as would have been the custom of the time, spend much time assisting her mother with the care of her five younger siblings, and she did not care to play with dolls.[22] Anna's mother only learned to cook at the onset of war when she was thirty years old, and Anna herself never took an interest in this family task. In fact, observing the time and energy cooking and other domestic duties required of her mother, Anna specifically determined not to spend her time in this way, preferring instead "the books in her father's study and his companionship there."[23] Although her mother did not demand that Anna assist with unappealing domestic duties, she did encourage her toward cultural pursuits, particularly music. To Martha's dismay, young Anna had little talent or interest in music and "refused to submit the discipline of scales and exercises, for while she liked to sing, she knew that she had no talent for the piano."[24]

When Anna was six, J. B. was appointed secretary of the Baptist Mission Board of West Virginia. He was called to help smooth the mission-related controversies that threatened to split Baptist congregations at the time. The new state of West Virginia developed rapidly after the war and this growth included the state's educational institutions. In particular, public free schools were being established. Anna had received private schooling as a very young child in North Carolina, but for the first time she took advantage of new opportunities in public schooling in West Virginia. The family remained in West Virginia until Anna was twelve, then moved first to Atchison, and then, less than three years later, to Leavenworth, Kansas.[25]

The moves to Kansas were fortunate for the Hardwicke children. The state's public school system was relatively well developed, having been established twenty years prior to the Hardwickes' arrival, and the state had supported a public university since 1866. At the time of the Hardwickes' arrival, Leavenworth, a city with a population of around thirty thousand, was home to ten school buildings, including a new high school. Anna attended the classical high school in Leavenworth. The school's principal was Harvard-educated W. W. Grant, a man who possessed the ability to inspire in his students his own love of the classics. At school Anna was in her element. She was "early capable of a concentration of mind on anything that interested her" and she idolized her teachers.[26] At school she could intensely focus on her interests, and in doing so, she excelled. She is reported to have had a "bluestocking mind," the term denoting a woman whose serious literary and intellectual interests outweighed the traditionally feminine accomplishments in the fine arts and fashion.[27] She loved words, and inherited her father's facility for public speaking. J. B. was at his best in the pulpit, and in Kansas he conducted revival meetings that gained the attention of newspapers and involved "dramatic but not over-fervid oratorical style."[28] A friend of Anna as a young woman described her as "most companionable with the girls," but noted that she may have lacked the coyness toward males that was expected at the time: "I have thought that her perfect frankness sometimes confused the beaus of the town."[29] As the minister's daughter, Anna taught Sunday school, an opportunity which provided for her a stage for her storytelling abilities as she brought biblical tales to life for her students.[30] At home she entertained her brothers and sisters with ghost stories, sometimes using the promise of a story to induce a sibling to run an errand for her.

Anna developed her talent in writing as well as in speaking during these years. At age eight, she collaborated with her ten-year-old brother, Samuel, on a romance novel. Although she shared that work only with her family, by fifteen, she had written a long letter which was published in the Southern magazine, *Happy Home*. The article revealed her sense of identity as a southerner as she at once defended and critiqued perceptions of southern women. She began by thanking the editors for "providing a true representation of literature as it is among the women of the South." She continued with the following assessment of the state of southern women's taste, education, and intellect:

> A mistaken idea is still prevalent, that the women of the South, though refined and beautiful, have not taste for any kind of reading but the society novel, fashions, and perchance, now and then a poem. Again and again, have I argued against this, but ignorance is bigoted. Before the war, our women were taunted with being mere dolls, the pampered pets of fortune, and playthings of men. But since they have shown themselves brave in the midst of terrible dangers, adapting themselves to every situation, this complaint is hushed. And now we hear the cry of weak taste and feeble intellect. . . . I think from the experience that I have had in both sections, that the Northern women, as a class, are more thoroughly educated than those of the South. But this is natural, since in the North, for years, every town and city has had its Public school, while in the South these are a modern institution. But this state of things will not last long. I notice in the schools of this State, that as a general rule the scholars from the South have quicker minds than the others, but often lack in application; they generally stand well in their classes. I would like to have some of your contributors write an article on the condition of the Public Schools in the South, as I am much interested in all educational matters.[31]

Anna signed the letter "Paris Lee," apparently claiming her southern patrimony in the choice of the name. She wrote authoritatively of southern scholars at fifteen although her knowledge must have been limited. Likely she drew on personal experience. Anna excelled academically in Kansas, then considered a northern state, and she herself, perhaps, was the quick-minded southern scholar to whom she referred. A note on the margin of the clipping in Anna's scrapbook, written by Anna later in life reads, "Written at 15. I was much more sure of many things then than I am now!! 1904."[32] Still, the issues she defined at fifteen—the changing role of women in American culture, the importance of education and public schools, even the sectional differences in the United States—were ones that would define her interests and activities for years to come.

Anna graduated from the Classical High School on May 31, 1878. With thirteen students graduating, the ceremony, the eighth graduation held, was the largest ever. The school offered courses in English, Latin, and science, as well as a classical course that focused on Greek and Latin classical literature, mythology, and culture. Anna's focus was the classical, and at graduation she delivered the closing exercise, an essay on epics, to a large, uncomfortable audience. A local newspaper reported that, "there must have been at least sixteen hundred persons inside the church," for "every available space within the church was taken." Seating was unavailable, and "all during the evening, the vast assemblage, packed almost like sardines in a box, stood." [33] The church was "most oppressively warm," although everything was done to render the audience comfortable."

In addition to her essay, Anna also delivered the parting words to "teachers, classmates and friends" in a feeling manner, which was responded to by a cordial approbation from the audience. "Wherein does the power of the epic poet lie?" she began, and she reflected, "Its truthfulness to nature, and its reaching out into almost every division of living and lasting human interests are the central points of its power. Human nature is the same, yesterday, to-day, and forever, hence what interested mortals of ancient days, will also interest us, for we have the same feelings, the same desires, the same longings that they had."[34] Anna continued by discussing how Gladstone may have used the Iliad to draw parallels with his own life and how he used lessons from the work in his own life. She suggested that everyone should try to find the "jewels hidden in these poems" and use them in to aid them in life."[35] Again we see in this speech, themes that would shape Anna's future for the long term. In particular, the importance of making a personal connection to historical and cultural themes and events constituted a line of thought that Anna would carry through the next decade and a half as she transitioned from the role of student to that of teacher and author.

TRAINING FOR TEACHING

Anna identified teaching as her intended profession early on, a decision likely influenced by her father's oratorical displays, her mother's love of assisting her children in study, and the public acceptance of teaching as one of few appropriate professions for women of the era. Upon graduation from high school, she aspired to attend college. Because private women's colleges, like Vassar, were clearly out of reach for her family, Anna set her sights on attending the University of Michigan, one of few public colleges at the time that would admit women. In fact, as a high school student, she dropped her middle name, McLaughlin, and replaced it with an unknown name beginning with the letter "J." Anna told no one the name the letter stood for, promising to reveal this secret upon her graduation from the University of Michigan. Her family, however, was without the means to send her to Ann Arbor and she never achieved her aspirations of a university education. Likewise she never revealed the mystery of the new initial that she took and kept.[36]

Shortly after Anna's high school graduation, her family uprooted once again, leaving Kansas for Bryan, Texas. Bryan was home to the state's new Agricultural and Mechanical College. Although the college did not admit female students, Anna remained an active learner and was fortunate to live near the college because she was able to access the school's library. She hired a private tutor for lessons in Latin and Greek. She also began her teaching career. In a building near the Hardwicke family's main residence, Anna opened a small private school, largely attended by her younger siblings. She conducted her school during the summer, and a friend recalled that she led her pupils in a recitation of "The Charge of the Light Brigade" unperturbed by the heat of Texas's summer months.[37] While in Bryan, she lectured for the local Academy of Science on the history of Christianity in England. In her lecture, she found significance in the fact that Christianity was introduced to England twice, both times by a woman.[38]

Texas's educational system in the late 1870s was extremely underdeveloped in comparison to other states. In fact, in 1870, U. S. commissioner Hon. John Eaton Jr. called Texas "the darkest field, educationally, in the United States."[39] The years immediately following the Civil War saw much contention over the issue of public schools in Texas. The Radical Republicans who came to power after the war installed a system that was widely unpopular, although some of its tenets seem quite acceptable today: compulsory education, a centralized system, and taxes to pay for the system. Still, Texans objected to having the system imposed from without, and to the northern influence. The schools used northern textbooks and many of the teachers hailed from the North.[40] The unpopularity of the Radicals encouraged Texans' distrust of government and slowed educational progress in the state for years. Texans widely viewed the education of children as a private affair, and state intervention as an infringement on personal liberty. Plans for a compromise system failed when Governor Oran M. Roberts declined to sign a bill that allocated funds for public schools. Dr. Barnas Sears, representing the Peabody Education Fund, traveled to Texas in 1877 to confer with Dr. Rufus C. Burleson, the Texas representative of the Peabody fund. Sears determined that Peabody funds would be best used for teacher training. Two years later, in 1879, Texas's first tax-supported teacher training institution opened in Huntsville on the site of the old Austin College, a Presbyterian school that had moved to Sherman.[41] The school, Sam Houston State Normal Institute, was established by the state with aid from the George Peabody fund. Two students from each district and six from the state at large, selected by competitive exam, would be admitted each year as "state students." These students' tuition, room, board and laundry were paid by the state. In return, students agreed to teach in Texas for as long as they attended the normal institute with state support.[42] In the early days of the school, the institute offered a year-long course.

For young Anna Hardwicke, lacking financial support from her family for university study out of state, the state support at Sam Houston Normal Institute offered her an opportunity for education as well as for training in a desired profession. In 1879 she sat for the examination for her district with just three or four others.[43] Anna outscored competitors from her senatorial district with a perfect one hundred on the examination. For an academically talented, ambitious young woman without means to pursue a university education, the scholarship was a prize opportunity. From all accounts, Anna took full advantage of this opportunity and became one of the Normal's top students.

Sam Houston Normal Institute (SHNI) endured a rough beginning. Within days of the opening ceremony, Principal Bernard Mallon died and was replaced by H. H. Smith of Houston.[44] Despite rumors of internal trouble and disorganization during the institute's first year, Anna would remember fondly her time there. She boarded at "the old Lee homestead" which she described as being a "long, long way from the Normal." Years later, she would reminisce about the long walk to and from the Normal Institute through the pine forests of East Texas "and the fragrance of the narcissus blossoms that lined the walk leading up to the house."[45] Pennybacker also remembered the Sam Houston faculty fondly: "Dr. Cooper impressed me with his profundity of knowledge; Mrs. Mallon with her gentle womanliness and innate refinement; Mrs. Whiteside with her energy and determination to succeed; Mrs. Reynolds with her big-heartedness and magnetism; Dr. Smith with his enthusiasm for teaching and his belief in the ability of youth."[46] Anna absorbed the values promoted by the Normal Institute, particularly those related to teaching as a profession. Years later she wrote, "I love to think also that I went out from the Normal with an abiding conviction of the dignity and honor of the teaching profession."[47]

The purpose of a normal institute in the 1800s was to train teachers in the "Normal Method," one that entailed the development of subjects and the provision of instruction according to "the natural method of the mind."[48] This method involved systematic presentation of subjects rather than the teaching of isolated facts. The educational ideas of European educators Friedrich Froebel and Johann Heinrich Pestalozzi were in vogue, and Anna surely encountered the methods of object learning, a method that promoted a progression from the concrete (the object) to the abstract. Later in life, she would describe how she used this technique in her classroom. However, a survey of articles in educational journals of the time, as well as research by others, indicates that oral recitation of facts in the Lancasterian method remained one of the primary methods of instruction in schools of the time. Anna's own articles about teaching indicate that she led her students through oral recitations in addition to conducting object lessons.[49]

Sam Houston Normal Institute was created by the Texas legislature to train teachers for Texas's newly developing public school systems. The small and mainly rural schools of the day did not require teachers to be single subject specialists. A teacher of that time was considered fortunate to obtain a position in one of the state's newly developed city graded schools. In such a setting the teacher was responsible for teaching every subject at a particular grade level. By contrast, country teachers in ungraded schools were responsible for teaching every subject to students at every level of schooling.[50] In both cases, teachers were expected to teach multiple subjects. Consequently the curriculum of Sam Houston Normal Institute was necessarily broad, to account for the broad range of knowledge that teaching demanded. Students took examinations in elocution, natural philosophy, mental philosophy, and astronomy, among other subjects. Physical education was included, even for female students, and a reporter, commenting on the educational exhibit at graduation, proclaimed the "young lady students in fatigue uniform" performing calisthenics the exhibition's "most interesting" feature,[51] although female normal school students across the country were required to participate in calisthenics and "exercise requirements generally did not make distinctions between men and women."[52] SHNI also offered a model school in which students practiced teaching. In the spring of her year at the Normal, Anna was one of very few students selected for a teaching position at the model school, for which she was paid twenty dollars a month.[53] For Anna, this work was a critical part of her training as a teacher. She would later assert: "It would not be possible to recount what I learned while teaching under supervision"[54]

In the later nineteenth century, social life at normal schools was "remarkably lively."[55] Involvement in "all sorts of events and organizations" allowed normal school students to deepen "their understanding of social capital" and build "strong ties with other students, faculty, and administrators." The normal schools "created a microcosm of middle class society" that was largely devoid of the idea that the public sphere of industry, commerce, and politics belonged to men and the private sphere of the home to women."[56] Campus events "featured displays of student abilities in oratory and music, and student-sponsored socials, excursions, and picnics were common."[57] Literary associations and other formal associations thrived, and at the "many gatherings and events," students "formed social networks and learned the benefits of association building." Male and female students took part, and "the notion of a separate female sphere was absent as all students took the stage in literary societies' public rhetoricals, oratory contests, and debates."[58] As was typical of normal institutes of the time, SHNI offered opportunities for extracurricular participation. Anna, whose love for literature and drama would continue throughout her life, remembered the keen impression "our amateur dramatics" made upon her as a student.

Although women in normal schools had remarkable freedom to participate fully in most campus activities, school customs reflected some aspects of the belief in separate spheres for men and women. "Principals and guest speakers at the most formal ceremonies were usually male," in keeping with Victorian belief that men were better suited for the public sphere.[59] This differentiation in roles was the case at Sam Houston State Normal Institute as well. As she had been in high school, Anna was an exemplary student. With a ninety-nine average, she tied for the rank of first in her class of twenty-one female and twenty-five male students. Harry Estill, who later would become the president of SHNI, also earned an average of ninety-nine.[60] At graduation ceremonies on June 16, 1880, Anna and another young woman were awarded Peabody medals for "superior scholarship and meritorious deportment." Despite being among the top students, however, they were not invited to speak at graduation ceremonies; that honor being reserved for male students. Harry Estill and Thomas U. Taylor, who later would become an important figure in the engineering department at the University of Texas, spoke as valedictorian and salutatorian, respectively.

PERCY V. PENNYBACKER

Normal institutes offered opportunities for students to build networks of personal and professional connections.[61] Anna certainly formed many lasting relationships during her normal school year, including friendships with top male students, Estill and Taylor. In addition to Estill and Taylor, newspaper descriptions of the first SHNI graduation mentioned another promising young man, Percy V. Pennybacker.

A close runner-up in rank, with a ninety-eight average, Percy was not only a strong student, but he became Anna's romantic interest as well. By all accounts, Percy was an excellent match for Anna. Percy resembled Anna's father: tall, with a long, full beard in the fashion of the day, although blond and blue-eyed. He was counted among the most striking in appearance of all the students at the Normal: "A young man of splendid physique, tall, graceful, and well-proportioned."[62] Anna, for her part, was petite and pretty, with light hair and sparkling eyes. They made a handsome couple. Both were noted for their good humor, warm demeanor, and social grace. Like Anna, Percy was a superior student, devoted to the cause of education, and already on his way to leadership within the profession. He was, as well, a good choice for Anna socially. Born in Paris, Texas, February 17, 1856, he attended the graded schools at Kansas City, Missouri, and then a private academy in Paris, Texas, before coming to Huntsville. Before his arrival at Sam Houston Normal Institute, he gained experience teaching at the National School for the Cherokee Indians. He had taken a one-month temporary position with the school, but was offered a regular teaching position based on his good performance.[63] Whereas Anna's family consisted of Baptists, Percy was an Episcopalian, but the religious differences were not an issue in their relationship. Percy's father, Dr. G. M. Pennybacker, descended from the Pannebacker family of Pennsylvania, a family with long-standing military ties. Percy's mother, Julia Egbertine, had died in 1873 at the age of thirty-eight, after suffering a long illness.[64] His family was financially secure, able to provide him with opportunities beyond what Anna's family could provide for her. Percy was educated at a private academy and, after graduating from the Normal Institute, he would travel and study overseas. That Percy was able to study abroad, as well as his inheritance of some property upon his father's death, suggests that his family was financially well settled. Later in life, Anna would remember her years at Sam Houston State Normal Institute and realize, "all my recollections are tinged more or less with melancholy because it was at the Normal that I met my husband, and many others who have passed over the great river."[65]

The friendships and professional connections she would make at Sam Houston Normal Institute would be important parts of Anna's later life. Many of her classmates would become leaders in the field of education in Texas. H. F. Estill would teach at the Sam Houston Normal Institute and write history textbooks for the state's school children before assuming the presidency of the institute. Thomas Taylor would help to establish the college of engineering at the University of Texas, and Sue Huffman Brady in Fort Worth would become the first female superintendent of schools in Texas.[66] Anna, too, would achieve success in teaching, and along with Percy, gain statewide prominence in the field.

Chapter Two

1880–1900

Called to Teach

ANNA HARDWICKE FELT CALLED to the teaching profession from a young age and frequently expressed gratitude for the calling. "I entered the Sam Houston Normal Institute," she would later write, "because it offered the best opportunity to continue my education and to give me preparation for the profession I had most wanted to follow, that of teaching." Because she considered "any child fortunate who has a strong bent in any one direction," she counted this calling one of her blessings.[1] Anna was fortuitous not only for having a strong bent in a particular direction, but a strong bent for the teaching profession in particular. The years during which she prepared for and engaged in her teaching career were years of immense growth for the profession. Between 1870 and 1900, the number of teachers in the United States increased 300 percent, as the student population doubled. The rapid increase brought career opportunities for women that they could find in few other professions at the time, as the ratio of female teachers increased from two-thirds to almost three-quarters of the profession.[2] Although the feminization of the profession provided desired occupational opportunity for women, it was driven largely by financial inequities. School boards could hire female teachers for a little more than half what a male teacher would be paid. Female teachers' advancement opportunities also were distinctly limited in as much as many male teachers were channeled into administrative roles from which women largely were excluded.[3] Thus the profession offered both new opportunities as well as limitations to the women rushing to join it.

In Texas, as in other areas of the United States, educational leaders debated the roles and value of women teachers. Some of these arguments have a contemporary ring, as they stress the necessity of a gender balance in the field. Male teachers of the 1800s surely felt threatened by the onslaught of women into the profession, in part because they worried about the effects on professionalization and pay. Articles in the *Texas School Journal* during the 1880s and 1890s stressed fair hiring based on an applicant's qualifications. However, fair hiring practices were advocated not to support women entering the field, but in defense of males purportedly being overlooked for teaching positions. The belief that women in particular benefited from nepotism and a political spoils system when it came to teaching positions, whether true or not, was widespread.[4]

The status of Anna's relationship with Percy Pennybacker upon graduation in 1880 remains unclear. They were not yet engaged. However, shortly after graduation, both left Huntsville for Bryan, Texas. There Anna became a teacher, and Percy was employed as superintendent of the fledgling public school system. For Anna, this position may have been a sharp disappointment and evidence of the gender discrimination she would face most of her career. She had been considered for a teaching position at SHNI, but was passed over for the position, purportedly because of her youth—she was just nineteen at the time. Perhaps this reason was accurate; however, youth and inexperience were often used as excuses for not hiring females in leadership roles in education.[5] If she was disappointed with her teaching position, she apparently never revealed this feeling, although she is on record as having been sorely disappointed about not getting the position at SHNI. In later years, however, she would view the events as having been for the best.

EARLY YEARS IN A NEW CAREER

The City Free Graded Schools of Bryan were newly established when Anna Hardwicke and Percy Pennybacker arrived. As Percy assumed the superintendency, he faced public resistance because some members of the community opposed public schools supported by taxation. Public school systems had not gained universal acceptance in Texas by the 1880s and the imposition of a system by Radical Republicans in the post–Civil War years had created especially bitter resistance among some Texans. Opposition largely focused on whether educational expenses should be carried through property tax revenue. The state had set aside some of its land for public schools, and many Texans believed that revenue from that land should be sufficient to fund schools. Other Texans rejected the idea of state support for schools altogether, believing that education of children was the responsibility of individual families.[6]

However, in Texas, some opposed not just public, but any, primary education for the general public. Quoted in the *Texas School Journal* in 1885, R. L. Dabney, professor of moral philosophy at the University of Texas, argued that universal primary education would lead to "strikes, communism, and socialism," as primary education led to an "initial grade of knowledge and intelligence, just adequate to the suggestion of a number of unsatisfied desires." Dabney asserted that the primary schools and the newspapers "play[ed] into each others hands" in assisting trade unions, organizations Dabney believed to be dangerous.[7] The state superintendent of education, B. M. Baker, defended public education in his response: "The system [advocated by Dabney] would make educated lords of a few men, and abject serfs of millions, for only the rich can send their sons and daughters to colleges and universities." Baker argued that "the common schools fit the millions for a wise and earnest exercise of the duties devolved upon them as citizens under the constitution and laws of our government. We do not believe that education, however limited, begets crime; we believe it is the enemy of disorder."[8] Thus teachers and administrators in the new public schools systems, the Pennybackers among them, faced not only organizational and pedagogical challenges, but the challenge of promoting the value of public schools to the tax-paying public.

In Bryan the Pennybackers clearly were aware that they were charged with promoting the value of public education. In the Bryan district's first annual report a year after he assumed leadership of the district, Percy Pennybacker specifically reported that the school system had made progress in convincing the public of the efficacy of the graded system and the value of a public school system. "Prior to the inauguration of the Graded system there were those among your citizens who, from want of information or other cause were skeptical concerning the merits of said system as above others, who also give preference to private as above public schools," he wrote, continuing on to note his progress in persuading them: "I believe you are not with out good cause to think that many of said doubts and preferences have been removed."[9] Along with some public resistance to the establishment of a public school system generally, Percy faced problems that could be expected with the opening of a new school system. In what must have been a public relations challenge for Percy in the school system's first year, the names of some eligible students did not appear on the assessor's rolls. Those students were unable to attend unless their families paid tuition, a fact which did not sit well with the families. In addition, the perennial challenge of managing student behavior faced the new superintendent and teachers.

Although Percy noted in his first annual report that his focus was on instruction rather than on discipline, he mentioned neither methods nor subjects of instruction at all. Rather, a good section of his annual report outlined his behavior management strategy. "Prior to the opening of the schools, I frequently heard it said that the boys of Bryan were unusually bad," he recalled, but noted that he had not found them so. Although "it is true that many of them are innately mischievous," Percy argued, "that is different from being bad." He continued to share his positive approach to behavior management with the public, noting, "There is much in the manner in which boys are managed. The policy of the present management is to have few rules; to make each pupil feel that his example is worth something; to attach as much responsibility to his position as possible; to let him feel that you rely implicitly upon his honor; to teach him to do right for the sake of right and because it is mean to do otherwise; to let his conduct be regulated by such motives as these rather than by fear."[10] Possibly Percy sought with this article to assure the community that he shared what he perceived were their views on the discipline of children. Conversely, he may have felt the need to explain and promote a disciplinary policy based on cooperation and social inclusion rather than punishment because the ideas were new to some in the community. Despite a generally liberal attitude regarding discipline, Percy noted that corporal punishment was used when necessary, "most often for fighting after school." Percy also made it clear that in some cases, family and community values (or both) conflicted with school values. The attitudes that led some boys to fight he blamed on the attitudes of parents who encouraged their boys to fight to preserve their honor. Boys caught fighting would tell him, "Pa said if a boy called me so and so to whip him." Against this view, Percy countered with his own belief "that it requires more courage not to fight than it does to do so."[11] Percy's views about what constituted proper school behavior were clearly not shared by the entire community, and he had to promote his views about proper conduct to the general public. He spent a good portion of his first annual report doing so.[12]

Anna Hardwicke, too, faced challenges during those first years. Young and notably small of stature, she had to use all of her resources to control and motivate the "innately mischievous" boys of Bryan. Her classes in the new public graded schools were large and student progress slow. Anna taught between forty-five and fifty-four students at a time for most months of that first year, the numbers dropping only when a measles outbreak struck the community. Of those enrolled, only about half, twenty-five students, took the end-of-year exam to move to the next grade. This statistic actually suggests Anna's strength as a teacher. Schoolwide, of 290 registered students, 86 were examined for promotion, and just 62 passed their exams and were promoted to the next grade.[13] Despite the challenges, the school district grew during Anna and Percy's two-year tenure. Attendance in the second year grew to 300, with 211 taking exams and 147 being promoted.[14]

A school flyer announcing the beginning of the district's 1881 school year indicated that the schools opened on September 19 that year, and that the school year began with students reporting for exams. As superintendent, Percy Pennybacker taught eighth grade. Mary O'Brien taught sixth and seventh grades; Mrs. T. N. Cavitt, third; Laura English, second; and Mrs. S. G. Yates, first grade. The Bryan schools were segregated during Percy and Anna's tenure there, and about half as many black students attended as there were white. The colored school employed two teachers, John N. Johnson for the grammar grades and D. F. Taylor for the primary grades.[15] Anna taught third and fourth grades her first year at Bryan, and cycled up with her students to teach fourth and fifth the second year. The curriculum for fourth and fifth grades included familiar school subjects. Grammar, language, reading, writing, spelling, arithmetic, and geography were specifically named in the school flyer. As was common at the time, textbooks were a teaching tool heavily relied upon by teachers. How Anna incorporated the textbooks into lessons, and what her teaching in Bryan entailed beyond these subjects is unknown, although one might guess she supplemented book work with object lessons, literature, current events, and other classroom activities as described in accounts of her later teaching.

Anna and Percy became engaged in December of their first year in Bryan.[16] Percy, already in his mid-twenties, wanted to marry quickly, but Anna, still a teenager at this time, thought that they required further education. With Anna's encouragement, Percy left Texas for Europe to pursue further studies after having served in Bryan for a total of two years. At the time, aspects of the U.S. school systems, particularly universities, were being modeled upon the German school system. Germany was home to some of the world's most prestigious universities, and Percy chose to study at one of these, the Royal University of Berlin, as well as the College of Modern Languages at the Sorbonne in Paris, France, concentrating in French and German. While overseas he also traveled across Europe and North Africa, "visiting England, France, Belgium, Germany, Switzerland, Austria, Italy, Sicily, and Tunis.[17]

Anna, too, left Bryan in 1882, not for European study, but for the less-enviable opportunity of returning with her family to Carthage, Missouri.

Although she expressed regrets at leaving Texas, she adapted quickly to life in Missouri. Articles she wrote and had published in local papers detailed her "Texas sickness" at having to leave the state that she, by then, considered home:

> Though, on his arrival, one may see little to admire, much to condemn in the country and town life of the Lone Star state, yet if he remain there six or twelve months a change comes o'er the spirit of his dream. He makes acquaintances, is charmed with the frank, generous people, finds their interests are his interests, becomes identified with them—in short acts as if he were 'native to the manor born.' Send him away and he finds it hard to stay; a magnetic attraction seems to draw him ever Texas-ward and it has been darkly whispered that this feeling, if not yielded to, produces the same effect that nostalgia does on the Swiss.[18]

As was typical for her, Anna kept busy in Carthage, a town of sixty-five hundred with "all the appurtenances of a city—gas, waterworks, telephones. . . . park, public libraries, churches of all denominations, schools &c., &c."[19] There she began a teaching position in the local schools. Despite her Texas sickness, she clearly admired Carthage, a town that she felt prided itself on beauty over commerce. She wrote of it in the local paper, "Picture a miniature Utopia with the impossibilities thrown out and a few disadvantages thrown in and you have an idea of this gem of a town. . . . her citizens pride themselves rather on the beauty, both natural and artificial, than the commercial standing of the place, hence each property owner takes the greatest care of house, yard and shrubbery."[20]

Public schools in Carthage were well developed for the time and, like the rest of the town, picturesque. Writing again for the local newspaper, Anna described "two handsome brick school buildings situated in fine groves" which served the primary and grammar grades, as well as a high school "where the languages and higher branches are taught."[21] Anna taught in Room 1 of the Carthage public school and the local press reported events from her classroom. She organized a classroom newspaper, *Gathered Pearls,* appointing students as subject editors, and conducted monthly lyceums, programs to which the general public was invited. Anna assigned students major roles in preparing for the events. A president and secretary were appointed to conduct each lyceum as well as a decorating committee to decorate the room appropriately.[22] Press reports indicate the programs were well attended. One such program focused on the works of Longfellow, and included recitations of a long list of Longfellow's literary works, including "The Story of Evangeline" and "The Story of Miles Standish." The programs were well received, with local press reporting: "The interesting programme prepared showed the teacher to be a live, energetic worker, leaving nothing undone for the advancement and best development of pupils."[23] The year's final program gained still more press attention, as an article noted the "large crowd assembled yesterday afternoon to witness the closing public exercises of that room for this term" and described the scene in some detail: "The room was handsomely decorated with flowers of every description," the article noted. "A large cross of ferns was suspended above the teacher's desk, and a magnificent horse-shoe adorned the wall. . . . The entire four walls were literally covered with pictures, flags, drawings, and bric-a-brac of every description—all being very tastefully and neatly arranged."[24] Exercises consisted of "recitations, declamations, etc., all of which were very good." A debate concluded the program. The topic was "Who is greater: the poet, the statesman, or the warrior?" and the newspaper noted, "It was decided in favor of the poet."[25] Anna's popularity extended not only among the press and public but among her students as well. Even after Anna had resigned her position, her former students welcomed her to a reception in her honor at the "mansion" of one of the classmates, to "sing old class songs," conduct recitations, discuss the fortune of school life, and tell ghost stories. The reporter noted, "Miss Hardwicke should feel much complimented to know that she has won the hearts of her pupils so thoroughly that neither succeeding teachers nor absence can cause her to be forgotten."[26]

In addition to teaching, Anna developed herself as a writer. She submitted articles to national educational journals during these years, and she served as literary editor for the local newspaper, the *Carthage Press*. To this paper she contributed long articles on literary topics as well as shorter pieces on various topics of local interest. In addition, her travel articles, including those detailing her trip from Texas to Missouri and trips she took during the summer break, appeared in small local papers. Anna's ability to connect to an audience through humor would serve her well throughout her lifetime, and her published pieces from this period demonstrate that this aspect of her style clearly had developed by the time she was in her early twenties. Her writing style incorporated facts and her opinions in a way that was personal, highly descriptive, and humorous. She described, for example, a wait in a West Texas train depot: "Some sage has said that solitude and quiet produce thought and thought produces philosophers. This being the case, Garret, the station at which the Waxahachie tap connects with the Central, will in time produce Platos, Aristotles, Hamiltons and Mills enough to supply the entire state and have besides a surplus to bestow on the country at large."[27] Her humor here arose from irony born of a sense of culture unmatched by physical surroundings, not necessarily surprising for a young woman with a classical education traveling in rural Texas in the late 1800s. Other articles again show the sense of irony regarding physical difficulties and indignities, as she writes about Texas pests, joking, "Then, too, we miss another feature of a Texas summer—the mosquito. He loveth not this section of the country, but gives up the field to his first cousin, the fly, as if the Egyptian plague were repeating itself." She continued in the same tone, "It is a sight to excite one's sympathy when some Arabi Pasha of the fly nation makes an attack upon the enemy! No sooner does he succeed in entering the sacred precinct than the entire population, master, mistress, a maid and child open on him an artillery of fans, brushes and dusters."[28]

In 1884 Anna published several biographical articles in the women's department of the *Carthage Press,* at times writing under the pen name Cousin Patty. The famous figures she featured included Shakespeare, the Cary sisters (Alice and Phebe) and Margaret Fuller. The latter is of particular interest. Pennybacker described Fuller in much the same way that her own biographers would later describe her—stressing early accomplishments (she notes that Fuller was reading Shakespeare at age five), a girlhood spent in close study, and the importance of her father in her development. Anna might have been describing her time in her own father's study when she wrote of Fuller: "That she had much for which to thank her father's care is shown from the fact that she wasted no time in reading useless books or in wrong methods of study." Anna, who herself studied elocution and was known as a skilled conversationalist, noted of Fuller: "Possessed of few qualities that men admire in women, she yet won the regard of Emerson, Carlyle, Greerly, Alcott [and] Channing and held spell bound, by the magic of her conversational power, the greatest minds of the day."[29] Anna's description of the conversation classes Fuller offered to women foreshadows events in Anna's own life. She wrote that Fuller organized a conversation class for women only (gentlemen "seemed to throw a restraint upon the ladies") which had three aims: first, "to pass in review the departments of thought and knowledge, and endeavor to place them in due relation to one another in our minds"; second, "to systematize thought, and give a precision and clearness in which our sex is so deficient chiefly, because they have so few inducements to test and classify what they receive"; and third, "to ascertain what pursuits are best suited to us, in our time and state of society, and how we may make best use of our means for building up the life of thought upon the life of action.[30] Pennybacker also addressed Fuller's views on women and femininity, noting that she claimed "not only equal power with man—for of that omnipotent nature will never permit her to be defrauded—but a chartered power, too fully recognized to be abused. There is not danger of woman unsexing herself. Nature has pointed out her ordinary sphere by the circumstances of her physical existence."[31] At the time she wrote this article, Anna was just beginning to become active in the women's club movement. Later in life, she would, like Fuller, meet with other women to discuss culture, society, and women's roles within each. She would encourage women to develop their ability to think and act systematically and to express themselves clearly. Also like Fuller, Pennybacker would argue both women's equal power with and differences from men.

In addition to publishing frequently in the local newspaper, Anna took pleasure in performing before an audience. She practiced her elocutionary skills whenever possible. A newspaper account of a recitation she performed gives a sense of her well-developed skills. For her recitation, she described "two armies bivouacked within hearing distance of each other," and the newspaper report commended her ability to touch the emotions of former Civil War soldiers: "Miss Hardwicke's recitation was a beautiful word-painting—[she] is a charming elocutionist—without affectation or mannerism, and with thorough command of her voice, even to the nicest intonation. In listening to her one forgot the rusty opera house, the distorted Shakespeare overhead, the appointed plank ceiling and the cramped up narrow chairs, and was transported back 20 years to the scene she painted with warm, fresh, living colors." The article notes that she was "vociferously applauded."[32] The ability to reach an audience's emotions that she evinced as a young woman would remain with Anna for life. In her work as a teacher and as a clubwoman, she would frequently be called upon to inspire an audience and to motivate them to action. It was a skill at which she excelled.

In addition to paid work teaching and writing, Anna read and studied widely. Her surviving scrapbooks document her broad interests at the time. While Percy studied at the University of Berlin, Anna hired a tutor to teach her German, and she featured articles about Germany prominently in her scrapbook. She collected articles both from German-language newspapers as well as articles in English about Germany and German culture. Gender roles and education, in Germany and at home, were also common themes of the articles in her books. Sometimes she wrote in the margins of the articles, as in one that described the role of women in Germany. The article noted that women in Germany performed hard labor and worked in fields, on construction sites, and in fire departments carrying water. The English-language article's author saw this as a sign of German women's oppression, writing, "Everywhere there is laid on her the menial drudgery that must be done, but which men will not assist in doing, nor for the performance of which will they provide mechanical appliances as American men do. Everywhere she is robbed of proper compensation for her labor."[33] Anna corresponded regularly with Percy during his travels, often writing in German. In the margins of this article, Anna questioned: "Is it true?" but if she asked this question of Percy, the scrapbook does not hint of his response.

Other articles in the scrapbook presented arguments about women's capacities and place in society. One described French "savant" M. Delauney's work, "the purpose of which is to show, by a scientific examination of all existing data on the subject, that woman is intellectually, as in every other respect, on a lower stage of development than man, and therefore, inferior to him." Delauney's arguments were based on women's anatomy and physiology. Women's flatter feet, less developed frontal lobes ("the seat of the higher faculties") and voluminous occipital lobes ("which especially preside over the life of sentiment") evidenced their inferiority. "In its totality, according to Professor Wagner, the brain of a woman is in a state more or less embryonic."[34] One wonders how Anna, with her record of superior academic achievement, received the news of her intellectual inferiority. Nothing indicates that she accepted this view. However, she certainly understood the belief that women had inferior reasoning abilities to be part of the cultural landscape in which she lived and took this into account in her work. Later in life she would emphasize, on the one hand, woman's ability to reason as well as feel, and, on the other hand, the necessity of young men attaining an education so that their educated wives would not surpass them.[35]

Like gender issues, racial issues were widely discussed in the public discourse of the time. A scrapbook clipping indicates that young Anna followed the debates about the meaning and roles of the races in the United States. One article she took pains to save promoted education as the solution to racial problems in the United States and justified the social and political oppression of blacks by whites on the basis of black ignorance. "The negro was the source of our national trouble. Consciously or unconsciously he had been the cause of discontent among us for the last fifty years," the article asserted. It continued, noting that "the trouble was not over yet, though they were emancipated," and explaining, "It was now pretty generally acknowledged that the troubles of the south arose out of a bad local government and a suppression of the suffrage. Both these things were permitted to continue not because the negro was black, but because he was ignorant, and therefore so easily corruptible. President Garfield said that the remedy was education."[36] The article noted as well the great progress made by blacks in education and property ownership during the short time of their emancipation. The ideas expressed here were ones Anna shared. While she never supported overt violence against African Americans, she also did not fight against segregation and discriminatory policies. She voiced support for African American efforts at racial uplift generally and for the efforts of African American women in particular, but it was support from a distance and sometimes in word only. She condemned overt violence and the expression of racial hatred, but when policy decisions related to race came before her, she often took the conservative, segregationist approach. Later in life, she would express to a northern colleague, "Social equality is simply unthinkable to me. Mixture of blood is a most obnoxious thought."[37]

In addition to her language studies and reading on current events, Anna took on a more formal program of study through the Chautauqua Literary and Scientific Circle (CLSC) during her time in Carthage.[38] The CLSC was a self-study course originated in 1878 by Dr. John H. Vincent, cofounder of the Chautauqua Institute of Chautauqua, New York. Already the curriculum director of the thriving educational retreat, Vincent recognized a desire for further education among those not fortunate enough to have been able to attend college. Working with prominent educators, Vincent developed syllabi for a four-year course of study he believed analogous to a college education.[39] Despite debate regarding the value of this sort of education, Chautauqua enrollees formed local study clubs called Chautauqua Circles at an incredible rate in the latter part of the nineteenth century. Between 1878 and 1894, ten thousand local reading circles were established across the country.[40] Anna, as a member of the class of 1889, must have begun her course in 1884. She described the purpose and format of the study course to readers of her newspaper articles in a passage that may have been copied from Chautauqua promotional material: "This new organization aims to promote habits of reading and study in nature, art, science, and in secular and sacred literature, in connection with the routine of daily life (especially among those whose educational advantages have been limited), so as to secure to them the college student's general outlook upon the world and life, and to develop the habit of close, connected, persistent thinking."[41] Anna noted that the CLSC course involved individual study, usually consisting of a recommended forty minutes of reading nightly, as well as meetings with local circles. Written reports and annual examinations were requirements of a CLSC diploma.

Although few records document the details of Pennybacker's earliest club work, through her affiliation with the CLSC, she would likely have studied and discussed a broad range of topics, including English and Greek history, English literature, astronomy, human psychology, and the Bible with her fellow club members. Appreciative of the opportunity for self-culture (and perhaps appreciative, as well, of a column topic), Anna promoted the value of the CLSC to her readers. She noted that the CLSC had thirty thousand members who were eager to share the good word of opportunity presented by the study course: "Those whom the circles' helping hand has rescued from the slough of mental despondency, haste, like the leper of old, to spread the good tidings, that others may seek and find the same aid."[42]

As a member of the CLSC, Anna participated in Carthage's active literary association. The association consisted of five literary societies: the CLSC, the NNC Club, the Stratford, the Shakespeares, and the Alphas. At annual meetings, members of the societies gave readings and vocal performances. Anna received positive press reports for her recitation of "La Cica" at one of these meetings. Of her performance, the press wrote: "Attractive presence, excellent characterization and perfect elocution comprise it in a nut shell."[43] In addition to participation with the CLSC, Anna also founded a club, the Omega Society, although little information about this organization is available.[44]

In 1883, Anna left her position with the public schools of Carthage to accept a position in Lexington, Missouri, at the Baptist Female College. The Baptist Female College was a prestigious school for young women at the time, and Anna was considered to have obtained an excellent post.[45] Although some reports have her teaching there just ten weeks, she likely stayed for the full term. That summer, Anna made her first trip out of the country, traveling to Canada for a month-long course in expression.[46] Later that year, upon Percy's return from Germany, Anna joined him in Tyler, Texas.

TYLER, TEXAS

In Tyler, Texas, as in Bryan, Percy once again accepted the position of superintendent of a young school district. Upon accepting the position, Percy hired Anna as the principal of the high school. She earned

$800 per year, a handsome sum for a woman at the time and much more than she would have made as a teacher in the district.[47] Teachers in Tyler earned $45 per month in 1885 although, as one teacher noted in the *Texas School Journal,* "hopes [were] entertained for better salaries another term."[48] A little more than a month after the school year opened, on October 31, 1884, Anna and Percy were married in a small ceremony in Tyler.[49] They were married on a Friday; school classes were cancelled for the day in honor of the wedding. Anna's father traveled from Missouri to attend the exchange of vows, and twelve of Anna's students comprised the wedding party.[50]

As had been the case upon his graduation from Sam Houston Normal Institute, Percy's career advanced more quickly and he gained more stature within the profession than did Anna in the first years of their marriage. As a man holding the superintendency of schools, he enjoyed enhanced status as a matter of course. At the time, however, for Anna, as a woman, even to hold the high school principalship was surprising to the people of Tyler.[51] In addition, Anna's continuing to teach after marriage appears to have been rather unusual for the period. Married women comprised just 4.5 percent of the female teachers in the entire nation, and only about 5 percent of married women in the United States worked outside the home as of 1900.[52] Furthermore, this trend seems to have been on the increase at the time, suggesting that the percentages may have been smaller in the 1880s. In fact, in many cases, "public opinion restricted the workplace to those married women who labored out of emergency or dire necessity. Teachers whose husbands drew a respectable income did not fit this category and had to fight to remain employed."[53] How Anna was able to continue teaching after marriage is a bit of a mystery. Was public opinion more liberal in Tyler, Texas, than other parts of the country? Did her superintendent husband insist upon her continuance? Was the need for qualified teachers, or was Anna's talent, enough to outweigh prevailing social norms? A friend remembered Anna at the time as unlike many of the women in Tyler at the time: "Early responsibilities voluntarily assumed had given her initiative and self reliance unusual at that time for the young women of Tyler, Texas, an always conservative town."[54] Anna's opinion about the position of women teachers in schools is a similar mystery. No record exists of her identifying gender discrimination as a major problem in her career. Possibly she accepted that positions of authority would, even should, go to men. In any case, Anna, a "vivid, enthusiastic young woman,"[55] seems to have made the most of the opportunities available to her without comment on those that were not. She seems, as well, to have been content to work in close partnership with her husband in a relationship that was in some ways unusual (her career) and not in others (his advancement into other leadership roles). The couple worked and traveled together for the first decade of their marriage, as well as sharing common interests, experiences, and work. Anna learned much from Percy during these years. Later in life, she would credit Percy with having taught her to be an efficient administrator. In addition, early descriptions of Percy's active participation in teacher organizations parallel descriptions of Anna in a similar role later in life.

PERCY PENNYBACKER AS SUPERINTENDENT OF SCHOOLS

Continuing in Tyler the success he experienced in Bryan, Percy gained recognition as a leader in the emerging field of Texas education and particularly in the administration of graded schools.[56] The Tyler public school system had been formed in 1882 when prominent members of the community called for a tax to benefit the establishment of a school system. The town "in usual progressive spirit" voted for the tax for a period of two years, and the school board appointed a superintendent, two principals, and a corps of teachers. The superintendent of the new school system faced duties "made more onerous by the newness of the system to Tyler and many inexperienced teachers," and the man selected first for the position resigned before the end of the first term, leaving his duties to the first principal.[57] The following year, a third man, J. C. Brooks of Tennessee, became superintendent, but served a tenure of just one year.[58] Thus, when Percy Pennybacker accepted the superintendency in 1884, he became the fourth superintendent of a school system that was just beginning its third year and was struggling for public support. Although the summer of 1884 had seen the school tax, decreased from one-half to one-fifth of 1 percent, passed by a larger margin than in 1882, the city remained divided about the necessity of public schools.[59] By March of 1884, however, Percy was credited with having secured the necessary public support. Leila Thornton, a Tyler teacher, wrote in the *Texas School Journal:* "The Tyler public school system was not permanently established till the fall of 1884, there having been hitherto much opposition from various causes, but now we are glad to state that under the efficient management of our superintendent, Percy V. Pennybacker, the school has given universal satisfaction. The people are no longer divided on this momentous question."[60] Thornton, who taught under Percy's leadership at the time, also noted that he was "popular with teachers and patrons of the district" and that the enemies of public education were "becoming less in number" as patrons gave "not only their good will, but hearty co-operation."[61]

As superintendent, Percy was challenged with the task of managing the behavior and educational progress of a large number of students as well as managing teachers and forming relationships within the community at large. Percy addressed these tasks systematically in ways unique enough for the time to warrant a brief article in the *Texas School Journal* describing them. Written by Anna, the article provided examples of the registration card that the district used to track students, and noted that attendance was tracked on individual student cards. Written excuses were required of students who had been absent. Percy also made student exam papers available in the superintendent's office and the public was free to examine them. His management of teachers began upon his selection of them. The *Texas School Journal* article also noted that "the Superintendent says that he attributes the general success and popularity of the schools to the fact that he makes amiability the first requisite in a teacher, believing that a cross, peevish woman had better mar the life of one man than of forty children."[62] Percy used positive motivation to encourage students to attend school promptly and regularly. According to Anna's article, he achieved success with this plan. The article noted that since the new superintendent took charge, absences and tardiness had "decreased considerably." The means used "are many," Anna noted, "each teacher adopting what plan she pleases. Grades 1, 2, 3, and 4 vie with one another to see which room can win the banner by having the least per cent of absence and tardiness. . . . This system of generous rivalry does more, perhaps, than any other one thing to secure prompt attendance."[63] Percy also published in the local newspaper the names of students who had been absent or tardy, a use of peer pressure as a negative rather than a positive motivator. "In some of the rooms," Anna reported, "the teachers have managed to establish such a public opinion among the pupils that a late pupil is disgraced in the eyes of his own comrades; this shifts the lad from the teacher's shoulders, and induces the scholars themselves to become disciplinarians."[64]

In addition to being an efficient administrator and effective motivator, Percy was well-liked and successful in his position in part because he either shared, or at least refrained from challenging, the values and way of life of the community. Tyler, in the heart of East Texas, insisted upon a racially segregated school system, and, by all accounts, the Pennybackers supported this system and its attendant inequities. Little is known about the operation of the black schools under Percy's leadership. His annual reports note little about these schools, perhaps indicating benign neglect or perhaps an understanding that his audience lacked interest in this matter.[65] The few reports that mention the system's black schools indicate that Percy did little to advocate for them. One incident, described in undated newspaper articles, involved the district in a controversy over the land on which Tyler's black school was situated. The property had been acquired by the Freedman's Bureau for the school, but had been used by two black churches, one Baptist and one Methodist. Later the Baptists displaced the Methodists and took control of the property themselves. Problems arose during Percy's superintendency when the black church and the school district both claimed ownership of the property, and a committee appointed by the school board could reach no agreement with the church. Percy noted in a report to the school trustees that the five acres on which the school sat had been purchased "several years after the war, and while the Freeman's Bureau was in existence." The land, he noted, was deeded to school trustees "for school purposes for the colored people" and the building was "erected upon the grounds by private subscription from whites and blacks."[66] The use of the property by the Baptist church irked white town leaders for reasons that were political as well as racial. The Baptist church in question purportedly removed their pastor because he voted Democratic. The headline of one of the local newspaper articles revealed the white community attitudes with regard to the church as it gloated: "The Colored Baptist Church. Not so wealthy as it thought it was—out of doors if the city does its duty to the public."[67] The report snidely observed, "It is the church that discharged its pastor without paying him what the members owed him, for voting for democrats at the recent election. The members of the church, it seems, intend to swindle their former pastor out of about $150 of his salary. Nice religion, isn't it? . . . The new mayor is very apt to see that this property is not used any further for sectarian purposes."[68] A board of education committee recommended that the district take control of the property and repair the building for use as the school for blacks: "In view of the above, and of the fact that the building now in use by said colored school is greatly in need of repairs, and that it is injudicious to use the same building for both church and school purposes, your committee recommend that the board of school trustees have said building placed in good repair so as to make it suitable and comfortable for the winter. . . . and that its use for any other except school purposes be forbiden [*sic*]."[69] In what appears to be a warning to Superintendent Pennybacker, the article continued, "If the superintendent of the schools does his plain, simple duty, the colored Baptist church will not meet next Sunday at its usual place of meeting."[70] Percy, apparently aware of public opinion, followed suit and forbade the Baptists from meeting on school property.

The facilities for "the colored school" became a public issue once again in 1889. Newspaper accounts described the black community with disdain (this time quoting Percy), and again Percy supported the segregated system. At the start of that school year, the school for black students caught fire and was nearly destroyed. The school, which had housed seventy-two, ninety-three, and ninety-six students respectively for the first three days of the term, nearly burned down. Percy reported the incident to the board, and blamed the carelessness of one of the black students for the mishap. In response, he recommended "the appointment of a committee to consider the advisability of your Board recommending the erection of the new building in the north part of the town. . . . to build a new school building for white students."[71] Because the white school was full, he reasoned, white students could occupy the newer, larger building, and the black students could be given the existing white school. Beyond reports of these two incidents, little information about Percy's administration of Tyler's black schools exists, indicating the lack of importance and attention given these schools by the town's white elite.

ANNA PENNYBACKER AS TEACHER

As her husband negotiated the political and organizational challenges associated with running the school district, Anna faced challenges of her own in the classroom. Conditions in Texas schools at the turn of the nineteenth century could be primitive. Some schools were conducted in the open air, some under crude structures that consisted of merely an awning constructed of sticks. More common was a simple one-roomed building constructed of wood. Texas teacher John Kocken noted that organization and classification were "one of the most difficult problems of a lifetime" in schools of the era, and described his experiences as a first-year teacher in a late-nineteenth-century Texas public school as follows: "The furniture consisted of long benches made without adjustment to pupils from seven to twenty years of age. Twelve-inch boards were attached to the long benches by means of strap hinges. . . . The equipment consisted of a very limited supply of blackboard, which was constructed of three pieces of one by twelve, framed and painted black."[72] The students, he noted, appeared with dogs, "every variety" of textbook, dinner buckets, and bottles of molasses and milk. Schools in Bryan and Tyler likely were somewhat better equipped than the poorer, rural schools of the state that Kooken described, but much was left for the teacher in terms of outfitting classroom and acquiring materials. The Tyler school in which Anna taught was housed in the former facilities of the East Texas Military Academy. In addition to her principalship, Anna taught sixth and seventh grades in the high school, which included all grades, five through eleven. All of the classes for the high school were conducted in the Big Hall which spanned the entire second floor of the three-story building and had served as the military academy's auditorium. A former student described the Big Hall as a large room with "long recitations benches in the front and its three classrooms partitioned off in the rear."[73] Anna's descriptions of her classroom, presumably one of the partitioned areas, indicate the amount of effort she put into making it comfortable and aesthetically pleasing. She and the other teachers ensured that classrooms were "more or less ornamented and made to look as cheerful and attractive as possible." She decorated with "curtains of red oil calico, flowers, hanging baskets, lambrequins over doors and windows, pictures of all kinds that tend to cultivate a love for the beautiful, portraits of distinguished men and women, busts of Washington and Shakespeare, mottoes made of gilt and silver paper, ornamented waste baskets," and "brackets, plaques, maps and drawings made by the pupils."[74] Some decorations for the room were donated by students or purchased with funds raised by personal donations from students in the class or a fundraising entertainment held by members of the upper grade who realized the large sum of fifty dollars in their fundraising. The money brought "steel engravings of classic, literary or historical scenes, and two large busts" to the classroom.[75]

Writing about schooling in the United States during the 1880s, educational historian Barbara Finkelstein notes that Americans of the time "charged teachers with the responsibility of providing the nation's children not only with the rudiments of literacy but with the qualities of virtue as well."[76] Teachers, according to Finkelstein, accepted the moral education of their students as one of their duties. All evidence indicates that Anna, too, assumed the responsibility of developing her students' moral sense. "It is my duty to train them morally as well as mentally,"[77] she wrote in a *Texas School Journal* article. As noted earlier, Anna's appointment as principal of the high school was unusual for the time, and the people of Tyler found having a slender young woman in that position a bit shocking. A former student wrote of the students' amazement to learn that they were to have a female principal, and described how they plotted to take advantage of the young teacher. Anna, however, won them over quickly with a warm smile, a sense of humor, and her ability to engage them in lessons by her storytelling abilities.[78] Anna's focus as a teacher was on the building of a sense of community within the classroom. She not only involved students in decorating the classroom, she made the history class "more spirited" by dividing her class into competing teams. Additionally she posted the daily written work of her students "in conspicuous places." She ran her classroom democratically. "I tell [my students]," she wrote, "that as our school is a little republic. . . . they may elect a legislature consisting of five of the best and wisest pupils, to pass laws concerning the crime of tardiness."[79] Still, Anna was not entirely progressive in her teaching and classroom management styles. With large numbers of students, maintaining control over the classroom was challenging to teachers of the day, and corporal punishment was common. Though no evidence exists that Anna used corporal punishment with her students, she did use classroom management techniques that focused on peer pressure and did not hesitate to shame a wayward student into compliance. Anna noted that in her school mischievous boys were forced to wear a bib. "One dose of this is generally enough for the urchins who wish to be thought boys and not babies."[80] From Anna's perspective, another aspect of inculcating moral behavior related to class struggle. She believed that both "labor" and "capital" must understand their rights and obligations toward one another. In her view, schooling could help ease class tensions. This argument is a neat reversal of the argument advanced by a University of Texas professor in the *School Journal* several years prior. His reverse position held that primary schooling encouraged class struggle because educated working people expected more out of life than they realistically would attain.[81] The argument establishes that Anna understood education as a force for social stability.

ANNA PENNYBACKER'S INSTRUCTIONAL METHODS

Like her classroom management techniques, Anna's teaching methods relied on engaging students in classroom activities. Finkelstein identifies three types of teaching styles common during the early progressive period: the intellectual overseer, the drillmaster, and the interpreter of culture. The intellectual overseer primarily functioned by assigning work and testing the student's comprehension of what was read, largely through recitations. The drillmaster, "managed to instruct their students without becoming involved in elaborate illustration and exploration" and the interpreter of culture "clarified and elaborated materials for and with their students."[82] Of these, Pennybacker would have been an early example of the interpreter of culture, and she promoted this way of interacting with students to others in the field. As was common in educational institutions across the country at that time, recitations were a regular form of both instruction and evaluation. In her classroom, Anna combined the recitation with object lessons (lessons arranged around specific objects) as well as opportunities for students to engage in thoughtful debate about issues. Students in her class engaged in hands-on activities, making maps of clay or models of historical figures.[83] Although her teaching style included many elements of what would be known as progressive education, in the mid- to late-1880s Anna's teaching was influenced not by John Dewey but by European educators Froebel and Pestalozzi. Anna certainly knew of these educators' work. In 1886, she presented on "Pestalozzi, His Life and Work" at the annual meeting of the Texas State Teachers Association (TSTA).

THE PENNYBACKERS' STATEWIDE STATURE

In addition to their duties in Tyler schools, the Pennybackers were active in educational affairs at the county and state levels. Percy, in particular, played high-level leadership roles in several educational associations, and the couple regularly traveled to educational conferences and conventions throughout the Texas and the region. In December 1884, for example, Percy and Anna traveled with other Texas educators for a meeting of the Texas School Superintendents Association held at the World's Exposition in New Orleans. In addition to attending the exposition, Percy spoke to this association on "Indifference in Texas to Higher Education: Its Causes and Remedies,"[84] and was soon after elected secretary-treasurer of the organization. The next month, January 1885, he became president of the newly formed Smith County Teachers Association, which was likely formed under his initiative. Percy dominated the program of the first meeting of this organization, encouraging teachers to attend the World's Exposition in New Orleans. In his speech he emphasized that the fair was of great importance to teachers "inasmuch as there are exhibits from all classes of schools from every quarter of the globe, which would enable him or her to gain something of intrinsic value." Percy also stressed the effectiveness of the exhibit, noting the "value of optical inspection by illustrating the difference between reading about anything and seeing it."[85] Percy linked the importance of the fair to the renewal of the post–Civil War South. Residents of the South, "who, not having yet recovered from the severe blow given them during the recent war, and being too poor to travel, can go to New Orleans and have all the world brought to them," Percy suggested.[86] For southerners, then, the fair was an opportunity to learn about new ideas and technologies taking hold in other parts of the world. For southern educators, the fair brought information about pedagogical ideas and methods being popularized elsewhere.

One idea the Pennybackers brought back was that of the exposition itself. The *Texas School Journal* reported that Texas educators were impressed by the school displays of the East and Midwest during the fair, and Percy found the exposition format so useful that he carried the idea of an education exposition back to Texas. In 1885, after his return from the World's Exposition, Percy proposed to the body of the Texas State Teachers Association that the organization sponsor an educational exhibit of its own to be held at the association's next meeting. In an article directed to Texas educators Percy outlined the reasons for holding the exhibit. "The coming exhibition will awaken more thought on education, and result in more direct and practical good to the profession of teaching, and to the children of the state, than any single movement theretofore set on foot in our state," he wrote. "It is intended that the exhibit, as an educational one, shall be universal in character."[87] The duty of every teacher, Percy continued, was to put forth his best efforts to have his work well represented. The teachers' association passed a resolution to form a committee of three men and three women to organize the exhibit. Percy served on the committee, and Anna assisted the endeavor through fundraising efforts. In 1885 she formed a dramatic club in Tyler that rehearsed and produced a play, the proceeds of which went in part to support the educational exhibit. The committee of three men and three women created a number of divisions for the exposition. These included separate departments for higher education, city public graded schools, country schools, private institutions, art education, industrial education, school architecture, schoolbooks, and school furniture. The first exhibition took place at the July 1886 meeting of the TSTA and was considered a great success. Reports noted that the "room was thronged always with teachers and citizens" and the quality of the displays surprised and impressed visitors.[88] After 1886, the exhibit became a regular feature of the TSTA annual convention.

THE TEXAS STATE TEACHERS ASSOCIATION

Percy was highly active in the Texas State Teachers Association during the later 1880s. He attended annual meetings in various cities of the state, actively participated in meetings, and rose to leadership positions. At the TSTA convention in Dallas in 1887, Percy played a prominent role. He responded to the address of welcome, was appointed to the transportation committee, and introduced a resolution that a committee be appointed to select the association's next meeting place and consider places where the meeting could be held permanently. He also appointed a committee of three, including himself, to investigate the possibility of the teachers' association preparing school textbooks and having them published by the Farmers' Alliance.[89] The year 1887 brought Percy several other honors and responsibilities. In addition to assuming the TSTA presidency, he was appointed the Texas member of the board of directors of the National Education Association, at the meeting of that organization in Chicago.[90] He was also elected vice president of the Sam Houston Normal Institute Alumni Association. In that role he addressed the eighth reunion of the alumni association in 1888.[91]

As president of the TSTA, Percy developed a personal vision for the association. He believed that it should be made more practical and less social. He also sought to expand association membership and attendance at the TSTA convention. In a speech before members of the organization, he noted that Texas had 10,000 teachers but that only 250 attended the TSTA convention and only 2,000 subscribed to the state's educational journal. He also noted that 90 percent of the attendees were from city schools. Percy also suggested important organizational changes. He believed that the TSTA addressed issues haphazardly and without study during its meetings. To enable issues to be addressed systematically, he proposed forming committees to study issues for a year and then report back at the annual conference. He suggested committees to cover manual training, uniformity of textbooks, and office tenure; committees to work on establishing more normal schools, promoting needed legislation, and securing more regular attendance; and a committee that would address how to make TSTA more practical. Percy also noted the absence of school trustees at the meeting and suggested inviting trustees, mayors, and state officials to attend TSTA meetings. Finally he noted dangers with regard to employment decisions: "Family, political or religious influences too often control the selection of teachers, not merit." These causes, he argued were "gaining power day by day."[92]

In addition to his service on committees and as an executive of various professional organizations, Percy also spoke regularly to gatherings of the TSTA and other organizations throughout the 1880s and 1890s. In 1889 he was a discussant on a TSTA panel debating the topic "What preparation ought to be required for entering college?" Percy argued against the position forwarded by professors Bringhurst and

L. A. Johnson whose position held that Latin and Greek courses were important preparation for college."[93] In 1890 Percy spoke at the Central Texas Teachers Association in response to a paper on "Teachers' Tenure of Office." He argued that teachers needed to "work up the school boards, and the patrons, and stir up the newspapers on the subject [of tenure]," as he emphasized the problem of hard-working teachers being replaced because of "a request for more money or to place someone with political connections."[94] In 1894, at the meeting of the State Association of Superintendents and Principals, held conjointly with the first meeting of the Southern Educational Association, he again urged teachers to address the public with their concerns: "We have still before us a great missionary work in organizing public opinion to make it effective."[95]

In the early days of her marriage, Anna seems to have been considerably less active in organizations than was Percy. She was not an official member of the Texas State Teachers Association in many years, even though, being female, she needed only to submit her name in order to join. Whether or not her lesser participation was due to personal preference or prevailing norms within the field is impossible to determine. Although some women held leadership roles in the teachers' association, men predominated both in executive positions and as speakers at the association's annual meetings. The program of the 1885 TSTA conference, for example, listed only three females among dozens of presenters: Miss Fannie Reese, Miss Nannie C. Breeding, and Mrs. Maggie Barlow. Women were not excluded from the TSTA, and even had the possibility of being elected to an executive position, as was Nannie Breeding in later years, but their place in the organization generally mirrored women's place in the schools of the time: they made up the bulk of teachers and the bulk of membership in organizations, but held executive positions far less often than men.[96] In smaller educational associations, as well, the men dominated. For example, the Smith County Teachers Association, of which the Pennybackers were founding members, was headed by men even though the women members outnumbered them. Despite the women's majority—the association boasted thirteen female and ten male members—men held the positions of president and first and second vice president, while females served as treasurer and secretary of the organization.[97]

Although she did not always maintain a regular membership in the educational organizations, Anna nevertheless presented at several annual state conferences of these groups and spoke on an incredible variety of topics over the years. The TSTA had held annual meetings for many years, but they had "been poorly attended and awakened no enthusiasm." In the mid-1880s, however, the association grew stronger and the meetings became livelier. The *Texas School Journal* reported, "In 1884, the one of the white teachers was a success; in 1885, the one at Waco a grand success, and in 1886, the one at Austin was in every respect one of the most imposing and learned gatherings in the history of the state."[98] At this successful meeting of 1886, Anna presented on "Pestalozzi, His Life and Work."[99] Several years later, in 1891, Anna presented "The School Should Shape the General Reading of the Pupil."[100] The next year she and Percy both appeared on the program at the TSTA conference: Percy presented with W. L. Bringhurst of College Station in response to E. M. Pace's "The Course of Study Demanded for the Intermediate Grades by a Strict Adherence to Educational Principles." His lecture was entitled "Modifications of Such a Course Demanded by Conditions of Life in Texas at the Present Time." Anna's speech was entitled "The World's Fair—What Should Texas Do in the Interest of Education?"—perhaps a reference to preparations for the upcoming World's Columbian Exposition to be held in Chicago the next year.[101] In 1897 Anna's address was titled "The Teacher Who Most Influenced Me." The Pennybackers did not appear on the TSTA program for 1898, but Anna presented that year at the East Texas Teachers Association on the topic of art in the classroom.[102] In 1895 Anna had presented her lecture "Teacher's Reading Circles" to the same organization.[103] In 1900, established as the author of a popular Texas history, Anna attended a meeting of the Texas Historical Association, speaking on "What the Texas Teacher Can Do for Texas History." The *Texas School Journal* reported that Anna's "words and injunctions in her talk to the teachers of Texas were strong and earnest and very beautiful. They gave inspiration to more than one young man or young woman in the assembly hall." The article noted as well Anna's exhortations to the teachers of Texas history, "To them if any, she declared, belonged the power, the privilege of molding the youth of our broad State into true, patriotic Texans."[104] In addition to presenting at meetings of the TSTA, Anna attended the meetings of other education-oriented groups. With Percy, Anna attended the meeting of the Southern Educational Association at Galveston in 1894. She served on that organization's committee to promote Mother's Day. Anna also served on at least one committee organized by the State Association of Superintendents and Principals. The committee's purpose was to develop an educational exhibit at the next state fair—in Dallas in 1895. Texas teachers had been dissatisfied with the weak exhibitions of the past and attributed the poor displays to the fact that there was little time between the opening of the school year and the opening of the state fair. Anna's committee began in February to urge teachers to begin planning immediately and to lay aside work for displays for the next fall. A note to teachers and school trustees suggested that they organize local exhibits and then send materials to the organizers of the state-level exhibition.[105]

SUMMER TEACHER INSTITUTES

Another sign of Anna and Percy's rising status in the profession was their role in training other teachers. Even their single year at the Sam Houston Normal Institute provided them with more training than most teachers of the time possessed. In Texas, as in most of the country at the time, many teachers possessed only a high school diploma and obtained a teaching certificate by passing a county examination. With so little preparation, teachers in the state required professional development. Teacher institutes were one answer to the problem of lack of teacher professional training, and they were popular across the country. These institutes were a useful form of teacher education in an age before teachers commonly pursued education beyond high school. Held during summer months, the institutes might last a week or several. In Texas, summer institutes were sponsored by the state, but teachers paid their own transportation and lodging while attending.[106] Competition for teaching positions at the institutes was stiff, but with their normal school training and growing prominence in the state, Anna and Percy were in demand as conductors of institutes. Percy began teaching at the summer institutes in the early 1880s, when he taught calisthenics at the normal institute in San Marcos before traveling to Europe.[107] Later, in 1885, he headed the summer normal in Tyler after trading with another educator for that particular city.[108] He held that position again in 1886. That same year, Anna conducted an institute in San Marcos, Texas, along with several other instructors. One hundred three teachers attended, and Anna instructed them in orthography, reading, and elocution. She was also in charge of the Friday evening entertainment.[109] In 1887 Anna again taught at the summer institute in San Marcos, this time teaching her favorite subject, history.[110] After the births of her children in the late 1880s, Anna appears to have stopped her work with summer institutes. Percy, however, continued accepting this work into the 1890s.[111]

Anna had strong opinions about the purpose of the summer institutes, which she shared in the *Texas School Journal*. Nationally, summer institutes generally consisted of three elements: a review of common-school subjects, with attention to the best methods of teaching them;

lectures on and discussion of the "organization of the schools, the classification of pupils, and the theory and practice of teaching"; and "public lessons on and discussions of broader educational topics, to take place in the evenings."[112] Unfortunately institutes often fell short of addressing these three elements because "the teachers' thin grasp of subject-matter knowledge necessitated thorough reviews."[113] Educational historian Christine Ogren notes, "While teachers' institutes did more to engender enthusiasm than to provide in-depth training, they reached a very broad number of teachers."[114] Anna's experiences with teacher institutes support Ogren's overall assessment of what the institutes were widely able to accomplish, but her understanding of the ideal role of the institute differed slightly from Ogren's three elements. Anna believed that "institutes have, or should have, two main objects, Instruction in Philosophy of Teaching and the Cultivation of an esprit de corps among teachers."[115] Despite this ideal, Anna recognized that the teaching force needed drill in subject knowledge. However, she insisted that this was "not the true institute." In her opinion the institute should focus less on factual content and more on philosophy and methods. "Not the what but the how and why, fall in the province of your institute conductor," she wrote in an article for the *Texas School Journal.*[116] According to Anna, the role of the institute was to encourage teachers to address these questions: "How shall I impart this to my pupils? Is this plan true to nature? Why does this plan succeed and that one fail? What relation does this study bear to the child's mental development? When should it be taught? What is its underlying principle?" Anna promoted "interpretation of culture" as the role of a true teacher, writing again in the *Texas School Journal:* "Don't you see the stimulus that comes from such work? Don't you see how it cries, 'away with imitation, down with your parrot drill: Give us teaching, pure and undefiled Nature's teaching'?" Because she believed that the institute should "season" theory with practice, Anna suggested that institute conductors give model lessons (the object) and let the teachers deduce the principles that informed the lesson—using the object method's principle of moving from the concrete (the model lesson) to the abstract (the underlying principles).[117]

ANNA PENNYBACKER THE AUTHOR

While Percy made his mark on the field of education in the state through leadership roles in multiple educational associations, Anna enhanced her reputation by writing articles for educational journals. From 1886 until around 1900, she regularly contributed articles on a range of educational topics to the *Texas School Journal.* As she did in her summer institute work, Anna emphasized the practical over the theoretical in her writing. She focused on concrete advice, including lesson suggestions and content, for practicing teachers. Her articles offered young teachers concrete plans for recitation or advice about comportment, organization, and classroom management.

She began her first series of articles for the *School Journal* in 1886. These articles consisted of monthly outlines for "memorial" lessons featuring a great historical, literary, or political figure. The articles were similar in content and form to the biographical sketches she had published in the *Carthage Press* a few years earlier, and represent a continuation of her interest in biography. Fittingly for a young woman who would write a history and become a political leader herself, for her first article she chose Macaulay, the English statesman and historian, an essayist noted for his powerful style of composition. Articles on Milton, Tennyson, and Longfellow followed in later months.[118] Pennybacker's biographical sketches focused on the heroic nature of her subjects—she wrote of their early talent and the hardships they overcame to achieve success. Throughout this series of articles and in several other articles about the teaching of history, Anna presented a pedagogical vision for teaching this subject. This vision emphasized great historical figures and used biography, seen as a primary organizing principle, for the teaching of history. Great men and women were to serve as exemplars for students, and the study of their lives was relevant for guidance in living one's own. With this emphasis on the individual, Anna viewed history as drama, with historical figures as key elements. Settings and plot were also important, but secondary to the human interest and action. Her methods for teaching history supported the idea that children were to enter and engage in history through identification with historical figures. Anna suggested classroom activities that included, for example, children role-playing historical figures and writing letters as if they had witnessed events firsthand. She also encouraged teachers to emphasize depth of knowledge and understanding rather than broad memorization of facts. Although memorization was still important and recitation a primary element in both instruction and evaluation, Anna emphasized comprehension and analysis. She encouraged teachers to organize student debates on current or historical events, and for classes to select the winners. Anna's methods counter Finkelstein's observation that teachers in her time period were not concerned that their students think independently about information and facts they were learning.

Another series of articles Anna wrote for the *Texas School Journal* began in 1890. These articles, "Letters to a Young Teacher," give a broader sense of her understanding of the teacher's role in preparing her students for life. Under the conceit that she was writing to a young, untrained, and inexperienced teacher named Helen, Anna offered ample and diverse advice based on her own ten years in the classroom. Included were tips on general professional and personal development, suggestions for the use and acquisition of materials and facilities, and advice on teaching content and procedure. These letters provide a picture of what life might have been like for teachers in the late nineteenth century and what Anna herself might have been like as a teacher.

In the first letter of the series, the narrator, an experienced teacher, responds to a letter or conversation in which the new teacher "bewailed" her "lack of normal training, experience, books, journals and, indeed. . . . everything that goes to make up a successful teacher."[119] The narrator reassures the fledgling teacher that despite the inadequacies in her training, with "fine health, youthful energy, happy disposition, bright mind and true ambition" she can succeed as a teacher.[120] The experienced teacher chides the "so-called" teachers who "think they need no educational journals, no works on methods or matter, no previous training for imparting what they know," noting that they fail in their duty to their students and keep back the profession. To address a lack of training, the narrator recommends that the young teacher study independently, reading from journals and books. Unsurprisingly, the narrator strongly recommends the *School Journal* first. With teacher preparation limited in the late-nineteenth-century United States, particularly in the Southwest, education journals like the *Texas School Journal* commonly served as an accessible form of professional development in lieu of more formal, distant, and expensive educational opportunities.[121] Of course, Anna is not unbiased here. Her articles appeared in the *School Journal,* and the journal was related to the state superintendent of schools, whose good favor Anna and Percy would have desired, especially after the publication of her textbook in 1888. The *School Journal* was important, Anna wrote, because it provided information about the work of other teachers, including how they were solving the problems that faced the profession. The journal also helped form a basis for professional pride. In it, she wrote the young teacher, "You will not only find a host of good things to help you in your work but will learn what your Texas co-laborers are doing, how the cause of public education is growing, the obstacles yet in our way and how to remove these obstacles; you need to be kept in sympathy with others workers [*sic*] for, by kind Nature's law, this awakens in you renewed ardor."[122] In addition to the *School Journal,* Anna also recommended *Popular Educator,* published in Boston and sold for $1.00 per year, and Raub's *Methods of Teaching.*

In addition to subscribing to professional journals, Anna encouraged the young teacher to participate in the state teachers' association.[123] Professional development for teachers at this time, she understood, could not mean merely individual professional development, but also included participation in the development of the profession generally. Anna explained that attending meetings of the association provided the young teacher with the opportunity to develop professional relationships and gain the spirit and inspiration to bring back to her classroom and community. The third important professional development activity the experienced teacher recommended was that the novice attend teachers' institutes. Again Anna stressed the importance of forming bonds with coworkers as they met annually (or more frequently) to improve their skills.

The young teacher in Pennybacker's series of articles is employed in what Anna represented as a school "typical of Texas style," a "rude box house mounted on stilts as if ready to walk off at a moment's notice." Still, given the conditions faced by others, the experienced teacher advised the novice to "'think of your mercies' and keep cheerful."[124] She advised the young teacher to improve conditions and offered suggestions as to how she could do so. Her suggestions ranged from using girlish charm to convince trustees to add windows to the classroom to appointing the room on a budget."[125] In addition to advising the young teacher on gaining the supplies and materials she would need to teach successfully, Anna provided advice for the teacher's physical and mental health. She wrote, "It really gives me the blues to see a fresh, rosy, bright-eyed young woman enter the school-room and hear the good folk say: "Poor thing; she'll soon begin to fade: those teachers don't stay pretty long." In what may have been one of her first forays into social reform, Anna critiqued styles in women's clothing that restrict movement or bind and restrict the body, giving as a negative example, Miss Prim: "In winter her skirts never weighed less than eight or ten pounds. . . . day after day she carried that load from her waist and went home completely tired."[126] By contrast, Anna recommended that teachers wear comfortable shoes and looser fitting, lightweight clothing. Appealing to the young woman's vanity, Anna argued that the key to maintaining youthful looks was to reduce stress and increase physical health. "Take plenty of exercise in the open air, and *don't worry,*" she advised.[127] She attributed the rapid aging of female teachers to a tendency to sit at home reading, sewing, writing, and worrying about their students, and she encouraged them instead to move about and be active socially.

In addition to giving recommendations for the young teacher's general professional knowledge and the management of materials and facilities, Anna offered specific advice about what and how the novice teacher was to teach. This advice on substance and procedure lays out a sort of curriculum for public school pupils. Anna believed that information about substance without the procedure would be useless to the young teacher, and she described substance and procedure for lessons in tandem. In addition to academic work that focused on classical literature, history, and current events, Anna encouraged the young teacher to teach her students social skills. Manners appropriate to the American middle class were an important subject of study that Anna discussed in more than one letter. She reminded the new teacher that children may come from families where middle-class manners were not exercised, and recommended that teachers teach table manners with the realization that the students' families may not practice them. "Be very careful," she warned the new teacher, "not to offend any one by making such statements as, 'No lady will put her knife into her mouth,' 'no gentleman will make a noise over his soup.' You can let them know what is proper without making them blush at the thought that deems their parents boorish."[128] She also suggested that the new teacher have students practice how to greet one another, to introduce a friend or honored guest. "We learn how to do a thing by doing it," she reminded the new teacher.[129]

In the "Letters to a Young Teacher" series, Anna suggested that teacher professional development should include not just individual attainment of skills, but active participation in the development of the profession. In her view, attitude—or "zeal"—was as important as professional knowledge and skills, and professional knowledge and skills were defined broadly to include substantial and procedural knowledge about academic subjects as well as social knowledge and behaviors (manners, for example) that the author views as essential for teachers' success. The letters addressed all aspects of a teacher's professional life and presented a view of schooling that encouraged a curriculum to address the students' educational needs broadly by including social and moral lessons, and lessons on health and practical living, along with the academic lessons.

Other of Anna's articles in the *Texas School Journal* offered both specific advice to teachers on content and methods, as well as Anna's views on a wide range of educational and social issues. Content and methods of teaching history were frequent topics of her articles and she provided the content information teachers needed to inform their lessons on historical topics. Anna encouraged teachers to engage student interest through appeals to emotion and imagination and through classroom activities that involved some active participation on the part of students. In particular she encouraged teachers to focus on heroes and great events, the study of which would inform, interest, and, ideally, inspire the children.

BIRTHS AND DEATHS: FAMILY CHANGES

Anna's and Percy's personal lives were as full as their professional lives during the 1880s and 1890s. In addition to establishing themselves as state leaders in education, they enjoyed an active social life. Anna was active in clubs, and the couple traveled not only to exhibitions and events in Texas and other states, but abroad to Europe as well, fulfilling one of Anna's long-time dreams. They also saw their family grow during this time. Their first child, a baby girl named Lorena, was born in 1886, but died five months later.[130] Son Bonner arrived two years later. In 1894 Percy accepted the superintendency of schools in Palestine, Texas, and in the fall he and Anna relocated to that city with their small son. In Palestine, Anna retired from teaching to care for her growing family. Their son Percy Jr. was born the year following the move, and daughter Ruth two years later, in February 1897.[131]

Although no longer in the classroom on a daily basis, Anna continued to be active in educational affairs during her time in Palestine. She continued to write for the *School Journal* and revised the textbook which she published in 1888. In 1897, a few months after the birth of her third child, Anna presented a paper entitled "The Teacher Who Most Influenced Me" at the Texas State Teachers Association annual meeting.[132] In 1898, when Texas teachers created a Chautauqua in Boulder, Colorado, Anna took charge of the Chautauqua Literary and Scientific Circle there. With her assistant caring for her children, Anna devoted her attention to "the work of the Chautauqua reading course; conducting the CLSC round table discussions, arranging for lectures on the allotted reading, selling the books themselves and in all way strengthening the tie with the New York Chautauqua." She molded the Colorado Chautauqua's woman's council into a club on the lines of the Chautauqua Woman's Club, with the intent that "women should learn from it how to conduct club business." Additionally she presided, prepared the programs, gave lectures, and directed social affairs.[133]

Along with his duties as superintendent, Percy ran both the couple's small publishing company and an employment service for Texas teachers which he promoted in the *Texas School Journal.*[134] In 1898 he was recognized in the *School Journal* as the senior school superintendent in Texas. At that time he had held the position longer than anyone else still employed in that position in the state.[135] As the 1890s drew to a close, however, the Pennybacker name appeared less frequently in the *School Journal.* Percy was ill with leukemia and, although he maintained his position as superintendent in Palestine until March 1899, he took a less active role in state educational affairs.[136] The last years of the decade were years of illness for Percy, who at times left Anna with the children to seek treatment outside of Texas. Sadly, the treatments failed, and in May 1899, Anna was summoned to Missouri, where Percy had sought treatment for his illness. She arrived in time to be with him at his death.[137]

Percy's death left Anna with three very young children to raise on her own. Prior to his passing, the couple had planned to move to Austin, Texas, where they believed they could provide better educational opportunities for their children as well as better promote their business interests. Newly widowed, Anna continued with these plans, moving with her children to Austin in 1900. Their lives there would be comfortable. Percy held several life insurance policies which provided money for Anna and the children upon his death, and Anna's own work with her textbook had provided a solid income. She had a large house built on Whittis Avenue, just north of the University of Texas. Although Anna would travel widely from this point in her life onward, this would remain her home until the end of her life.[138]

Chapter Three

PENNYBACKER'S *HISTORY OF TEXAS*

WHEN ANNA MOVED TO AUSTIN with her children, the Pennybacker name was a household word in Texas. With their involvement in educational affairs in the state, Anna and particularly Percy had gained recognition among Texas educators early in their careers. In the mid-1880s, Anna had embarked on an endeavor that made the Pennybacker name broadly recognized, not just among educators, but among the general public of the state as well. In 1885–86, while principal of the high school in Tyler, Anna began to write a Texas history textbook that, when completed, would be used throughout the state. Anna's decision to prepare this history of Texas for schoolchildren resulted from encouragement by a visiting teacher who was impressed by the way she approached the subject. Anna was a superb orator who was said to have captivated her students with her storytelling abilities.[1] At the suggestion she write a book, however, Anna reportedly laughed, as her "days seemed already quite full with the high school, private classes in expression, writing for educational magazines and social duties."[2]

With Percy's encouragement, however, Anna began the arduous process of writing her Texas history. Although few records of Anna's work on the first edition exist, documents that supported her many revisions indicate that the process of writing the book could not have been easy. Relying heavily on published histories written for a general audience, she adapted stories to suit her young readers. Anna did not have easy access to a substantial library. Consequently, she purchased books from remote dealers. For some information she relied on personal contact with individuals who had access to books she did not possess. In the days before photocopies, her contacts copied relevant information by hand and sent it to her by mail.[3] Although she relied most heavily on published secondary sources, Anna also solicited information from individuals or unpublished secondary sources. She corresponded, for example, with a former soldier in the Texas Revolution about particular battles, and with family members of significant figures in Texas's history, such as Adina de Zavala, the granddaughter of Lorenzo de Zavala, the first vice president of the Republic of Texas.[4]

At 244 pages, the first edition of Anna's textbook was compact, even slight, by twenty-first-century standards. She began the book with an account of La Salle's return to France from America and concluded with a description of Governor Sul Ross's administration through August 1888. The final seventy-two pages consisted of a copy of the Constitution of Texas and its amendments. Throughout the book, the text was accompanied by extensive footnotes. These notes often provided background information or anecdotes about the people or groups discussed in the main text, but some provided detailed accounts of the mythic stories of Texas history. One footnote, for example, related the story of Cynthia Ann Parker, who as a child was captured by the Comanches and lived among them for many years.[5] Each chapter or era concluded with a brief "Blackboard Analysis," a rough outline of the main persons and events of the chapter. Other than this guide, however, few pedagogical tools were provided. Anna suggested at the beginning of the book that students could be assigned to make their own relief map of Texas using putty on a wooden plank.[6] Nevertheless, the textbook lacked the extensive comprehension questions and student assignment suggestions that accompany present day textbooks. *Pennybacker's History* was used during a period that stressed what Miles Myers terms "recitation literacy."[7] Myers notes that students were expected to memorize and recite back for the teacher large portions of the text. Teachers in Texas schools of the late 1800s likely used Pennybacker's textbook in this way. Indeed, many Texans recounted to Anna how, even in adulthood, they were able to recite the first chapter of her history from memory.[8]

Anna's writing style in this first edition also differed dramatically from that of textbooks today. The opening paragraph of the book displayed her enthusiasm for romantic descriptions. "Some two hundred years ago, had one been in Versailles," she began, "he would have found Louis XIV on the throne, with all France delighting to honor the 'grand Monarque.' What sights were to be seen in the gay capital! The king's magnificent palace, with its beautiful grounds, playing fountains, blooming flowers, and singing birds, was the center of all life and pleasure." Anna introduced La Salle in similarly grand terms: "But one morning there were even more gayety and animation than usual, for wonderful news had come to the king and his court. 'la Salle . . . has returned from America!' was the announcement that caused such a stir among the royal household."[9] Anna stated in the introduction that she had attempted to "picture the events in our history in a style easy and natural, yet vivid," as teaching history "demands not only a live instructor, but also a live text-book."[10] Her style of writing, however, was both the subject of praise and of criticism, and later editions of the textbook demonstrated an evolution in her writing from this florid style to one that was more tempered and academic.

PUBLICATION AND MARKETING

The textbook was completed and published in 1888, the year Anna turned twenty-seven, and shortly after the death of the Pennybackers' first child.[11] At that time most textbook publishers operated out of northern states, and the Pennybackers found no publisher interested in issuing a Texas history for school children.[12] To get the book into print, the Pennybackers self-published it. They contracted with a local printing firm, paid the cost of printing, and marketed the book across the state. At the time the textbook was published, Texas uniform textbook laws had yet to be enacted. Each district decided which books would be used, and parents were required to purchase the books for their children. The Pennybackers marketed Anna's textbook by contacting individual schoolteachers and administrators in districts across the state. One method of promoting the book was a printed circular distributed to school personnel. The flyer included four pages of praise for the book by educators across the state. Those quoted in the circular touted the book's writing style, organization, and appropriateness for schoolchildren. Professor A. W. Orr of Omen noted the "happy style of the author, the logical arrangement of topics, the omission of unimportant statistics and the artistic appearance of the book."[13]

Percy's position as superintendent of schools in Tyler and Palestine, and his involvement in the Texas State Teachers Association, undoubtedly helped the marketing efforts. In 1895, as the second edition of the book was being published, Percy sent out professionally printed surveys to administrators of districts around the state which he signed "Supt. Percy V. Pennybacker, Palestine, Texas. The survey requested information about the number of Texas histories used in the school, which Texas history textbook was currently used, the names and addresses of the local dealers from whom the school purchased books, and the name and address of the respondent. The reverse side of the postcard offered space for additional comments.

The textbook, widely known as *Pennybacker's History*, gained immediate success. By 1898 it had been adopted by the newly formed state textbook committee, and the Pennybackers established their own publishing firm. Besides the original edition published in 1888, the Pennybackers and later Anna herself issued revised editions in 1895, 1898, 1900, 1908, 1912, and 1924.[14] Order estimates to Anna's publisher from the early 1900s indicate that during the textbook's run as the state-adopted Texas history, the Pennybackers sold nearly twenty-five thousand books per year.[15]

CRITICISM AND REVISIONS, 1895–1900

The Pennybacker textbook provoked debate about the nature and purpose of school history. For Anna, the purpose of studying history was to inspire patriotism. A textbook, she would write in later years, required accuracy, teachableness, and inspiration. It must "leave the pupil imbued with a spirit of true patriotism."[16] She and her supporters believed that her textbook's romanticism effectively conveyed the "true spirit of a true Texas" and inspired patriotism and love of the state in its readers.[17] The immediate success of her textbook indicates that many educators agreed. Nevertheless, Pennybacker had detractors. An 1891 review in the *San Antonio Express*, for example, excoriated the textbook as well as Anna's qualifications as a writer. In an article entitled "An Alleged History, Wonderful Powers of Invention Displayed in Narrative," William Bowen wrote, "I am simply amazed that any teacher capable of passing judgment on the all-important study of history should have been found who would adopt the book in its present state of inaccuracies, absurdities and palpable errors."[18] He cited a long list of details which Anna had incorrectly asserted in the textbook, beginning in the first chapter with La Salle's motives and travels. Anna's assertions that La Salle sought a new route to China and that he sailed down the Ohio River are just two of the many points with which Bowen took issue. Bowen also objected to Anna's omission of such information as the mysterious diplomacy behind the establishment of the Neutral Ground which Bowen attributes to General Wilkinson being bribed by "the Mexican diplomatist."[19] Also, he criticized Anna's writing, objecting in part to her "syntax" but reserving the bulk of his criticism for the text's absurdities, "the numerous irrelevant foot notes of a sensational character," an incorrect definition of the word "presidio," a bear-hunting dog, and a reference to Baron de Bastrop, founder of Texas's Bastrop County, as a "fairy Godmother."[20] Despite the extraordinary harshness of his comments, Bowen placed Pennybacker in good company with his criticism. In the same article, he railed against "Macaulay, Hume and Gibbon," noting that they, like Pennybacker, favored style over historical accuracy. "Fictitious stories are easier to get hold of than facts and the general public are more readily captured with romances than with facts—because the 'general public,' as a rule, is never a profound student," he mused. The debate about accuracy versus style and inspiration would continue for years, with Anna consistently arguing that her book was both accurate and inspirational.[21]

In 1893 and 1894, Anna began the first major revision of her textbook. Her decision to revise may have been a response to criticism such as Bowen's, but it also took into account demands of the market. Evidence suggests that she was losing business because her history did not continue to the present year.[22] Although Anna would update the textbook on a regular basis for the next few decades, this first revision was the most extensive. For this revision, published 1895, she solicited feedback on the first edition from educators across the state. In response, she received numerous laudatory comments about the book. Many respondents found the book so satisfactory that they saw no need for change or room for improvement.[23] Despite the generally positive comments, however, she also received many widely varied suggestions for improvement. Former SHNI classmate Harry F. Estill, who had obtained a position at the Normal Institute, found Pennybacker's book "a textbook par excellence" given "the place for which it is intended."[24] According to Estill, the book was appropriate for the fourth grade. Despite his high praise, however, Estill identified three areas of criticism that Pennybacker should address in her revisions. He wrote, "The criticisms that I have heard on the book are that (1) it is too elementary—'a child's book'; (2) it is incomplete, or not full enough; (3) the language in some places is too figurative or extravagant."[25] The question of completeness that Estill raised also appears in many of the other letters Pennybacker received in response to her query. The list of items her respondents thought should be added ranged from textual tools to help make the book more usable, to complete chapters about issues in Texas history, to specific details about particular events or people. By far the most requested additions to the textbook were maps. Anna included no maps in her original edition, noting that "any teacher may secure an excellent map of Texas, free of charge, by applying to Central Railroad offices."[26] Educators using her book apparently found this suggestion inadequate.[27]

The map obtained from the railroad would not allow students to "trace the heros [*sic*] of the early part of the story, in their movement across the territory." Respondents suggested adding a map for each chapter or era of Texas history.[28]

In addition to maps, Anna added a substantial amount of material to the revised edition, pushing its length from 244 pages in the first edition to nearly 400 pages in the revised edition.[29] Many of the additions addressed problems or requests written to Pennybacker in response to her request for feedback. She made corrections in response to many, but not all, of the criticisms lobbied by Bowen in his newspaper review, and included additions suggested by Bowen and those from whom she solicited feedback. Among these changes were reference dates at the top margins, a note about La Salle's burial place (the location is unknown), and a small footnote about the location of the Neutral Ground, provided at the request of several respondents.[30] Pennybacker also provided a key to pronunciation at the back of the book, and expanded the index. Some of the additions demonstrate Pennybacker's political acuity. Correspondence with several chapters of the Daughters of the Republic of Texas enabled her to add a section on that group's goals and activities. Similarly, she requested that ex-governor Sul Ross write an account of his term for inclusion in the book. Although he declined to write the passage, the textbook includes a glowing account of his heroism.[31] A similarly positive account accompanies the section on the sitting governor at the time of publication, James Steven Hogg.[32]

In response to Bowen's ridicule or the comments of supporters, Pennybacker also tightened up her writing style in the revised version. She adopted a more scholarly tone, added factual details, and limited obvious authorial opinion and bias. The following passages provide just one example of how her writing style changed. About Hayden Edwards' disputes with other settlers on his land grant, Pennybacker in 1888 wrote: "It happened that, scattered here and there over Edwards' land, were settlers who had come before he received his grant; these parties claimed immense tracts of land. Some of them were lazy, insolent Mexicans, while many others were criminals from the Neutral Ground. It is easy to see what troubles necessarily followed."[33] In the 1900 version, she revised this passage to read: "For years colonists, some with, but most without, legal rights had been settling in the country about Nacogdoches; Mexicans, Indians, rough characters from the Neutral Ground, and daring American adventurers, all claimed more or less of the land granted to Edwards."[34] Notably, the prejudicial words "lazy" and "insolent," which Pennybacker uses to describe Mexicans in the first edition, are omitted from the second, although Pennybacker is still clearly writing in support of Edwards and his colonists. The latter version also extends the account and offers greater depth of description of the events and controversies, including the views of the opposing sides. This move toward a more balanced, scholarly tone is evident throughout much of the revised edition, although Pennybacker clearly writes from an Anglo-American perspective. Notably, just one of Pennybacker's respondents critiqued bias in the textbook. T. V. Orr, principal of Liberty High School, perceived regional bias. He wrote, "On page 141. I find these words 'After our noble Lee surrendered:' etc. This savors of party feeling. And all things of this kind, should in my opinion, be avoided. Several of my pupils have objected to the phrase and dislike the book on that account."[35] This passage is rewritten in the later edition.

ADOPTION BY THE STATE, 1898–1913

The debate on accuracy versus inspiration in a history textbook was not the only controversy that surrounded the Pennybacker history textbook. Anna's foray into textbook publishing put her in the middle of a sectional debate about the content of history textbooks and the ways in which history, particularly the history of the southern states, could be cast. Historically, most of the country's textbooks had been published in northern states. Southern educators and other prominent southerners had for decades, even before the Civil War, objected to northern bias in textbooks of various subjects, and had advocated for specifically southern textbooks to represent southern culture.[36] Southerners understood their history and culture to derive not from the Puritans of New England, but from the Cavaliers. Some traced southern ancestry directly to classical Greeks and Romans. In addition to claiming familial and cultural ties to the Cavaliers and classical civilizations, southern romanticism "highlighted distinctions between South and North, lauded the ideas of chivalry and honor, and promoted a military tradition."[37] Post–Civil War, "military defeat and the burden of Reconstruction policies rendered Southerners deeply suspicious of any possible reintroduction of offensive textbooks which might cast aspersions on them and their recent experiences."[38] Despite high levels of distrust of northern publishers, however, the South produced few large publishers of its own.[39]

In Texas, attempts to control the depiction of southern history were invigorated in the mid-1890s in part as the result of populist threats to the reigning southern ruling class. Historian Fred Arthur Bailey dates the Texas campaign for a southern version of American history to the

1895 Grand Reunion of the United Confederate Veterans held in Houston.[40] Several years later, in 1898, residents of the Texas Confederate Home protested the first state-adopted history books on the grounds that they "expressed sentiments inimical to the ideas and prejudices of the South."[41] Soon the Confederate Veterans, the United Daughters of the Confederacy, and other Texas Confederate societies joined together in advocating for "unbiased" accounts of U.S. history. "Unbiased," to members of these Confederate societies, denoted texts that stressed the constitutionality of secession and the virtues of a "stratified society, properly articulated by class and race."[42] Depictions of slavery and the factors that brought about the Civil War were of particular concern to supporters of the Confederacy. These organizations demanded that slavery be presented as a benign and natural institution, and that the outbreak of the Civil War be attributed to northern financial interests rather than moral interest in freeing the slaves. Confederate organizations in Texas worked for the next several decades to ensure that southern views of history prevailed in the state. Their tactics included monitoring history books used in public schools and libraries, and advocating, with good success, the removal of books offensive to southern sensibilities. The two most prominent organizations, the Confederate Veterans and the United Daughters of the Confederacy (UDC), each appointed textbook committees whose job it was to review the books used in the state's public schools. Members of the Confederate societies notified school administrators of offensive textbooks, and school superintendents generally removed offending texts without resistance. In most cases, school leadership seems to have shared the views and concerns of the Confederate associations. A survey of school superintendents conducted by the UDC in 1907 indicated that most believed history should be taught, not from an unbiased standpoint, but from "a strictly Southern" point of view, although how many were likely to report otherwise to this organization is a matter of question.[43]

In the late 1880s, the Texas state legislature investigated various models of state textbook adoption. This effort was spurred in part by a desire to lower textbook costs and to address problems that arose from each school district adopting textbooks independently. However, the effort was also strongly supported by organizations wishing to control the content of textbooks and the curriculum of Texas public schools. The Texas Confederate Veterans, for example, claimed to have advocated for the law for decades before it was passed, acknowledging that it was created to give the organizations greater control over textbook content.[44] Despite the textbook law having prominent supporters in the Confederate societies, the Texas State Teachers Association vigorously opposed state adoption and/or publication of textbooks. In a "memorial" presented to the House of Representatives, Twenty-first Legislature, the executive committee of the association called uniform textbook legislation "a species of paternalism of the most despotic type, and not in accord with the democratic principals of local self government."[45] The teachers lost this battle, however, and they were unable to prevent uniform textbook legislation from passing.

In 1897, the state of Texas adopted a law that established its State Textbook Committee, which would be responsible for selecting textbooks for all the schools of the state, exempting only cities with populations larger than ten thousand, and state colleges and universities. The legislation provided that publishers seeking adoption would submit their book to the state. The State Textbook Board, a group composed of the head of the State Board of Education, the state superintendent of education, the president of the Sam Houston Normal Institute, and the attorney general, would be responsible for selecting textbooks upon the recommendation of a textbook commission composed of five "persons engaged in the school business." The committee would select the best textbooks based on "the internal merits of the books irrespective of price." The board was to adopt the committee's first choice unless other books were offered at lower prices.[46] Revisions of the legislation in later years also required textbooks adopted by the state to be "unbiased," a restriction the Confederate Veterans sought to expand to all taxpayer supported schools within the state, including the exempted large cities and state-supported institutions of higher education.[47] Passage of the state textbook amendment succeeded in giving the Confederate organizations additional control over the textbook adoption process.

Although they profited from the bill, the Pennybackers were among those who opposed it. Percy argued against the bill on the grounds that it was undemocratic in that it usurped the right of local districts under local control to determine which books would be used in the school.[48] The effects of the bill on the Pennybacker textbook enterprise are difficult to determine. For the most part, Anna's textbook did not attract the attention, positive or negative, that U.S. histories were accorded by Confederate organizations. Whereas the Pennybackers' friend and former classmate H. F. Estill wrote a history of the United States that frequently centered in a decades-long, active debate about U.S. history books in Texas, Anna's book, by contrast, rarely was mentioned.[49] This lack of attention may have resulted from the fact that, in dealing with Texas history, she was able to keep her account of the Civil War brief and to avoid the controversial issue of its causes. The single mention of her text in a report of the UDC textbook committee merely notes it as the product of a southern author.[50] From a business perspective, because her book was the adopted Texas history textbook for fifteen years, she had captive buyers who were required to purchase it. However, she and Percy were now required to compete for adoption at the state level, and to abide by the regulations stipulated by the law. In addition, if the Pennybackers' textbook failed to win state adoption, the primary market for the book would disappear.

FAILURE TO BE RE-ADOPTED, 1912

Pennybacker's textbook was adopted by the state in 1897, 1902, and 1907. In the fall of 1912, the textbook faced re-adoption once more. Despite multiple assurances from Texas educators familiar with her book, Pennybacker clearly worried about the possibility of her book being passed over for re-adoption. Pennybacker's correspondence indicates that she began seeking information about the competing textbook and its publisher early on. By December 1911 she already was aware that she would bid for re-adoption against a new book published by Row, Peterson & Company of Chicago. The book's authors, she would learn, were Eugene Barker, Charles Potts, and Charles Ramsdell, all distinguished faculty members in history and government at the University of Texas. Having discovered the identities of the publisher and authors, she made inquiries among contacts in Chicago and New York seeking information about the content of the textbook, Row, Peterson & Company, the terms of its contract with the authors, and the bid the company would submit to the textbook committee of the state of Texas. After Percy's death, Anna had contracted with the A. S. Barnes Company in New York to print the book which she then marketed independently, thus retaining her rights to the book. Her publisher, John Barnes Pratt, president of A. S. Barnes, sent word that December that Row, Peterson & Company had purchased rights to the competing book and likely would support it with all of its resources.[51] This news spurred Anna to action. Employing a network of contacts across the state and country, she gathered as much information as possible about her competition and, throughout 1912, she waged a wide-reaching publicity campaign designed to win re-adoption for her textbook.

By the second decade of the twentieth century, Pennybacker had cultivated a reputation in the state and nationally as a charming, southern lady from Texas. Although conventions of femininity, in the South particularly, required women to foreswear political action, Pennybacker clearly knew how and was willing to engage in the political aspects of the adoption process. In fact she seems to have set the standards for intrigue and backdoor political maneuvering in this case. A letter from her publisher indicates how Pennybacker proceeded in her competition with the new textbook. Here publisher Pratt responds to Pennybacker's apparent request that he obtain and pass on to her confidential information about her rival, writing, "You give me a very difficult task, but I assure you that I will do all I can. It will take some little time to glean the information desired and I doubt very much my ability to ascertain the terms of the contract. Those things usually are kept pretty secret."[52] This same letter outlines Pratt's plans to prevent the submission of the competing Texas history by working behind the scenes with the Row, Peterson & Company. Pratt informed Pennybacker that he would ask for the adoption of his company's New Barnes Writing Books, and offered to approach Row, Peterson & Company with a deal that involved its dropping the Barker, Potts, and Ramsdell Texas history.[53] In a subsequent letter, Pratt regretted that he had been unable to find out much about the competing publisher other than that the firm had been rather "shaky" financially. However, Pratt outlined a "scheme" by which he and Pennybacker could learn more about the company. He would arrange a meeting between Pennybacker and a young author who had been an agent for Barnes, but was now going to compete with Row, Peterson & Company for the adoption of his English book in Texas.[54] The result of this scheme, or whether it was carried out at all, is unknown. Pratt, however, related success with a different deception which he described in a letter to Pennybacker. His wife, he wrote, "did a little detective work by going right to Mr. Row and passing as a pseudo author, interested in History, particularly in State Histories." Through this ruse, Mrs. Pratt, "By judicious handling, and without questioning. . . . elicited the information. . . . Mabel used her maiden name and the whole affair was handled beautifully."[55] The competing publisher, Mr. Row, revealed to Mrs. Pratt his logic for promoting a new Texas history. "He said that the Pennybacker History had been in use so long that it was about time a change was made."[56] Through her discussion with Mr. Row, Mrs. Pratt confirmed that "the three authors of whom you have knowledge have prepared the book." She also determined that the book would be about three hundred pages, with illustrations, and Row & Peterson were to assume "all the costs whether the book is adopted or not." Because of this arrangement, Pratt writes, "You will have a big fight on your hands and I wish I knew how to help you."[57] This news dampened Pratt's determination to fight Row, Peterson & Company's backing of the Barker book. In the same letter, Pratt delicately backs away from his earlier offer to persuade the publisher to drop the Barker, Potts, and Ramsdell book in exchange for support for their language book. Pratt notes that he might not submit his writing books (which he was going to use as leverage) after all, as he is "not much of a gambler in these State adoptions."[58]

Perhaps as a result of the discouraging news about the strength of the competing book, Pennybacker went all out in asking her friends and contacts to seek endorsements from superintendents in support of her book. In the early years of the new century, Anna had attained a prominent position in women's clubs at the state and national levels. Her connection with women's clubs gained her many contacts who were civic-minded and politically active, and Pennybacker mobilized this network in support of her textbook. She used her contacts from Texas women's clubs to pressure their prominent husbands for support and pressed friends to approach school trustees, superintendents, and teachers with the request that they write a recommendation for her textbook. The following excerpt demonstrates the politics, and in particular, the gender politics, involved in just one of these requests. A woman named Paulina reported her encounter with an unhelpful school board member: "Mr. Brooks is a boor, entirely unfitted by breeding and scholarship for the position he holds." Paulina continues to explain, "He was a candidate when Mr. Lefevre was elected, and imagined I had a strangle-hold on the two women who were then on the school-board, and took it as a personal affront when I didn't control their votes for him." Ever since "he has been in power," she noted, "he has made himself as disagreeable as possible about anything that I was concerned with."[59] Despite socially and politically difficult situations such as that described above, Pennybacker supporters used all their influence and power of persuasion to elicit the desired recommendations.[60] Some supporters acknowledged that their reason for writing the recommendation were related to their association with Mrs. Pennybacker and her past support, rather than the merits of the book itself. One supporter wrote, "I am doing this on account of the service you have rendered the cause of education and out of my regard to you for cordial cooperation given me while in the campaign of the Conference for Education in Texas."[61] Pennybacker's supporters offered to lobby for her at the highest levels of state government. Jessica Sayers wrote, "The Governor thinks something of me—I taught his boys—so he may care for my opinion if he has anything to say here."[62] Anna also had her brother, Sinnette, then a Waco attorney with connections to the governor, approach the governor on her behalf.

The political influence of the women's clubs garnered Pennybacker support from many parts of the state, but engendered resentment and backlash in at least one school superintendent. W. F. Jourdan of Del Rio wrote to Pennybacker's competitor, Professor Eugene Barker, complaining that he had been "besieged and beset" by clubwomen until he gave a qualified endorsement of Pennybacker's text. Acknowledging that he had not yet seen the Barker text, he wrote that he had "not a doubt that your new text is superior to the one now being used in this state," and suggested, "I have a plan already worked out and agreed upon between the President of the leading 'Woman's Club' here and myself whereby we expect to start something through a set of resolutions attacking no one, but setting the 'Clubs' right if possible before the Governor and the 'Text Book Commission' yet-to-be. . . . I have no motive in view whatever other than to get the best books for the children."[63] Barker's response was ambivalent. He wrote that he would appeal for adoption of the book solely on the grounds that "the school children of Texas would derive greater profit from its study than from the study of any other text which is now available." However, he complied with Jourdan's request for a copy of his textbook and wrote, "I hope that you will like the book, and that you will be willing to help secure its adoption."[64] Jourdan's eagerness to support Barker's book without having seen it undermines his statement that he is interested only in the welfare of the children, and his desire to set the women's clubs "right" in front of the governor more than hints of his resistance to Pennybacker's political power.

Although the team of writers responsible for the competing textbook was comprised of prominent academics at the University of Texas, Pennybacker's supporters portrayed the competition in regional terms. That Pennybacker was a Texan and a southerner worked strongly in her favor among some supporters, as the regional conflict was depicted in terms of North versus South. When one recommendation came back less positive than expected, Pennybacker had a supporter address the offender. Her associate wrote of the conversation: "I told him that you you [*sic*] were going to . . . come in [*sic*] competition with people possibly from Maine, Rhode Island and Connecticut, and that we could not afford to have a Texas girl, or woman, run over by a bunch like that, and her business taken away from her, and when I got through he [Prof. Orr] promised to write you another letter this evening, and I think I can guarantee that it will suit you a little better than the other one, and I hope will do you more good."[65] A Mrs. E. Reid similarly cast the situation in terms of southerners versus northerners, leaving the impression that southerners were more inclined to support the book without question, out of regional loyalty, whereas northerners sought the appearance of an unbiased attitude:

> I believe the party in question is inclined to our side of the matter too; but wished to see a copy of the other book, purely, so I took it, as the confirmation of an unbiased attitude. . . . Conditions here are different from those in most sections of Texas, in that this town is a settlement of Northern people imported to run the oil refining machinery, etc., and their friends, even the merchants are from Kansas, New York and Pennsylvania, especially Pittsburgh; I don't think the Southerners are in the ratio of as low as 1 to 50—my own husband is a New Yorker; & their sympathies are entirely with the things of their former home. . . . I can't recall on the instant a single Southerner of any influence in the town, I believe though the party in whom I am particularly interested is a native Texan' nay how I am pretty confident of success.[66]

As she revised the book through the years, Pennybacker took care to solicit the input and good will of southern women's organizations such as the Daughters of the Republic of Texas. She added sections on this organization to her textbook, praising their work in establishing the home for wives of Confederate veterans.[67] Anna herself qualified for membership in the UDC but for years had declined to join. In 1909, however, with the help of the UDC's Mrs. Dibrell, also an active clubwoman in the state, she was admitted to the Albert Sidney Johnson Chapter 105.[68] Her joining does not seem to have been related to the textbook issue, but rather to her efforts toward the establishment of a Texas State Library and Historical Commission.[69] However, being a member of the chapter of which Mrs. O. B. Colquitt, Texas's first lady, had served as treasurer likely helped her textbook campaign. As sitting governor in 1912, O. B. Colquitt was a member of the state textbook committee. Unsurprisingly, Pennybacker found support among the UDC when seeking re-adoption. Prominent UDC leader, Miss Katie Daffan, who also served as superintendent of the Texas Confederate Woman's Home of Austin, wrote Pennybacker a letter expressing confidence that there will be "no difficulties in [your textbook's] path, for. . . . so long as you live I see no reason why any body should write a Texas school history."[70]

Pennybacker's competitor, Professor Eugene Barker, understood her influence with the women's clubs and he sought to counter it by sending excerpts of his book to a number of the clubwomen, and a copy of the book to Katie Daffan whom he recognized as "a big gun in the Daughters of the Confederacy."[71] As chairman of the history department at the University of Texas, Barker had raised the ire of the president of the University of Texas with his assignment of Henry W. Elson's *History of the United States of America* in history classes at the university in 1911. In 1912 Barker was negotiating with wealthy Austin banker and University of Texas contributor George W. Littlefield, as well as "prominent Confederates and Daughters of the Confederacy," to "endow a manuscript collection dedicated to southern materials."[72] Barker's textbook depicted the events leading up to the Civil War in decidedly Confederate fashion, and, not coincidentally, the sections that he suggested his publisher send to Daffan and other Texas clubwomen were those describing the Civil War era.

Pennybacker's description of Texas's decision to join the Confederacy was brief. She mentioned only Texan fears that the slaves were on the point of uprising and notes that, although Governor Houston opposed secession, the "great mass of the people had no sympathy with the Governor's views" and the legislature, called to special session, voted to join the Confederacy.[73] Barker, by contrast, elaborated the Confederate position in greater depth, giving an account that represented the views of the Confederate societies in every aspect. He wrote that in the country's early days "no one saw any harm in slavery. It was thought to be a good thing for the Negroes to bring them from the 'Dark Continent' of Africa to the civilized country of America, where they would be better fed and better clothed, and where they could learn to be Christians."[74] Then he devoted three-quarters of a page attributing the North's abandonment of slavery to it being unprofitable since "most of the land there was poor, and the fields were small." He also described the southern justification for keeping slaves: "Much of the best land lay along the river bottoms, and these were so unhealthful that it was thought that white men could not live there. Slaves were absolutely necessary, therefore."[75] According to Barker's history, the Civil War was fought because southern states believed they had a right to secede whereas the North objected.[76] In total, Barker devoted four pages to Texas's decision to join the Confederacy, Pennybacker just three paragraphs.[77] Barker realized he had little chance of swaying the women from supporting Pennybacker. "These club women are already enlisted against us, of course, and only here and there will one change her mind," he wrote to his publisher. Still, he hoped that "a little concrete information of the character of the book such as these pages would give would make their opposition less vigorous, and might even gain us some positive help."[78]

Pennybacker's fears about the fate of her textbook were realized on October 18, 1912, when the textbook committee selected the competing book instead of her own. A letter from a friend informed Pennybacker that the vote was eight to three in favor of Barker, Potts, and Ramsdell, with only Mrs. Little, Mr. Garrison, and Governor Colquitt voting for Pennybacker. The vote was more uneven than expected; even some who were believed to be Pennybacker supporters voted in favor of the competition.[79] Despite the blow, Pennybacker immediately began petitioning for her book to be added as a supplemental text, painstakingly informing her supporters that using her book as a supplement was still within the law. The continued publication and sale of her textbook into the 1920s demonstrates that it remained a popular book for at least another decade. However, after the textbook was displaced as the adopted text, sales declined from a high of around twenty-five thousand per year during the period of adoption to around five thousand per year in the 1920s.

At the same time Pennybacker was waging her campaign for re-adoption of her textbook, she entered the national spotlight as nominee for the presidency of the General Federation of Women's Clubs (GFWC) and was elected to this position. While her national stature undoubtedly helped her gain prominence and useful contacts across the state and country, her dependence on the highly political textbook adoption process may have influenced or limited the view she expressed as president of the General Federation. In a speech at the organization's national convention in 1912, Pennybacker claimed that although she herself supported women's suffrage, she did not advocate the General Federation of Women's Clubs endorsing such a potentially divisive topic. Pennybacker's position was carefully designed so that she would alienate neither conservative southern clubwomen nor suffrage supporters from the northern and western states.[80] Embroiled in a highly politicized textbook competition in her own state, however, Pennybacker may have had further motivation not to be a strong advocate for suffrage. In one of the letters detailing his plans to help her gain re-adoption for her textbook, her publisher praises a speech she made regarding suffrage. "I note your statement published this morning in the New York Times," he wrote, "If you will permit me, I should like to give expression to my admiration for the splendid position which you have taken on the subject of suffrage. I should think that the calm judgment of the Convention would reflect your statement and I trust it will.[81] In the end,

Pennybacker would lose the textbook adoption, but would win the GFWC presidency, a position of national prominence.

Pennybacker would attempt to have the textbook readopted again in 1919, with equally poor results. By 1919, she was spending much of her time outside Texas, working with war efforts at the national level. Unable to conduct the textbook campaign herself, she recruited her friend, fellow clubwoman, admirer, and author of a 1916 biographical appreciation, Helen Knox, to campaign for her. At Anna's request, Knox approached Mrs. Walter Benson, whose father had been an agent for a major publishing house, and Annie Webb Blanton, then serving as the state's first female state superintendent of public education, for advice on promoting the textbook.[82] Both advised that Pennybacker send circulars and visit as many teachers in the state as possible. In addition, each suggested that she contact a book publisher or distributor for assistance. Blanton expressed particular optimism that the textbook commission might readopt the Pennybacker textbook.[83] Despite the encouragement from Blanton, however, the attempt to have the book readopted failed. The specific influences on the textbook board and the politics behind its decision will likely never be known, as there are no records of the meetings. However, Knox speculated that the rejection could have been political, retribution, perhaps, for Knox's political involvement in struggles at the University of Texas. Knox also speculated that the lack of support from a major publishing house was also to blame. "Whether I was the obstacle, or graft, or Mr. Marr's influence, I cannot say," she wrote, continuing, "I can't help but feel that we were too innocent for the intricate ways of political commissions, and I believe that if you ever get your book in, it will have to come through the greased channel of a contract with some of the experienced publishers."[84] Pennybacker never sold the rights to her book to a major publishing house, nor did she hire one to represent her book. In the end, Knox's prediction proved correct. Despite efforts to have the book adopted in 1924, the Pennybacker history would never again be the state-adopted history book. Nevertheless, Anna continued to publish and update the book into the 1920s, and it was used in schools as a supplement to the state-adopted text throughout the decade.

THE TEXTBOOK'S IMPACT

Pennybacker's History presented Texas history to Texas schoolchildren for over forty years. In so doing, it helped to propagate and perpetuate a romanticized image of the state's history in the minds of at least two generations of Texans. Though Pennybacker's textbook is now largely forgotten, many who studied it are not. In the early teens, as part of her re-adoption campaign, Pennybacker included in a brief a statement of support from a young history professor at South Western Training School in Georgetown, Texas. The young professor outlined the qualities a textbook required to be teachable. Foremost among these was the ability to "arouse in the pupil ambition to emulate the great history makers . . . to make students admire the noble and heroic."[85] That professor, J. Frank Dobie, would himself become one of Texas's great mythmakers, a "spokesman of Texas and southwestern culture."[86] Twenty years Pennybacker's junior, Dobie likely first encountered Texas history from *Pennybacker's History of Texas*. Dobie would become a founding father of Texas literature and one of the state's major literary figures for decades, and exert widespread influence on succeeding generations of Texans.[87] Anna's textbook influenced not just the generations of young Texans who studied it as schoolchildren. The renown generated by the book, as well as the financial security it brought, helped to shape her future. After Percy's death, she moved the family from Palestine to Austin, Texas, in part to better promote the book. In Austin, the history textbook author joined the Austin American History Club. Her connections with this club would soon propel her into prominence among clubwomen at the state and national levels.

Chapter Four

THE TEXAS FEDERATION OF WOMEN'S CLUBS

IN ADDITION TO HER WORK as an educator and author, Anna became increasingly involved in the growing women's club movement during the last decades of the nineteenth century. She became active in this movement early, at a moment in history when such clubs were poised to enter a period of enormous growth and increasing influence across the nation. Active in women's clubs for the rest of her life, Pennybacker would live through many of the early years of public resistance to the clubs that arose from largely male resistance to women operating in the public sphere, an era that clubwoman Helen Knox called the regime of "ostracism and suspicion." During Pennybacker's career as a clubwoman, public opinion generally swayed in favor of clubwomen, and clubs experienced what Knox called a regime of "power and recognition."[1] Pennybacker would become one of the leaders to effect this change.

PENNYBACKER'S EARLY CLUB WORK

Pennybacker joined her first women's club in her early twenties, when, from 1882 to 1883, she lived and taught school in Carthage, Missouri.[2] This first club was affiliated with the Chautauqua Literary and Scientific Circle (CLSC). As described in chapter 2, Chautauqua enrollees formed local study clubs, Chautauqua Circles, at an incredible rate in the latter part of the nineteenth century. Between 1878 and 1894, for example, ten thousand local reading circles were established across the nation.[3] The growth of the Chautauqua Circles paralleled that of women's clubs and in fact these Circles may have been the origin of many women's clubs across the country. In his 1921 history of Chautauqua, Jesse Hurlbut, long-time head of the CLSC, speculated that if one traced the history of women's clubs, "it would be found that nearly all of the older woman's clubs arose out of Chautauqua Circles whose members, after completing the prescribed course, took up civics or politics, or literature." "It would be an interesting study," he noted, "to ascertain how far the General Federation of Women's Clubs of America was an outgrowth of the Chautauqua movement."[4] Mary Terrell, a founding member and the second president of the Texas Federation of Women's Clubs, similarly attributed the development of women's clubs, particularly in the South, to the Chautauqua movement.[5]

For Pennybacker, then, as for many women of her time, Chautauqua was the entree into club life. Pennybacker continued her interest in the CLSC and in club work as a young wife and teacher. In February 1885, while living in Tyler, Texas, Pennybacker organized her own club, the First Literary Club.[6] By Pennybacker's own account, this club was Tyler's first, and she would later correct those who claimed that honor for another club.[7] According to biographical and autobiographical accounts, Pennybacker found only seven women in the city "brave enough to join."[8] However, at least one other club, the Quid Nunc, formed shortly thereafter and by 1888 a *Dallas Morning News* article about Tyler would report the formation of a Mendelssohn Club in Tyler to join "the many clubs and circles our city boasts," indicating that there were perhaps more "brave" women in the town than Pennybacker mythology recognized.[9] In addition, Pennybacker's claim that she founded her club in 1885 may be mistaken. The *Dallas Morning News* from that period reported that Pennybacker was one of the founding members of the CLSC women's club in Tyler in March of 1886. Whether or not the CLSC club was a new club or the same First Literary club Pennybacker later remembered beginning a year earlier remains unclear. The *News* reported that Pennybacker was voted president at the CLSC club's first meeting and named seven women besides Pennybacker who attended the founding meeting. Pennybacker served as president for the club's first year and participated in its meetings for several years more. Notably the *News* also reported that in the same week Pennybacker formed an amateur theater club that would meet in her home to rehearse for a performance of "Among the Breakers," the proceeds of which would be donated to the Douglass Rifles, which was a military-style marching organization, and to a fund supporting the state educational exposition that had been proposed by her husband, Percy.[10] The existence of other clubs in Tyler calls into question Knox's comment that the number of women in Tyler courageous enough to join a club was extremely limited.

In fact Tyler seems to have had a number of clubs, and members included the social elite.

The membership of a woman from Tyler's prominent Herndon family is likely the reason that Pennybacker's CLSC club's activities were well documented on the society page of the *Dallas Morning News*. These articles provide a glimpse of what club meetings entailed. As was typical of Chautauqua organizations, the members studied topics from literature, history, geography, and science. At one meeting in January 1887, for example, the women addressed topics that included "Warren Hastings and the Christian Church" and "The Siege of Lucknow," and a biography of Clive. At a meeting in February 1887, Pennybacker, still a high school teacher, spoke on "Education in England."[11] The club also studied Macaulay, the historian to whom Pennybacker would be so unflatteringly compared in a review of her history textbook in 1891. Following the pattern of women's clubs nationwide, the topics addressed by this club soon expanded to include civic issues. By June 1887, at least one meeting was spent presenting quotations on health and studying topics that included the sanitary conditions of Tyler, "Homes as Education," and civil engineering.[12] One newspaper account noted that the meetings were organized as a class: "Though the teacher asked numerous questions and entered rather into detail, yet the members were ready with their answers."[13] Club members typically recited a quotation from a topical work in answer to roll call. They then presented papers on or recited from famous works, conducted a book table, and discussed current events before dismissing to socialize.

Despite the class-like setting, the club's studies were neither dry nor exclusively academic. The meetings conjoined study with a strong social element. Although men were not permitted to become members, the female members planned to invite men to bimonthly evening entertainments. The women provided the food for these meetings "cooking club" style: a meal was planned and women drew the name of the dish they were expected to bring. Members voted on the best-prepared dish, with the winning cook declared the "belle of the ball."[14] To celebrate the beginning of 1887, the CLSC clubwomen assisted at a New Year's Eve party at the home of W. S. Herndon, a prominent railroad attorney. Accounts of the evening indicate a lavish party in a refined setting: elegant parlors with rare paintings and marble mantels were bedecked in holly, ivy, and mistletoe.[15] In addition to holiday celebrations, the women found ways to celebrate literary heroes in creative ways that remind one of the activities Pennybacker included in her classroom. Clubwomen celebrated, for example, Macaulay's birthday in November of 1886, and in the winter of

1887 planned a party with the work of Charles Dickens as the theme, "each member and each guest to personate some one of the novelist's immortal creations."[16]

When the Pennybacker family moved from Tyler to Palestine in 1893, Anna again associated herself with at least one women's club. Although little evidence documents Pennybacker's specific club activities during this period, according to Knox she "found a little club sorely in need of reorganization."[17] Subsequently Anna served as president of Palestine's Self Culture Club, a club which later was "instrumental in Palestine's acquisition of a library grant from Andrew Carnegie."[18] In both Tyler and Palestine, then, Anna led the formation and organization of individual clubs, drawing from the CLSC model of self-education. Anna also appears to have been a force at the local level in organizing local clubs into city federations in both Tyler and Palestine.[19] While organizing local clubs during the 1880s and 1890s she would have witnessed the creation of both the General Federation of Women's Clubs and the Texas federation. However, she does not appear to have been instrumental in forming either of these two organizations. Nor do records indicate that she was a leader of stature in the state or national federation prior to the turn of the century.[20] That would change upon her move to Austin in 1900.

FEDERATED WOMEN'S CLUBS IN THE UNITED STATES

To understand the scope of the women's club movement during Pennybacker's life as well as the impact of her participation in the movement requires an understanding of the history of the women's club movement leading up to that time. The movement began in the mid-1800s when groups of women began to meet with an eye on self-improvement. The focus of the early clubs was largely educational and literary. Excluded from men's clubs and literary societies, women created their own organizations along the same lines. The movement quickly spread to smaller towns and among less wealthy women. For these women, many of whom had not been able to attend college, the club system served as a less-formal educational system as well as a social network.[21]

The General Federation of Women's Clubs was initiated in 1890 by Sorosis founder, Jane Cunningham Croly. Croly, a prominent female journalist who wrote under the name Jennie June, conceived the idea of forming a woman's club when she was excluded from the Press Club of New York's dinner for Charles Dickens in 1868.[22] Croly and a handful of other female journalists created Sorosis in response.

Twenty-one years later, Croly called a convention to honor her club's anniversary. She invited representatives of clubs from across the region and the country to federate in a national organization. The purpose of the national organization, as stated in its constitution, was to "bring into communication with each other the various women's clubs throughout the world, in order that they may compare methods of work and become mutually helpful."[23] Because many of the organization's leaders were socially prominent, the federation "acquired a fashionable, societylike reputation" and quickly became the national organization for American clubwomen.[24] The growth of the General Federation from its first biennial in 1892 until the 1912 biennial was impressive. In 1892 the organization counted twenty thousand women as members. By 1912 official figures compiled by the federation put the number at eight hundred thousand.[25]

The federation gave the women's clubs national visibility and power and encouraged a trend that was already underway—the shift in emphasis from self-improvement to public affairs that started when the literary clubs saw the need to establish libraries.[26] Even before the turn of the century, federation leaders began to promote an ideal of education that emphasized putting knowledge into action within one's own community. In 1896 GFWC president Ellen Henrotin called the women's club movement "one of the educational factors of the century," noting that "it has enabled women who could not leave home to proceed with their education through classes and in the department club." Henrotin at that time added that the clubs offered a special opportunity to "transmit into action" with "decision and courage" the knowledge acquired in their joint studies.[27] Sixteen years later, in her history of the General Federation, clubwoman Mary I. Wood remarked, "The club movement, in its early days a literary movement, is fast becoming a great civic force; and the club is very rare indeed to-day in which the subject of civic betterment is not discussed."[28] Leaders, often "public-spirited society women and club women experienced as activists," shaped programs that "stressed women's responsibilities in the public sector." Leaders tended to be more progressive than the larger membership.[29]

The departments of the General Federation in the second decade of the twentieth century reflected the clubs' origins as cultural forums in which women met to discuss literature and the arts. Among the eleven departments were those devoted to art, "literature and library extension," education, and music. By the second decade of the century, however, the growing civic activism of the clubs was revealed by the larger number of departments which focused on social and political issues: Civics, Conservation, Civil Service Reform, Home Economics, Industrial and Social Conditions, Legislation, and Public Health, for example.[30]

WHAT CLUB WOMEN WERE UP AGAINST: OPPOSITION TO WOMEN'S ORGANIZATIONS

Women's clubs were not always welcomed or accepted. From their earliest days, the clubs often ran counter to prevailing ideologies of femininity. Ex-president Grover Cleveland's 1905 article in the *Ladies' Home Journal* typified the arguments against women's clubs. In it he asserted, "I believe it should be directly declared that the best and safest club for a woman to patronize is her home."[31] Promoting the "Real Path of True Womanhood," Cleveland wrote that "no woman who estimates motherhood as less than her highest, holiest function and privilege is fit to be a mother" and described a "good wife" as "a woman who loves her husband and her country with no desire to run either." Cleveland argued that "any discontent on the part of woman with her ordained lot, or a restless desire on her part to be and to do something not within the sphere of her appointed ministrations" were "perversions of a gift from God."[32] The discontented woman who joined a club, he continued, corrupted the "wives and mothers within the range of companionship" and "as an aider and abettor of woman's clubs . . . must bear her share of liability for the injury they may inflict upon the domestic life of our land."[33] In an argument that presaged more contemporary antidrug campaigns, Cleveland warned against "the club habit," and made it clear that, in his view, participation in even one club threatened home and community, if only because, in not having bad effects, it made the danger seem benign. That Cleveland's article also addressed women's suffrage, noting its "dangerous, undermining effect on the character of the wives and mothers of our land," demonstrates how closely the national, highly charged issue was associated with women's clubs, even at a time when the clubs themselves declared neutrality.

Given that they faced accusations of destroying the country's social fabric by abandoning their domestic duties, clubwomen had to disavow any potentially self-serving political involvement and argue for social usefulness and selflessness of their activities. This focus on working for the good of the community rather than for other ends was more than a political strategy, however. Clubwomen defined their own culture, opposing what they saw as corrupt, masculine values of the political and industrial realms, and proposing an alternative set of values based on "higher ideals of life and purer modes of existence."[34] Founder Croly declared of the movement: "It is not a creed, a dogma, or a hobby—only the spirit of unity in the bonds of newly discovered love."[35] The idea of a separate and distinct female culture was commonplace in the late nineteenth and early twentieth centuries. Writing of the phenomenon, historian Ted Ownby notes, "Those who embraced the so-called cult of domesticity believed that women felt affection more deeply than men, both in their love for other people and in their love for God. Men had to stifle their emotions to meet the cold realities of the workplace; women let their emotions flow freely in the familial and religious spheres."[36] The "cult of domesticity" in the South, argued Ownby, was linked to Evangelical belief systems that pitted domestic values of harmony, self-control, moderation, and the suppression of individual will against southern ideals of masculinity and southern male culture. Southern honor, writes Ownby, "demanded self-assertiveness, aggressiveness and competitiveness" and male culture included violence (for example, fighting and hunting) combined with public drunkenness and gambling.[37] Again and again, clubwomen used rhetoric derived from cultural beliefs of the time and were both supported and limited by these beliefs. Pennybacker, as a southerner and the daughter of a Baptist preacher, was particularly astute in working within a cultural framework that pitted domestic and/or Evangelical values against "masculine" values of commerce, competition, self-assertiveness, and violence. Her rise to prominence was due in large part to her skill in manipulating this cultural framework to accomplish her goals, even as the framework shaped those very goals.

THE TEXAS FEDERATION OF WOMEN'S CLUBS

Inspired by the formation of the GFWC in 1889, clubwomen across the United States began to form state federations. Under General Federation president Ellen Henrotin, who traveled across the country encouraging clubs to organize at the state level, twenty-six state federations formed between 1894 and 1898.[38] Texas clubwomen, too, recognized the value of federating at the state level during this period. In the late 1800s, the Texas Federation of Women's Clubs, like many state federations of women's clubs, was in its embryonic stages. In 1894, following the example of women's club involvement in the World's Columbian Exposition in Chicago, Texas women organized a "Woman's Congress" at the state fair in Dallas. Female speakers, including sculptor Elizabet Ney and Woman's Christian Temperance Union state president Helen

Stoddard, presented topics related to women's roles in society, education, and temperance, as well as art and literature. The women were careful to cultivate as proper a public image as possible. Concerned that the name "Women's Congress" would carry political connotations, the women changed the name to the State Council of Women of Texas.[39] However, attempts to organize further stalled for the next three years, until the Texas federation was organized in 1897. That year Texas clubwomen held their first federation meeting in Waco at the invitation of the Woman's Club of Waco. The 1897 meeting differed from the 1894 congress in a way that demonstrated the progress being made by Texas women acting in the public sphere. The congress of 1894 had been held at the state fair, allowing many women to travel to the meeting accompanied by husbands interested in visiting the fair. The 1887 meeting did not coincide with another event, and women were more likely to travel alone or with female companions. For many women, traveling across the state unaccompanied by a male was a novel experience. Social norms of the nineteenth century dictated that women, especially southern women, be chaperoned by a trusted male when traveling.[40] A later clubwoman described how her predecessors, unused to traveling alone, yet anxious to present themselves in their finest attire, struggled with heavy trunks.[41] Later clubwomen would acknowledge the precedent set by these early clubwomen who "gained courage from each other" as they learned to travel independently and speak publicly.[42]

The gathering of women faced some public disapproval. Even the bishop who offered a prayer suggested public hesitancy about the advisability of women organizing in clubs. He is said to have prayed at an early meeting, "Lord, though we are in doubt about this movement, Thou canst bring good out of it."[43] Still, the women persisted, naming their organization the Texas Federation of Literary Clubs and defining their purpose for organizing: "to advance and encourage Texas women in literary work, to promote and encourage fraternal intercourse among literary clubs within and without the state, and to secure all the benefits resulting from organized effort."[44] The lofty ideals behind the organization reflected the women's middle- and upper-middle-class ideals of true womanhood: "This Federation stands for mutual help and mutual advancement," declared clubwoman and historian Stella Christian. "It stands for higher ideals of life and purer modes of existence. It stands for moral, social, educational and artistic development. It would eliminate the selfish, egotistic idea, which has so long dominated our social and economic fabric, and substitute therefore the sentiment that good to others is the greatest good to ourselves." Christian was careful to note, however, that clubwomen were to embrace "the lowly duties that lie nearest to us, and that make up so great a part of every wife and mother's [duties]."[45] The women adopted a constitution, formed committees, and elected Mrs. Edward Rotan of Waco president. Because most of the clubs were literary in nature, focusing on self-improvement and education, the women declared: "The keynote to this work is education, not merely that which lies in books, but that higher and nobler sort that elevates and improves every human faculty—that inspires everywhere a love for the good, the true, the beautiful."[46] However, because books were so expensive as to limit the size of even large private libraries, the women decided to focus on making books widely available by establishing public libraries throughout the state. The women remained aware of the importance of maintaining a proper public image. Terrell reported that at the first annual meeting, "the president outlined the policy of the organization in a manner that disarmed critics and won the support of the men of Texas."[47] The women also recognized that "healthfully educa[ting] public opinion" was an important part of their work.[48]

When the state federation was formed, Pennybacker lived in Palestine where she completed periodic revisions of her Texas history textbook and cared for three very young children and, most likely, for her husband, Percy, who was terminally ill with leukemia. Evidence that Pennybacker attended these early meetings of the Texas federation is nonexistent. Records of the federation suggest that she was not involved in its formation. Most likely her other obligations prevented her from dedicating much time to club work. Although she was not a prominent founder of the new organization, she probably was affiliated with the TFWC beginning with its first annual meeting in April 1898 when her Self Culture Club of Palestine joined the federation. By the autumn of 1898, Pennybacker was personally acquainted with the state federation's leaders and had won their respect. In October of that year, TFWC president Rotan asked Pennybacker to chair the program committee for the next state convention. In Rotan's opinion, as she expressed it to Pennybacker, this was an important position, "one of the most important," and it demanded enough work that it would be split with another clubwoman. Rotan explained the lack of federation funds to support Pennybacker, should she accept the offer, explaining that the federation collected only $3 per club for fifty-five clubs, and paid out $100 to the editor of the club columns in the *Dallas Morning News*. However, Rotan offered to personally pay Pennybacker $25 for the work, expressing her strong belief that Pennybacker would get the job done. The lack of records documenting the administrations of the first two TFWC presidents makes difficult the determination of what role Pennybacker played in the early years of the federation, beyond being known and trusted by early presidents.

Though the extent of her involvement in the TFWC during its earliest years is unclear, Pennybacker's role in the state federation would change quickly after Percy's death in 1899 and her subsequent move to Austin in 1900. The move ostensibly was to secure better education for her children, but being in Austin, the state capital, allowed Pennybacker to better manage the politics surrounding her textbook.[49] When she moved to Austin in September of 1900, Pennybacker promptly joined one of the city's most prominent clubs, the American History Club. Membership in this club, which was one of the eighteen original clubs to charter the Texas Federation of Women's Clubs, offered her opportunities for greater visibility and participation in the Texas federation.

In April of 1899, Mary Terrell of Fort Worth replaced Mrs. Edward Rotan, the federation's first president, as TFWC president. Terrell was a founding member of the state federation and served as first vice president during Rotan's administration. Because of her support for the creation of libraries across the state, Terrell would become known as the "Mother of Texas Libraries." She would also become Pennybacker's long-term friend and advisor. During her TFWC presidency, Terrell appointed Pennybacker to her executive committee. Pennybacker attended board meetings under Terrell, participating in the success of an administration that saw hundreds of thousands of dollars granted to Texas libraries from the Carnegie fund, initiated a federation-supported traveling library, helped to secure state support for a state college for women, and affiliated the Texas federation with the General Federation of Women's Clubs.[50] Pennybacker, well-known for her Texas history textbook, assisted the History Committee of the TFWC in developing an outline for a reading course in Texas history.[51] Terrell's administration of the Texas federation organized departments that were formed at the 1899 annual convention. These departments demonstrated the growth in scope of the clubwomen's interest, and covered public libraries, household economics and sanitary science, reciprocity, education, music, art, history, literature lecture, village improvement, and club extension.[52] A legislative department, however, was intentionally omitted, as the women continued to avoid overt politics. As Terrell would later explain, "No 'lobbying' would be permitted, but when one considered that the husbands, fathers, brothers and sweet hearts of clubwomen, were men of influence in affairs of state, it was conclusive that the clubwomen were not without ways and means of influencing legislation."[53] To effect political change, federation leaders issued circulars asking that clubwomen use their influence at home and in their social circles. Thus, without direct access to the vote and lacking overt political power, the clubwomen explicitly adopted a strategy of "silent influence" over the more politically powerful males within their social circles.

LEADING THE TEXAS FEDERATION

In 1901 Terrell and others began to encourage Pennybacker, then president of the Austin American History Club and a member of Terrell's executive board, to consider a run for the presidency of the Texas federation. Pennybacker expressed reluctance to stand for this post, citing business and family duties. Terrell encouraged her, noting that she could set her own speaking schedule and could expect clubs around the state to work around her schedule. She also reminded Pennybacker that she had appointed her to her executive committee to learn the ropes, and that she hoped she would use her knowledge in service to the organization. Another clubwoman, Belle Smith, informed Pennybacker that her name was mentioned as a favorite by clubwomen across the state.[54] Despite her initial reluctance, Pennybacker changed her mind and permitted herself to be nominated for the TFWC presidency at the organization's state convention in Dallas, in May of 1901. The reason for her change of heart is unclear. Perhaps she had expressed reluctance only as a matter of social convention so as not to seem overly ambitious or political. Clubwomen demonstrated a strong tendency to publicly decry politics and any actions that could be seen as self-seeking.[55] An apparently nonpolitical stance contrasted well with the more overtly political self-promotion of another candidate or candidates. After her election, Pennybacker would be congratulated by a former TFWC president for winning without overtly seeking the position. Perhaps, as well, Terrell's urging upon her the importance of the position swayed Pennybacker. In a letter suggesting her candidacy, Terrell reminded Pennybacker of the opportunity the state federation presented women: "The possibilities of the State Federation for good—if wisely ministered are great—the individual clubs do not comprehend the opportunity that it affords—an opportunity for which we will be responsible."[56]

The details of the race for president are difficult to determine. Richmond suggests that Pennybacker's candidacy arose from a race in which "the exigencies of Federation politics demanded the candidacy of a dark horse for the presidency."[57] Pennybacker ran against Eleanor Brackenridge, one of the wealthiest and most prominent women in the state, in a race whose internal politics have been suppressed, likely due to the need to appear above politics, a need which induced clubwomen to obscure overt political battles. Brackenridge, who lived most of her life in San Antonio with her brother George, a powerful businessman and philanthropist, was herself one of the state's wealthiest and most powerful women. She was also the more experienced candidate, having served as first vice president under Terrell. She was one of the strongest supporters of the clubwomen's work to have the state create a college for women, had undertaken much legislative work for the women's college, and had become a member of its first board of regents.[58] However, indications are that Brackenridge was pushing an agenda not fully supported by clubwomen, likely on the grounds that it was overly political. At the time of the election, Brackenridge was encouraging Texas women to examine laws that pertained to women, presumably with the intent to advocate changes in laws that created hardships. Additionally Brackenridge was a strong suffrage supporter. Brackenridge's agenda may have been perceived as too radical for the women of the state federation. In a letter urging Pennybacker to accept a nomination for the race, president Terrell stated that her "successor should be an earnest, strong, *conservative* woman—who would carry on the administration as the organization had sought to start it [emphasis mine]." Terrell also warned, "Our president should not be so devoted to the interests of some other organization, that there would be danger of the Federation being used to tow some other craft into harbor."[59] The latter comment reflects federation concern that leaders of other prominent organizations, for example, the Daughters of the Confederacy, the WCTU, or the state's suffrage organization, not use the TFWC as a tool to promote those organizations' agendas. Terrell also cast doubt on Brackenridge's competence for the role of federation president. She wrote Pennybacker that while she thought of Breckenridge as "an earnest, good woman," "my relations with her for the last two years—leads me to think she is entirely wanting in all qualifications except earnestness." Terrell suggested that Brackenridge was physically and mentally incapable of the organization and focus required to lead the growing state federation: "The office requires constant, systematic thought and work is a heavy responsibility—and too great a burden for a woman of her age and frail health—yet personal vanity, and with all her fine qualities, she has not a little, and the local influence may bring her to agree."[60] Despite strongly encouraging Pennybacker's nomination privately, Terrell did not publicly endorse Pennybacker, or any other candidate, believing that, as sitting president, to do so would be inappropriate. Privately, however, she assured Pennybacker, "Candidly and of course confidentially . . . unequivocally . . . you are my first choice."[61]

The Texas federation held its fourth annual convention in Dallas, Wednesday through Friday, May 1–3, 1901.[62] Pennybacker made an impression during the convention meetings as a delegate of the American History Club. Richmond notes that "she expressed herself frequently," and was a strong backer of a resolution to support the building of a women's dormitory at the University of Texas. Speaking before the assembly, Pennybacker contrasted the situation of female university students to that of males, noting that it could cost a girl twice what a boy would pay to secure lodging and board while at the university.[63] A contentious debate about how nominations for federation officers should be made also enabled Pennybacker to gain the attention of the assembly. A proposed amendment would have created a nominating committee to assemble a ballot based on tickets submitted by individual delegates. With some in the assembly calling the amendment undemocratic and fearing the creation of a "political machine," Pennybacker argued that the new procedure actually would make the process more democratic and pleaded for the women to strive for harmony and avoid "wrangling" over the issue.[64] The amendment passed, and Pennybacker established her reputation as a level-headed peacemaker in line with the clubwomen's feminine ideals.

A situation similar to the vigorous debate on nominations occurred just prior to the nominations for TFWC offices. Terrell reminded the assembly that the federation was a "God-appointed medium for some great purpose" and that the "good women of Texas would see that it prospered without regard to who was president." She urged her fellow clubwomen not to "allow this occasion to be marred by any show of feeling."[65] Directly prior to the nomination Pennybacker again issued a plea for harmony among the women.[66] Although Pennybacker's name had not been officially offered as a candidate, after her plea, clubwoman and journalist Kate Smith wasted no time in nominating Pennybacker. Despite the months of consideration on the parts of Pennybacker, Smith, and Terrell, Pennybacker was nominated without having officially declared interest, giving the appearance of a spontaneous nomination. Three other women, including Eleanor Brackenridge, were nominated, and three ballots were taken before one candidate secured the majority of the votes.

Pennybacker was elected third president of the Texas Federation of Women's Clubs on May 3, 1901. According to the *Houston Post,* her plea for harmony won her the election.[67] However, as the pre-meeting canvassing undertaken by Belle Smith indicated, Pennybacker was favored even prior to the convention. Interestingly, Mary Terrell later wrote Pennybacker that she had voted for Brackenridge. She did not explain her vote although she promised an explanation would come later. She also remarked that she thought the convention alone would have been too much for Brackenridge who was in her mid-sixties by then. Voting procedures may explain Terrell's vote for Brackenridge. TFWC voting procedures required that delegates write the names of themselves and their club on their ballots;[68] likely Terrell did not want Brackenridge to learn she had voted against her, a situation which admits the extent of Brackenridge's power and prominence within the state.[69]

Pennybacker extended the proverbial olive branch to Brackenridge soon after her election to the presidency by inviting Brackenridge to attend the meeting of the executive board. Despite Brackenridge's claim to be at peace with the election, however, her testy reply to Pennybacker's invitation suggests that she was unhappy with the results. It also suggests that the issue behind the campaign was a push by Brackenridge to examine laws related to women. Brackenridge wrote: "If I have anything to say to the board, I can write it. The effort I made at Houston to get the subject of our laws—and their benefit to us as women brought before the Federation was a failure—As an Education subject it was stillborn, so to speak. Events have brought the matter before the public—it may be that you can take it up and handle it to the good of humanity."[70] Brackenridge's ideas were considered too political and divisive for many clubwomen and that sentiment led to the more moderate Pennybacker's election. Despite some bitterness at her defeat, Brackenridge offered somewhat begrudging support for Pennybacker: "The field is new, the paths untried and you are without experience—but time has been given you, the energy you have, and earnest purpose and a wise selection of methods and a power such as the word had never known before is created," she wrote.[71] This occasion would not be the last time that Pennybacker would take a position for which Brackenridge was in the running. Nearly two decades later, Carrie Chapman Catt would bypass Brackenridge, a longtime suffrage advocate, and appoint Pennybacker to a trusteeship of the Leslie Commission, a prestigious committee of the National American Woman Suffrage Association.[72]

As TFWC president, Pennybacker took the helm of a young and growing organization that had experienced remarkable success in its early projects. The TFWC was establishing libraries across the state, its original purpose. When Pennybacker assumed the presidency, the TFWC consisted of 108 clubs with approximately 2,250 members statewide[73] More than two-thirds of these clubs reported establishing—or work toward establishing—libraries.[74] Furthermore, the Texas state legislature had just passed legislation funding the TFWC's second great project, a state college for women. From the beginning, Pennybacker relied on the support of Terrell who continued to advise her throughout her TFWC presidency. Terrell offered Pennybacker suggestions for the delicate task of appointing committees (each section of the state, city, and club had to be represented fairly among these appointments). She also warned of potential problems with factions within the TFWC, particularly, for a reason now unknown, the Texas Division of the United Daughters of the Confederacy. Apparently appreciative of the support, Pennybacker followed Terrell's advice and continued work along the lines already established during the Terrell and Rotan administrations, while further developing projects of importance to her.

Prior to Pennybacker's election, Terrell advised Pennybacker that the new president should take a tour of the state each year in order to visit clubs as widely as possible. Personal contact, she advised, would be the best way to awaken interest in the federation by the state's women's clubs. It would also, Terrell argued, "conduce to a solidarity of interest."[75] Pennybacker followed Terrell's advice. She made personal visits across the state and preached the gospel of the club movement. These statewide visits helped the TFWC to nearly double in size during the two years of Pennybacker's presidency. The organization grew from 108 clubs with more than 2,250 members to 135 clubs with more than 3,400 members during Pennybacker's first year in office, and increased to 175 clubs and 4,220 members by the end of her second year as president. The argument Pennybacker made for federated club work drew from Christian Evangelical values. One correspondent, assigned to promote federation membership, noted, "It is hard to answer the question 'what will the Federation do for us' without preaching a sermon and as Emerson's 'Compensation' is the best sermon I know, I quoted from it largely."[76] Pennybacker herself exhorted clubwomen to remember that "that club prospers most which asks not 'What do I gain from the Federation?' but 'What may I give to the Federation.'"[77] In addition to traveling within the state, Pennybacker also traveled to the annual meetings of women's club federations in other states in order to promote the work done by Texas clubwomen and to raise the state federation's visibility.

During her TFWC presidency, Pennybacker established herself as a woman who could not only inspire unified effort, but also organize a large and growing organization. An executive board meeting in the fall of 1901 enabled her to demonstrate her organizational abilities.

To address the swift growth of the Texas federation and problems that arose due to the great size of the state, the board, under Pennybacker's direction, divided the state into five districts, each to be presided over by a TFWC vice president. This restructuring, like committee appointments, was a delicate procedure inasmuch as various regions of the state required fair representation. The districting plan enacted permitted each district to be represented by a vice president at the state level and to have each vice president represent her district at the GFWC biennials. Additionally this plan minimized the travel necessary for clubs to meet with other clubs by instituting district meetings. It also made it easier for Pennybacker to have contact with clubwomen across the state by speaking regularly at district conventions.

In keeping with the issues that she had addressed at the state convention, Pennybacker focused her administration on the promotion of education. In fact, her TFWC administration became known as the "Educational Administration," as she was seen as having "swung the Federation forces squarely into line for the betterment of the educational facilities of Texas."[78] The focus for her presidency was perhaps defined even before it began. The night before the election, Pennybacker spoke to the assembly on "the social relation of teacher and parent," following State Superintendent of Education J. S. Kendall's address, "What Can and What Should the Clubwomen of Texas do for the Schools of the State?" Kendall encouraged clubwomen to go into the schools and "see that they were properly heated and ventilated and that the walls were hung with pictures of the best for youth."[79] In her speech, Pennybacker encouraged clubwomen, many of whom were upper-middle-class, middle-aged women, to bridge the divide of age and social standing and entertain local teachers in their homes in order to establish a friendly and supportive social relationship. She also encouraged women to create European-style salons in their homes to serve as centers of culture for their community, including teachers.[80]

As TFWC president, Pennybacker continued this emphasis on education. Following Kendall's lead, she focused particularly on the improvement of school facilities. In the first months of her presidency, Pennybacker sent a form letter to heads of schools across the state, asking what the Texas federation could do to support schools. The full range of responses is unknown, but one respondent requested that clubwomen provide small libraries for each grade in his school district.[81] Pennybacker was more general in her recommendations for clubwomen across the state. Early in her administration, Pennybacker urged each club in the state to devote two weeks in February to assisting the public schools.[82] This effort seems to have been successful. As Pennybacker herself reported to the General Federation in 1902, nearly all 135 clubs in the state cooperated to do "something tangible" for the public schools. The results of this cooperation between clubwomen and public schools included the beautification of school facilities: planting trees and adding artwork, including busts and pictures, to classrooms. Perhaps Pennybacker's speech on the "social relation of parent and teacher" inspired the clubwomen, who, during education weeks, entertained teachers and visited schools in "the proper spirit" (of helpfulness, not criticism).[83] Pennybacker also strongly supported higher education efforts, particularly for women. By the end of her first year as president, she had obtained funding for scholarships for women at several colleges in the state: $60 scholarships for study in the literary department and the music or elocution department at Baylor Female College; free tuition and a reduction of $43 in board for study in the literary department at Southwestern University in Georgetown; a $60 scholarship for study in the literary department and a $54 scholarship in the art department at Fort Worth University (Texas Wesleyan).[84] She continued work that had begun toward a scholarship fund to support women students at the University of Texas. Requesting donations from clubwomen, she raised more than $2,000 in the first year of her administration, not, as a fellow clubwoman pointed out, by holding "silver teas, lectures, and bazaars," but by individual donation. Giving money "in a dignified way" from their own purses rather than through "schemes" to solicit funds from the public was precedent-setting for Texas clubwomen.[85] By the end of Pennybacker's term, the administration had met the organization's $3,500 goal for the University of Texas scholarship fund for women.[86] The TFWC, under Pennybacker's administration, first invested the money, then donated this fund to the university, so that the responsibility of selecting the recipients would lie with the university rather than the federation.[87]

Even before she was elected TFWC president, Pennybacker supported the construction of a women's dormitory at the University of Texas. At the Dallas convention at which she was elected, Pennybacker seconded the resolution that the TFWC lobby the legislature on behalf of regents for an appropriation of $55,000 to construct the women's dormitory.[88] As president, she continued to emphasize the importance of this work. Twice she sent letters to the president of each club in the state urging clubwomen to lobby their legislator and any other prominent people in support of the dormitory. Her letters outlined the reasons for the dormitory, comparing the relative costs of room and board for male students living on campus and female students, who were forced to pay more for accommodations in the town. Along with the argument for equity, Pennybacker also argued that a women's dormitory would provide an arena for young women to socialize in a setting controlled by a lady manager, as opposed to entertaining in their single off-campus rented rooms or visiting public halls in town. Pennybacker encouraged clubwomen to contact their representatives, and personally contacted every member of the legislature to request assistance with this project. Like many of the issues Pennybacker would face as TFWC president, the girl's dormitory debate had a racial component. The university's president, William Prather, argued for the dorm on the grounds of racial equity, writing Pennybacker that he'd been examining "all the acts of the Legislature in regard to our institutions of learning" and had discovered, "that the funds of the University have been used in days gone by to establish the negro Prairie View Normal in which dormitories, furniture, and a piano have been provided for the use of negro girls." Prather argued that the white girls should receive the same consideration: "I feel that it is time the rights of the white girls of this country should have recognition before the legislature. When I think of the struggles our girls have unselfishly made by concerts and otherwise to raise a fund to present to the University the only piano which we own for chapel service, and the Legislature has appropriated the public funds for the same purpose for the colored girls, I cannot view with much patience this discrimination."[89] The campaign in support of the women's dorm was successful. In October 1902 the legislature appropriated $50,000 for the Woman's Building. In August of the next year, when the building's cornerstone was laid, copies of Pennybacker's letters in support of the building were placed inside, along with copies of the state constitutions and other documents related to women's clubs and the state. When finished, the dormitory offered what would be considered lavish accommodations by today's standards for $17 per month room and board. The accommodations included a large parlor and assembly hall, a gymnasium, and a swimming pool. Prather's argument for equity with the colored girls must have been successful, for the parlor had its piano. A lady manager ensured that the girls abided by the rules of conduct. Whether the building and the supervised lifestyle it offered was amenable to female college students is unclear. However, the building was popular with the girls' family members, at least some of whom used their prominence within the state to secure lodging for the girls.[90]

While supporting efforts to raise money for education within the state, Pennybacker also worked to gain financial support from benefactors outside the state. Just four months after the General Education Board was formed in 1902, Pennybacker was corresponding with this organization, seeking support of TFWC projects, including the women's college. The General Education Board was a foundation created by John D. Rockefeller to support public education in the United States. Particular attention was to be given to establishing and promoting public school systems in rural areas and in the South. Money would be provided to develop training institutes for teachers and collect and disseminate to the public information about educational matters. By July 1902, Pennybacker had requested money for the TFWC scholarship program, but was told that the board would visit each state and study educational needs extensively before agreeing to provide funding. However, Wallace Buttrick did express interest in the federation's educational work and suggested that the board's representative would meet with Pennybacker or other TFWC leaders upon visiting Texas.[91]

Another method of raising money for public schools gained attention during Pennybacker's presidency when a poll-tax amendment was introduced into the state legislature. The proposed amendment required that potential voters pay a poll tax prior to registering to vote. While a poll tax was already established in state law, those who failed to pay were not prohibited from voting as they would be on passage of the amendment. This was a controversial proposition. First, the amount of money that would go to the schools was a matter of debate. While some estimated that the poll tax would bring in as much as $400,000 for the state's public schools, the number suggested by the state superintendent of instruction was smaller.[92] In a letter addressed to the clubwomen of Texas, Pennybacker suggested the sum would be $70,000, based on estimates of 160,000 men who did not pay the poll tax. In a detailed argument addressed to the clubwomen of Texas, Pennybacker traced the source of public school financial problems to mismanagement of public lands designated for raising public school funds: parties who had leased or purchased the lands defaulted on payment. Current state funding of $4.75 per child, Pennybacker argued, did not adequately provide for educating all the children of the state. "The Constitution," she noted, "requires that public schools be sustained six months in the year, but under the present conditions that is absolutely impossible except in the districts where a local school tax is levied." Under the current system of funding, she continued, "Nine-tenths of the children of the State are educated in country schools that are entirely dependent on the State and county for support." For this reason, she concluded, "It is the duty of every citizen to do all in his power by ballot or by influence to develop and strengthen not only the town but the rural schools."[93] Pennybacker joined her detailed financial argument with an appeal based on the ideals of southern womanhood: "We, as women, cannot neglect the best interests of our schools, for upon these schools depends the education of our children. Is it not our duty to use our influence—remembering however, that all action must be guided by judgment, gentleness and the quiet dignity of Southern womanhood—toward securing the adoption of this amendment and thereby increasing the efficiency of our public schools?"[94] The "quiet dignity" Pennybacker advocated carried the weight of specifically feminine ideals as well as a more general political strategy. The clubwomen generally adopted a policy of exercising indirect political influence to avoid appearing overly political. In the case of the poll tax, at least one prominent clubwoman objected to the TFWC's involvement in lobbying on the grounds that the issue, and the TFWC's strong stance, were too political. In an argument that reveals much about the gender politics of the day and demonstrates why some clubwomen were so opposed to being overtly involved in politics, Mary D. Bonner warned Pennybacker: "It is political to the core, and whenever we women enter politics in Texas our influence is dead." Bonner noted the effectiveness of clubwomen's covert influence: "The legislature has been very kind to the Federation because we have remained off of the men's dominians [*sic*]. . . . whenever we trespass, no matter how little, our influence with them will be gone. I am not at all in favor of the women trying to do any thing that will be impossible for them to accomplish."[95] Bonner's analysis of the clubwomen's position within Texas political culture explains much of the reticence among clubwomen to be more aggressively political. They believed that conforming to the social strictures of southern womanhood rendered them more powerful (if indirectly) than directly asserting their goals. In the case of the poll-tax amendment, however, the policy of quiet, indirect support for the change was also adopted by male supporters, due to the controversy that surrounded the issue.

Although Pennybacker continued to support the poll tax with arguments based on the amount of money raised for schools by this amendment, those who corresponded with her prior to its passage indicated that much more was at issue with respect to this bill than money for schools. This correspondence also indicates that Pennybacker was fully aware of the reasons others supported the amendment. Although the bill's supporters publicly maintained that money for schools was the important result of enforcing the poll tax, the significance of the amount of money to be raised by the amendment was a point of contention, In a letter to C. A. Arnold which was found among Pennybacker's papers, State Superintendent of Schools Arthur Lefevre revealed the semi-hidden purpose of the amendment. The amount of money raised for schools "is really trifling and could well be thrown into the sea," he argued, because "everybody who pays any tax at present pays his poll tax." The "hope and purpose of the law" was not to collect more tax money, but rather to ensure that "ignorant negroes, and Mexicans, and corrupt whites in the large cities should cease to determine elections in Texas by their purchased votes."[96] Thus the bill was seen by supporters as a means to reform voting irregularities in the state: requiring the tax to be paid ahead of time would eliminate vote buying at the polling places. As LeFevre's comments indicated, this issue carried a significant racial component as well. Indeed, the measure was widely understood as one that would further limit the black vote. Although no records exist that Pennybacker agreed, she clearly knew of these arguments. Clubwoman Kate Perry Womack wrote Pennybacker about the poll-tax amendment in October of 1902: "We hope it will be carried here. Especially do we need some change in the voting where the negro is such an important factor."[97] At least some poor white Texans strongly opposed the amendment. This opposition arose from the recognition that poor whites would be practically disenfranchised along with poor blacks. That some blacks would be able to pay the tax made the sting much worse for whites facing disenfranchisement. Pennybacker received a letter from an ex-Confederate soldier, J. S. Waldrop, who accused Pennybacker of being a "bourbon machinist" based on her support for the amendment. Like the amendment's proponents, he raised the racial issue, arguing vehemently against being disenfranchised because of poverty, while blacks who could afford to pay the tax would be allowed to vote.[98] Waldrop's argument, like Prather's racially charged argument in favor of a girl's dorm at the University of Texas, indicates the resonance the claim that "Negroes were given advantages that whites were not" had with the public at the time.

Whether or not Pennybacker believed her own arguments about school funding as she supported the poll-tax amendment is unclear. She continued to argue in favor of the amendment on the basis of its support of schools, but she also adopted the political strategies suggested by Lefevre in his letter. After publishing at least one article in support of the poll tax in July of 1902, at Lefevre's suggestion, she and the Texas Federation of Women's Clubs adopted a strategy of quiet support for the bill. LeFevre suggested that publicizing the bill would create public controversy and arouse opposition. Perhaps the heated letter accusing her of being a "bourbon machinist" who would put blacks above poor white Confederate veterans convinced her of the potential opposition to the amendment. In any case, at Lefevre's suggestion, Pennybacker requested that the *Dallas Morning News* pull an article she had written in favor of the amendment. In doing so, however, she was accused of betraying the democratic ideals she and other clubwomen spoke so strongly of during their annual meeting and elsewhere. A letter to Pennybacker from Luther Clark of the *Dallas Morning News* chided her for adopting Lefevre's strategy. Clark strongly disagreed with the strategy. He argued to Pennybacker that agitation was the best strategy to pass the amendment, and criticized Pennybacker's decision to go along with Lefevre, on the grounds that democracy demands open, public discourse: "Even if this were not the most successful method, it is at least the open and democratic way of settling properly a public question."[99] Despite these considerations, clubwomen fell in line behind Pennybacker. She received numerous letters from clubwomen who supported the amendment but said they would not agitate for it, and when the amendment passed, Pennybacker credited the clubwomen's "quiet, unobtrusive" efforts in support of it.[100]

Pennybacker's relationship with the press in the case of the poll-tax amendment reveals the close relationship between Texas clubwomen and the newspapers. It was a mutually cultivated relationship, as clubwomen saw the press as a means of furthering their educational goals across the state, and the press, by publishing club news, appealed to a wide section of middle- and upper-middle-class women. Mary Terrell, who had designated the *Dallas Morning News* the official organ of the Texas federation during her administration, acknowledged that "the newspapers have been the unfailing friend of club effort."[101] Pennybacker, too, understood the importance of the press early in her presidency, and in the weeks following her election as TFWC president had already invited representatives of the *Dallas Morning News* to meet with federation representatives. The *News* for its part, expressed its willingness to meet federation executives, writing Pennybacker, "The Woman's Department of the Daily and Semi-Weekly News is open to the club women of Texas and it is the earnest desire of the publishers to make it second to none in the United States."[102] Other papers, eager to earn the designation of official organ of the Texas federation, also solicited her goodwill early on. Reporter Kate Friend, for example, tried to broker a deal with Pennybacker to confer the official organ status on a competing paper, arguing that the Dallas paper should be excluded because it employed a male as club editor.[103] In the end, Pennybacker selected the *Dallas Morning News* as the TFWC official organ, accepting the argument that its wide circulation was best to reach "the masses" and "especially the women of the country." In addition to being widely circulated, the *News* employed columnist Pauline Periwinkle, a strong club supporter. Periwinkle was the pen name of Sara Isadore Sutherland Calloway, herself a clubwoman and one of the organizers of the first Texas woman's congress in 1894. Through her columns and work with the federation, Periwinkle promoted many issues of interest to clubwomen.[104] In later years, she would advise Pennybacker on how to handle the press, as Pennybacker's use of the press to influence public opinion would continue into her presidency of the General Federation of Women's Clubs a decade later.

FOR WHITE WOMEN ONLY

Although clubwomen did not like to address the issue of race directly, the issue became explicit for the Texas federation during Pennybacker's TFWC presidency. The issue of race was raised at the national level by eastern clubs who either already had or were open to having African American members and wanted to ensure that the General Federation would permit their membership. White southern clubwomen, however, largely were appalled by the suggestion that they would interact with black women as social equals. At the Milwaukee biennial convention of 1900, the race issue erupted when black clubwoman Josephine Ruffin attempted to take her seat as a convention delegate. Ruffin, a journalist and publisher of *New Era* magazine, represented three organizations at the biennial, the Massachusetts Federation, the New England Woman's Press Club, and Boston's New Era Club, a black women's club which Ruffin herself had founded in 1894. Georgia's Rebecca Douglas Lowe, GFWC president, had admitted Ruffin's New Era Club to the federation not knowing that it was comprised of black members. When Ruffin arrived at the biennial, she was assumed by many to be a white woman due to her fair skin. However, news of a black delegate spread quickly, and when Ruffin tried to take the stage as delegate, she was attacked physically by at least one white woman, who ripped Ruffin's delegate badge from her clothing. Federation leaders scrambled for a way to revoke the New Era Club's federation membership. The board finally denied the New Era Club's membership on a technicality. Lowe had admitted the club, as she had many others, without the required ratification of the board of directors. Because that ratification was not obtained, according to GFWC leaders, the club had never actually been admitted. A heated dispute about whether Ruffin would be allowed to take her seat as delegate ensued, with lines of the debate drawn largely along sectional boundaries. Northern delegations, including Massachusetts, Wisconsin, Illinois, Pennsylvania, and Utah, as well as Missouri's delegation, supported Ruffin's representation of the New Era Club. Southern delegates vehemently opposed it. In the end, Ruffin was allowed to represent the Massachusetts federation and the New England Women's Press Club, but not the black women's club. Insulted, Ruffin declined to participate. The Ruffin incident brought the issue of black women's participation in the General Federation to the fore during the Milwaukee biennial, but further action on the admissibility of black women's clubs was delayed until 1902 to enable state federations to have more time to discuss the matter.

Although Pennybacker did not attend the Milwaukee biennial, as president of the Texas federation she would be confronted with the "color question" prior to the 1902 biennial in Los Angeles. In the fall of 1901 the issue loomed large because it was sure to be introduced at the upcoming GFWC biennial in the spring of 1902. Two state federations, Massachusetts and Georgia, had generated widely different plans for addressing the issue, and these plans were being widely discussed among the various state federations. Each plan reorganized federation membership procedures. The Georgia plan explicitly limited the federation to clubs comprised solely of white members, specifically by introducing the word "white" into the bylaws. This plan also excluded state federations (such as the Massachusetts federation which Ruffin was to have represented) from membership in the federation, admitting only individual clubs. The Massachusetts plan, by contrast, allowed membership only of state federations, with each state determining its own membership policies. Thus the General Federation would admit colored women from states which admitted colored women, but not from those that did not.

Although it was a highly sensitive issue, Pennybacker, as the Texas federation president, determined to address the "color question" in her state with what she termed "dignity and level-headedness." She wished to ensure that her state federation determined a position on the matter and presented a unified position before the other states at the biennial. Recognizing that, as one correspondent wrote, "Southerners will not belong to a body on equal footing with colored people, although our own Congress, Senate and President do," Pennybacker and her

TFWC board unanimously supported the Georgia plan's clause which stated, "The biennial shall be composed of white women only." However, they rejected the reorganization of the federation membership policies that this plan would have entailed, instead supporting the current system of allowing clubs to join individually or through their state federations. This "states' rights"–style plan ostensibly left the issue of black women's club membership to the individual state federations or local clubs to decide. One Texas woman rationalized, "There is positively nothing in there to keep the negro out."[105] However, the plan ensured that even if northern clubs were to admit black women, white southern women would not be expected to interact with them, as the plan forbade their attending the biennial conventions. Kate Friend, Texas reporter for the *Clubwoman,* explained the Pennybacker administration's logic:

> Settled as it is by home seekers as well as by capitalists from every state, nay from every country, Texas cannot be classed as a "Southern state." [Pennybacker] entered into the subject of the color question with no vestige of personal prejudice against the Negro club woman, but rather from the calm deliberation that the two social elements cannot mix with advantage to either element, and that the Negro club had a mission not in the same line as the white club of today. Yet appreciating the fact that the isolated cases of the North were not what the southern clubs would be called upon to confront, deference was paid the Northern sister, in leaving her free to settle the question of the Negro club member herself. . . . The prospects are that Texas will be well represented at the biennial. The club women go united in their opposition to the seating of a negro delegate in the biennial, but without the slightest tinge of sectional feeling.[106]

This explanation reveals much about the position of the Texas federation with regard to the race issue. First, clubwomen wanted to avoid addressing racial issues directly. This issue challenged their self-image as a democratic organization, their mission of seeking to unite women across the country, and their sense of dignity and gentility. Second, few would directly acknowledge their own prejudice. Arguments were made in terms of generic "women of the South" rather than in personal terms, and obvious personal prejudice was denied. Third, they denied sectional bias, even while practicing it. The above passage is most remarkable in denying sectional sensibilities and even that Texas was a southern state, especially given the great pride taken by Texas clubwomen in their southern heritage and the fact that in years to come they would celebrate Pennybacker's GFWC presidency as a triumph for the South.

THE TEXAS CYCLONE

However much Pennybacker's handling of the race issue seems to deny the obvious and betray the progressive and democratic ideals she and other clubwomen expressed elsewhere, it was, in her context, well respected.[107] In the spring of 1902 Pennybacker had the opportunity to attend her first General Federation biennial. As TFWC president, she led the Texas delegation and reported to the General Federation the accomplishments of Texas women. She also demonstrated her ability as a leader who could manage a large organization and avoid discord over potentially divisive issues.

For the first time, Texas's delegates to the GFWC biennial traveled together, reserving lower berths in five Pullman cars. Pennybacker later recalled that it was the first biennial for most of the twenty-two Texas delegates, including herself. The Texas delegates arrived in Los Angeles ready to act in unison. According to Pennybacker the delegates were "eager to do the right thing in the right way and to reflect credit on Texas," and determined to vote "as a unit." They met each day on the train for a conference at which they "discussed thoroughly each proposed amendment to the constitution and the merits of each candidate."[108]

Arriving on the West Coast, the delegates were greeted with, as Pennybacker later remembered, "flowers, perfume, gentle breezes, sunshine, smiling faces and loving welcome." They met in a convention hall decorated with sixty thousand calla lilies. As president of the state federation, Pennybacker found a basket of orange blossoms waiting in her chair.[109] Although the press noted that the only black women at this biennial were the restroom maids, the "color question" clearly was on everyone's mind. The *New York Times* predicted the imminent demise of the federation if the issue could not be resolved in a manner satisfactory to the southern states.[110] The *Los Angeles Times* made light of the impending debate on race with an article entitled "New Color Question More Trying Yet." The article read in part: "The much-mooted question of color, which was to have been left in the background, has been brought prominently forward and seems likely to overthrow the Simpson Annex." "It is not," the article continued, "really so much a question of color as of hue; and the aggravating part of it is every woman under the present circumstances turns out the same shade, a sort of jaundiced yellow."[111]

Light coming through the canvas canopies apparently was less than flattering and left the complexions of the white attendees looking yellow.

Pennybacker played a highly visible role at the biennial proceedings and in particular in the discussion of the "color question." Remembering the biennial in a later speech, Pennybacker was deliberately vague. She avoided any specific reference to race as she described a revelation: "One day early in the convention there came up a question for discussion on which the delegates were divided. From the gallery came the wonderful voice of Jane Addams of Illinois. Far back on the left one spoke in perfect diction; it was May Alden Ward of Massachusetts. From the extreme right some one from Georgia pleaded her side." The diverse voices apparently brought insight. Pennybacker continued: "All at once I realized what the Federation meant. I realized that we were the women of the Nation, no north, no south, no east, no west, but the women of the United States of America called in solemn council. From that moment I have never forgotten the potentialities and responsibilities of the organization."[112] According to Pennybacker, she became impatient with the lengthy discussions of race and other issues: "More than once, the discussions became tedious; the same thing was said over and over again, valuable time was wasted." As a result of her frustration, she "moved the previous question," which in parliamentary terms, means to end debate on a question and force a decision. She moved the previous question three times that day and continued to do so in upcoming days when the discussion threatened to carry on with no resolution in view.[113] The press took note, labeling her "Mrs. Previous Question Pennybacker." The *Los Angeles Herald,* playing on her initials, published a poem entitled "Mrs. P. Q. Pennybacker of Texas: The Previous Question Delegate."

> Some woman made a motion to amend the last amendment;
> Then a lady tried amending it some more.
> Still another made a motion to amend the whole thing over,
> Till the chairman didn't know who had the floor.
> Then rose a thoughtful woman with a sapient suggestion —
> The Pennybacker (Texas) lady moved the previous question.
> Anon another muddle grew apace and made delay,
> And amending of amendments started in;
> The press gang yawned and said things that they didn't put in print
> And that no one heard amid the swelling din.
> Then rose that self-same woman, waved her arm, made same suggestion—
> O precious Pennybacker, with your move for previous question!

The fountain of all wisdom only knows what might have been
(While the press gang simply shudders at the thought)
If this lady with the motion hadn't been on hand to call
The end of every Shattuck round they fought.
God bless the thoughtful woman with her always wise suggestion—
The Texas Pennybacker dame who moved the previous question.
(SWG).[114]

The vagueness of many accounts of the proceedings makes difficult any determination about which questions that Pennybacker specifically supported, but she clearly was involved in the several debates held during the convention about black women's clubs. All indications are that Pennybacker did move the question when the race issue came up for debate. The *Los Angeles Times* reported that at one session Jane Addams tried pass to a resolution requiring a three-fifths vote of the membership committee against a club in order to reject it, but that this amendment failed. The article reported that "Mrs. Pennybacker of Texas lent efficient aid in expediting the business of the session by moving the previous question, whenever debate threatened to become too long-winded."[115] A magazine reporter reported that the "move the previous question episodes" had been prearranged. Reports claimed that, having moved the previous question on several preceding days of debate, Pennybacker encountered GFWC president Dimies T. S. Denison prior to yet another session involving the inclusion of black clubs. During their conversation, the president laughingly told Pennybacker, "You have been a great help by moving the previous question. We are going to be awfully tangled today. When I raise my handkerchief to my lips, you move the previous question, will you?" Pennybacker was indignant over the charges, but they were consistent with her practice of quelling debate on contentious issues.[116]

Under Pennybacker's leadership, Texas clubwomen attended the 1902 biennial unified in their support for their "solution" to the "color problem," and their cohesion made a strong impression among the delegates of other states. Mary Terrell wrote in 1903 that the "strong and numerous" delegation of Texas clubwomen at the Los Angeles biennial, "in ability, tact, and personality, challenged the admiration of that assembly, and placed Texas near the first rank as to quality of her club material."[117] Additionally, the 1902 biennial provided Pennybacker a stage to showcase her speaking abilities. As TFWC president, Pennybacker delivered a report from Texas. Her reception indicated that she had captured the attention and admiration of the delegates. Reporters noted,

"There must be a great many admirers of Mrs. Pennybacker outside of Texas, also, for when she came forward to speak there was a demonstration that has not been excelled thus far during the entire convention."[118] Her skill and energy in public speaking won her the moniker "Texas Cyclone." The *Los Angeles Times* reported, "Mrs. Pennybacker is about as small of figure as the State of Texas is large, but she seems to have all the genius of that vast State concentrated in her own small person. Her oratory is of the spontaneous kind, that stirs the blood and works up an audience to the highest pitch of enthusiasm." Of her oratory, the reporter exclaimed, "Even a stoic would become hilarious under the sound of Mrs. Pennybacker's ringing voice. She is a veritable cyclone when she gets started up, and it does not take her long to get a move on. No wonder that woman is having her own way down in Texas when she has such an able and energetic champion of her cause."[119] Under Pennybacker's leadership, the Texas clubwomen impressed federation leaders so much that Mary Terrell, Pennybacker's mentor, was appointed to one of the General Federation's standing committees, a first for a Texas clubwoman. Texas clubwomen's rise in stature at this biennial, in part fostered by the group's cohesion, set the stage for Pennybacker's rise into national leadership. However, as Texas's clubwomen gained national stature, the exclusion of black women from the General Federation was formalized.

In the end, the biennial assembly adopted a compromise membership plan that avoided major reorganization as well as explicit mention of race. The plan left the question of black women in clubs to individual state federations and made eligibility for the General Federation contingent on the approval of a newly created membership committee. Although black women were not explicitly excluded from the federation, most members understood that the membership committee would ensure that no black women's clubs would be admitted. This plan effectively segregated the General Federation of Women's Clubs for decades.[120]

In her *History of the Texas Federation of Women's Clubs,* Stella Christian credited the organization's first presidents, Rotan and Terrell, with giving the organization life and enthusiasm respectively. Pennybacker she credited with providing stability. Indeed, Pennybacker effectively strengthened and expanded the organization, promoting a wide variety of progressive causes. During her presidency the federation furthered the cause of education in the state. In addition to raising money for scholarships and promoting a women's dormitory at the state university, the TFWC worked for laws making education compulsory, and limiting child labor. It supported the formation of kindergartens and industrial and manual education programs in public schools, and sought to strengthen the relationship of women's clubs and school teachers. In January of 1903, when the cornerstone for the College of Industrial Arts in Denton, now Texas Women's University, was laid, Pennybacker spoke at the ceremonies. By the end of her term as president, both the women's college in Denton and the women's dormitory at the University of Texas were helping make possible increased educational opportunities for Texas's young women. The organization also supported educational opportunities that were not school-based. Under Pennybacker's administration, the TFWC furthered the creation of libraries throughout the state, and supported the formation of a traveling library and traveling art gallery, statewide lecture series, and the State Library Association. Pennybacker continued to be active in the state federation after her term as president ended. She served on the executive board of her successor, Mrs. E. P. Turner, and consulted with federation leaders for at least the next decade.[121] Her success in Texas would propel her to the national stage, as she held positions of increasing prominence in the General Federation of Women's Clubs.

Chapter Five

THE MOST POWERFUL POSITION A WOMAN COULD HOLD

PENNYBACKER'S SUCCESS as president of the Texas Federation of Women's Clubs led her to broader involvement in women's clubs and to positions of greater national visibility with the General Federation in the years after her TFWC presidency. As her TFWC presidency came to a close in 1903, she traveled to Colorado to assume leadership of the Boulder Chautauqua Women's Council. Her mission there was to turn the women's council into a functioning women's club, "with a regular organization after the order of the New York Chautauqua."[1] Upon her return to Texas that fall, she was offered the presidency of the World's Fair Texas Women's Board. A group of Texas women believed they had made a poor showing at the World's Columbian Exhibition in Chicago in 1893 and pledged to do better at the St. Louis exposition in 1904. Although Pennybacker turned down the presidency of the Texas Women's Board, she remained involved with the leaders of this organization.[2] The General Federation had scheduled its 1904 convention to coincide with the St. Louis exposition to be held to commemorate the hundredth anniversary of the Louisiana Purchase.[3]

As she had in previous years, Pennybacker represented Texas as a delegate to this biennial convention. At this meeting, Sarah S. Platt Decker of Colorado was elected to the GFWC presidency, and Pennybacker was elected to her first national position, treasurer of the General Federation. Like her predecessor as treasurer, Emma Van Vechten of Iowa, Pennybacker also was appointed chair of the membership committee, the committee responsible for examining and approving the memberships of new clubs. That a single individual would hold both the treasurer and membership committee chair positions made sense. The work of the membership committee dovetailed with the work of the treasurer. As treasurer, a large part of Pennybacker's responsibility involved keeping track of which clubs had paid dues in a timely manner and were thus eligible to send delegates to federation meetings. Member clubs were required to pay dues, and often questions of membership depended upon whether or not dues were paid. However, Pennybacker may have been seen as particularly well suited for this position, not so much because of her organizational abilities, but because of her conservative handling of the "color question" at the 1902 biennial. As the Texas federation president, she had opposed the seating of black women as delegates and GFWC leaders may have expected that, as membership committee chair, she would be unlikely to admit clubs with black members. Furthermore, she was known for her tact, and others may have been secure in the belief that she would find a way to quell controversy and exclude the clubs with black members in what clubwomen would have considered a dignified manner. As chair of this committee, Pennybacker oversaw changes in the bylaws regarding membership. Among these changes were amendments that required new clubs to submit upon application their constitution and bylaws that "show that no sectarian or political test is required for membership." Changes also set dues for clubs: $2.50 for clubs with fewer than twenty-five members and ten cents per capita for larger clubs, and clubs were required to pay dues by May 1 of each year.[4]

As treasurer of the federation, Pennybacker was a member of the GFWC board of directors and as such consulted with other federation leaders on a variety of issues not limited to federation financial affairs. GFWC president Decker, known for her "long prospective view that overlooked some of the necessary steps between" and for "overstepping the strict parliamentary ruling that permits no presiding officer an expression of feeling, in order to point a moral or touch the heartstrings," relied on Pennybacker's "judicial mind" (Pennybacker, in Decker's view, was "never swayed by prejudice nor self-interest").[5] Pennybacker, for her part, served Decker well. She was an active member of Decker's board, participating in some of the major achievements of her administration. In 1904, for example, Pennybacker and fellow board member Mary I. Wood advocated the formation of a bureau of information, a central office from which information about the federation could be collected and distributed. Pennybacker explained the rationale for this office in a report, noting that relatively few members had the opportunity to attend a biennial to learn more about the work of the federation. "The great majority of our club women," she wrote, "have no conception of the magnitude of this work. Even though they may desire to know more of it, it is extremely difficult for them to get the information."[6] The bureau, which had been discussed for a number of years, would be responsible for coordinating the exchange of information between the General Federation and individual clubs across the country. Individual clubs and clubwomen could address questions to and receive information from a single source rather than try to determine which of the many officers and committees to address with particular concerns. The board agreed about the importance of the bureau and authorized its formation in 1905. Mary I. Wood, who, with Pennybacker, authored the report advocating the bureau, took charge of the office and would run the bureau for years to follow.

The bureau of information became important, not only in communicating information (largely study outlines) about the General Federation to other clubwomen, but in collecting and disseminating information about the organization to a larger public audience. Specifically, the bureau served to counter public criticism of the General Federation. For example, when *Ladies' Home Journal* editor Edward Bok, who had published Grover Cleveland's anti–women's club article in 1905, criticized women's clubs, the bureau of information was ready with a response. Bok accused clubwomen of focusing on self-education instead of contributing to their communities, and ridiculed their scholarly efforts as badly executed, mocking presentations of "papers copied from encyclopedias and ill digested."[7] In response, Wood prepared statistics that demonstrated "the club movement of today is a social movement" and showered Bok with examples of clubwomen's work in civic improvement, education, libraries, parks, and public health.[8]

When the bureau of information was organized in 1905, Wood chaired its executive committee and Pennybacker was the committee's second member. Pennybacker likely was appointed because of her advocacy for the bureau and because she had already been consulted about how to counter negative images of clubwomen in the media. In November 1904, Decker had included Pennybacker in plans to collect statistics about clubwomen in order to counter negative portrayals in the media, noting that a similar strategy had worked to help dispel similar negative images of college-educated women. Decker wrote Pennybacker: "We meet everyday in papers and periodicals and conversation the charge that the women of the clubs are single women, or unhappy in marriage, not mothers, etc."[9] Decker believed statistics would disprove this stereotype. The bureau provided a means to counter media images which portrayed clubwomen as unfeminine, unmotherly, and unsuitable for marriage, by disseminating carefully screened information about the federation and its membership.

In addition to working to form the bureau of information and improving the federation's public image, Pennybacker was consulted by leaders of other women's organizations regarding an alliance of national women's organizations. In July 1905, during the convention of the American Institute of Instruction in Portland, Maine, representatives of several national women's organizations met to discuss an alliance to further educational work. Besides the General Federation representatives, representatives of the Daughters of the American Revolution, the Women's Christian Temperance Union, the American Association of Collegiate Alumnae (ACA), and the Congress of Mothers attended this meeting.[10] The General Federation committee outlined the proposed goals and principles of this alliance as follows: "It shall be our aim to bring about such an equalization of educational advantages that any child in any nook or corner of the nation may receive as good an education as any child in the most favorable locality now receives."[11] The conference would work to further compulsory school laws, well-equipped and cared-for school buildings, properly prepared teachers with at least normal school credentials, minimum professional requirements, and a minimum salary. Members sought expert supervision of schools, and schools that focused on knowledge, efficiency, character, training for the hand, and instruction in moral principles.[12] Attendees at this meeting agreed to approach their own national organization regarding the alliance. The GFWC representative to this meeting, chair of the GFWC Education Committee, schoolteacher Mary Abbot, approached Pennybacker with the plan that Pennybacker subsequently presented to the GFWC board of directors.[13] As a result, the board agreed that the GFWC should join the alliance. By 1906, the GFWC, the ACA, the National Congress of Mothers, the Southern Association of College Women, and the National Council of Jewish Women formed the Educational Department of National Organizations of Women.[14] These women's organizations worked with the National Education Association (NEA) to coordinate educational activities nationwide and eventually would become the NEA Department of School Patrons.

Pennybacker continued her work with the GFWC through the first decade of the century. In 1906 she addressed the GFWC membership on President's Night at the biennial in St. Paul, Minnesota. Four women spoke, each representing a section of the country, East, West, North, and South. Naturally Pennybacker represented the South. Reports of the event relate that her "words were full of flaming affection and tenderness," as she drew vivid pictures of her "high hopes for the South of a new day as it should be merged into an America unified by common ideals."[15] At this meeting, Pennybacker was selected to be auditor for the General Federation. She also was appointed program chair for the 1908 biennial to be held in Boston. As program chair, Pennybacker arranged addresses on the historical city and excursions to famous localities. The governor of Massachusetts received the GFWC members in the State House and the Boston Symphony played on the convention's opening night.[16]

Having suffered a health scare in 1907, Pennybacker had determined to retire from club work after she was relieved of her GFWC duties. She planned an extended trip to Germany. The trip, however, would not be as relaxing as expected. On the voyage to Italy, her ship, the *Slavonia,* sank. Pennybacker and the two of her children with whom she was traveling were rescued, and eventually they arrived safely in Germany.[17] The trip provided her with the opportunity to visit a sanitarium, at which she was treated by a German doctor for problems with her health.[18] Despite these treatments, however, she suffered bouts of fatigue and loss of appetite upon returning to the United States.

DEVELOPING THE GFWC ENDOWMENT FUND

Although her doctor apparently recommended a lighter schedule, Pennybacker returned to her busy schedule upon her return from Germany. The GFWC had grown to nearly a million women. Yet, with dues of just ten cents per capita, the federation hardly had the money to cover operating expenses. GFWC executives used their personal funds for travel and lodging when they attended board meetings or visited the states. During her term as GFWC president, Sara Platt Decker had discussed with Pennybacker the possibility of establishing an endowment fund for the organization.[19] In the spring of 1911, Pennybacker was selected as field chair of the newly formed GFWC Endowment Committee. The federation had determined to raise $100,000 through donations from clubs and individuals across the states. Pennybacker believed that the first step in raising this money was "to convince ourselves in a two-fold sense that a $100,000 endowment is absolutely necessary."[20] She set out to convince clubwomen both intellectually and emotionally that the fund was needed. Intellectually, she argued for the fund by enumerating the expenses facing the GFWC. However, Pennybacker's exceptional talent was the emotional appeal—she understood how to address women's shared ideals and inspire them to contribute. The fundraising effort was organized systematically. Each state federation was assigned a field chair and a goal each state federation was expected to meet. Texas's goal was $2,000. In November 1911, Pennybacker appealed for the Texas federation's share of the money at the TFWC annual convention. Her inspirational talk was effective, and the money was raised in a matter of minutes. Her continued success as the chair of the endowment committee put her in the national spotlight once more.

The success of the Texas delegation to the GFWC biennial in 1902 put Texans, including Pennybacker, in prominent positions within the organization. GFWC leaders especially admired Pennybacker's success in raising funds for the endowment. In January 1912, Pennybacker's mentor, Mary Terrell, and other supporters approached her with the proposition that she run for the presidency of the General Federation of Women's Clubs. Pennybacker accepted the proposition with a few conditions. First, she insisted that she "should not be asked to turn over my hand to secure the position." Secondly, she refused to run an ugly campaign. "The whole contest should be conducted on a pervectly [*sic*] high and honorable plane," she insisted.[21]

CAMPAIGN FOR THE GFWC PRESIDENCY

Although nominations would take place at the 1912 biennial, which was to be held in San Francisco in June, Pennybacker learned before the meeting that her opponent for the GFWC presidency was Mrs. Philip Carpenter, a New York attorney and a woman Pennybacker considered a personal friend.[22] Carpenter's nomination was forwarded by Sorosis, one of the nation's oldest and most influential women's clubs, and she had the support of a particularly strong delegation from New York. Pennybacker was forwarded by the Austin American History Club. Compared to New York City, Austin, Texas, was a sleepy backwater town. Although Pennybacker's Austin History Club was prominent in its own city and state, it was little known at the national level. However, as the former president of the Texas Federation of Women's Clubs and the then-current chair of the federation's Endowment Committee, Pennybacker had gained renown as an efficient organizer and fundraiser who possessed the ability to inspire through powerful speeches.[23]

Both Pennybacker and Carpenter were so well supported by coalitions within the federation that at the San Francisco biennial the organization abandoned its traditional method of nominating candidates. Traditionally a nominating committee composed of representatives from each state selected a single candidate, then allowed other candidates to be nominated from the floor. In this case, however, the committee nominated both candidates, causing one reporter to comment: "The method was disappointing. . . . all of the honeyed speeches had to be forgone, all of the seconding had to be relegated to the limbo of things that are never said, while the nominating committee unblushingly looked on at the havoc their action accomplished."[24] Despite this reporter's view that the committee had caused havoc with its dual nomination, the committee's decision can be seen as an attempt to avoid the controversy that sometimes surrounded the candidates, divided the organization's members, and created an air of tension among attendees. In this case, the issue on the minds of the Eleventh Biennial attendees, but off the official program, was woman's suffrage.

Suffrage was such a defining issue in the race between Carpenter and Pennybacker that one reporter commented, "The vote will be tantamount to a vote on the question of suffrage."[25] Carpenter was well known as an ardent suffragist. During her campaign, she advocated that the GFWC officially endorse suffrage for women. Although many clubwomen were supporters of suffrage, many were not. Women in the southern states, particularly, resisted woman suffrage as too great a threat to the established social order. Southern ideals of femininity did not include women's participation in politics. That Pennybacker was a southerner herself brought her advantages in the campaign. She recognized southern concerns about suffrage.[26] In addition, southern supporters understood her position on issues of race to reflect their own beliefs. Pennybacker's stand on suffrage was that although she herself supported it, the General Federation should refrain from adopting a suffrage platform, and, rather, work to expand the organization. Her stated priority during the campaign was the unification and betterment of women nationally and worldwide. In particular, she argued a role for the federation in helping to reunite the sectional rifts caused by the Civil War. "Let me remark parenthetically that nothing has done more to unite the North and the South since the Civil War than this Federation," she told clubwomen. "It has brought together women from all parts of the country. They have learned to understand each other. When prejudice dies among women it will no longer exist among men. Aside from this, it has done more work of a charitable and philanthropic nature than I can begin to take time to tell."[27] However, under the plan Pennybacker promoted, sectional prejudice among white women would be overcome by avoiding measures that might lead to greater equality for black women, at least within the nation's largest women's organizations. Pennybacker's position on suffrage had been carefully developed by her campaign team to give her the political edge.[28] It suited the clubwomen's general stance toward the most divisive and overtly political issues and continued to emphasize the priorities established by previous leaders of the GFWC, particularly an emphasis on unity. Historian Judith McArthur writes of the clubwomen, "By disavowing and concealing their political side and emphasizing genteel sorority, clubs avoided alienating members who feared participating in 'unwomanly' activity."[29]

On July 2, 1912, "tumultuous cheering" filled San Francisco's Sutter Street Pavilion upon the announcement that Mrs. Percy V. Pennybacker had been elected president of the General Federation of Women's Clubs at the Eleventh Biennial Convention. Her supporters attributed her success to her genteel campaign style and great popularity among the Texas women. Campaign manager Mary Y. Terrell wrote:

> Our salvation had been being good, straight & above board. You were that way from principle—I from policy—for I recognized that we were no match for our opponents in the—of politics—but dear Lady there were times when my heart was in my boots—one of those was when I took stock of that Tex. delegation at Fort Worth—Such green stuff! and to go up against N. Y . . . But it was wonderful how that little crude delegation grew and developed. Each one did yeoman service, and stood as a stone wall in loyalty to you. Your opponent had not such support from her state—It was a great tribute to your personality.[30]

In addition to a successful campaign strategy based on de-emphasizing issues and strategies considered by clubwomen to be too political, Terrell credited Pennybacker's powerful public speaking ability for her victory. Mrs. Carpenter read her speeches and delivered them awkwardly. Pennybacker put her years of training and practice to work and spoke naturally and powerfully before the delegation. Terrell marveled: "Mrs. C-s speaking from manuscript helped us most. Funny isn't it—that such valuation should be placed on off-hand speaking!"[31]

PENNYBACKER'S GFWC PRESIDENCY

Pennybacker's assumption of the GFWC presidency gave her a nationally visible platform from which to advocate for the power of federated clubs and for progressive reforms. Pennybacker's administration continued its neutral stance on suffrage during the first two years of her presidency. Under her administration, the GFWC continued a general strategy of disavowing political activity while emphasizing sorority. Through a strategy of apparent conservatism which included avoiding controversial issues, expanding rather than overtly challenging expectations of feminine behavior, and carefully cultivating the federation's public image, Pennybacker became a force in developing power and recognition for clubwomen.

Pennybacker's administration of the General Federation of Women's Clubs was not marked by particular innovation. She was a conservative leader in the sense that she maintained the course set forth by previous presidents in terms of the issues and attitudes supported by the federation. In the earlier part of the new century, GFWC president Sarah Platt Decker determined that the organization needed "centralization" and she urged state federations and clubs to coordinate their local committees with national federation's committees.[32] As described earlier, Decker's administration also formed the bureau of information as "a central clearing house and base for operations."[33] Pennybacker continued the emphasis on focused and unified effort among the country's clubwomen. True to public perception of her as an efficient leader, she steadied the course of the federation during a time of immense growth. Toward the end of her first term in office, as she prepared to review the years of her administration at the 1914 Biennial, Pennybacker asked her board members what they felt were the major accomplishments of her administration. They listed growth, the endowment, the protection of the organization's power and reputation from exploitation by other interests and the protection of individual clubwomen from advertising schemes claiming federation connections.

Pennybacker focused on developing the organization and, in particular, on fundraising and encouraging new membership. The endowment fund which Pennybacker so successfully supported in Texas prior to her election continued to be a focus of Pennybacker's for the first term of her administration. Early in Pennybacker's first term, the fund's slow growth disappointed and frustrated members of the board of directors. In June of 1913, board member Grace Julian Clarke lamented: "I am growing really concerned about [the endowment]; it is dragging along at such a discouraging rate, and I fear will not be half in hand by the time of the Biennial, which would be disgraceful." Clarke noted that "with a constituency of a million women only about $34,000 of the $100,000 has been secured."[34] Having proven herself an adept fundraiser prior to her election by raising the scholarship fund in Texas and securing the state's portion of the GFWC endowment almost immediately, Pennybacker put these skills to use at the national level to complete the raising of funds for the endowment. Most of the solicitation for funds occurred at the state level. Pennybacker facilitated this process by encouraging and pressuring individual states to meet their quotas. She corresponded with state presidents regarding funds pledged and collected, and chastised those who did not seem to be doing enough to raise their quotas. Her administration also publicized the states' results in the official organ and at GFWC meetings. Pressure was put on states to meet their quotas or face public embarrassment when they were listed last on published records showing the percentage of quota each state had raised. Pennybacker also incorporated into her fundraising efforts the loss of beloved former GFWC president, Sarah S. Platt Decker, who became ill and died just days after making a stirring biennial plea for support for the endowment. To honor Decker, Pennybacker suggested dedicating the endowment fund to her memory and naming it the Sara S. Platt Endowment.[35] She encouraged clubwomen to show their love and respect for Decker by pledging generously to the endowment. Under Pennybacker's stewardship between 1912 and 1916, the remaining funds were raised and the endowment surpassed its goal of $100,000 by the 1916 Biennial.[36]

DISSEMINATING IDEAS AND DEVELOPING AN ORGANIZATION

In addition to developing the endowment that would enable the GFWC to fund its work, Pennybacker also worked to develop the organization in terms of the number of members. Expanding the federation meant promoting it, and early in Pennybacker's presidency the General Federation began a major publicity push. "This administration early saw the need for wider publicity, if we were to get into personal touch with the rank and file," wrote Pennybacker in a summary of her first two years.[37] In his history of American education, Lawrence Cremin devotes a chapter to the growing importance of the media of popular education in the last decades of the nineteenth century and into the twentieth century. Cremin notes a revolution in the "technology and the conception of the American newspaper," particularly, that "had profoundly altered the education that American newspapers proffered to the American public."[38] Newspapers became widespread and helped to set a national agenda for public discussion. Pennybacker entered office with a strong understanding of the educational power of the press and set to work harnessing it almost immediately.

From the beginning, Pennybacker and her colleagues discussed the most effective ways of reaching the nation's eight hundred thousand clubwomen as well as the "general public." Mrs. C. H. McMahon, chair of the press committee, advised Pennybacker that "it would be better to try and have the news of special and vital interest, go to the Newspapers immediately."[39] McMahon's opinion was supported by Mrs. Eli Hertzberg, president of the Texas Federation of Women's Clubs, who noted that clubwomen "like to have [news] fresh every week and not monthly, when it becomes stale." Distributing information through the newspapers had the additional advantage of reaching "the masses" and educating "the people up to club work."[40] Reports of the board, council, and executive meetings could be sent to the organization's official organ, the *General Federation Bulletin*.

THE *GENERAL FEDERATION BULLETIN* AND *GENERAL FEDERATION MAGAZINE*

The *General Federation Bulletin* was a monthly publication produced not by the federation but by a private concern under contract with the federation.[41] Almost immediately upon assuming her responsibilities as president, Pennybacker began using the *Bulletin* as a means of publicizing the organization and taking control of its public image. One way she would do this was to exert control over the material published in the *Bulletin*. At her administration's first meeting of the federation's board of directors in July 1912, Pennybacker placed herself on the *Bulletin* committee.[42] In August she began her monthly article, "The President's Message," and by September she had made arrangements for the various departments to contribute a description of each department and its work in order to familiarize clubwomen across the country with the organization's activities. She and the other board members also arrived at a policy that would prevent department chairs from publishing opinions that were at odds with the official stance of the organization.

Having the *Bulletin* as an official organ allowed Pennybacker a forum from which to promote the GWFC. Her relationship with the *Bulletin*'s managing editor, Harriet Bishop Waters, was strained from the beginning. In fact, trouble with Waters and the *Bulletin* was one of the most contentious and persistent issues Pennybacker faced during her GWFC presidency. Pennybacker and her administration wanted as much control as possible over the content of the magazine. Controlling the public image of the organization and avoiding controversy were priorities. However, without funds to create its own magazine, the federation had to rely on a contract with Waters who financed and published the *General Federation Bulletin* herself. As an independent publisher of limited resources Waters struggled often with financial and production difficulties, and Pennybacker's administration was almost immediately dissatisfied with her work. Upon the death of past GWFC president, Sara Platt Decker, just after the 1912 Biennial, Waters neglected to publish a tribute from the board of directors in a timely manner. Furthermore, she consistently had difficulty producing and mailing out the magazine on time. The situation distressed members of Pennybacker's administration who were concerned that the habitual tardiness did not promote the public impression they wanted to maintain.

Pennybacker also disapproved of several of the articles that Waters published in the *Bulletin* shortly after Pennybacker's election. The September 1912 issue of the *Bulletin,* which featured an article introducing Pennybacker as the new president, also featured an article by Frances A. Kellor outlining the platform of the Progressive Party. A full-page registration form at the front of the magazine read in bold print, "Why Every Woman Should Be a Progressive," and exhorted women to join the party.[43] Pennybacker received complaints about the political nature of the articles, not from conservative women who wished to remain apolitical, but rather from the more politically active women, such as Helen Varick Boswell, who headed both the General Federation's Political Science Committee and the Department of Women's Work of the Republican National Committee.[44] Waters explained that the article was to have been published in an edition that included pieces by members of all the major parties, but the other parties had failed to submit materials in time. Articles about the Republican, Democratic, and Socialist parties would run in later issues, but the controversy would cause Pennybacker to review the federation's contract to determine what level of control the federation was given over *Bulletin* content and later to revise the contract to provide the board more editorial control.

With the federation's press committee chair, Mrs. C. H. McMahon, proposing to distribute most information through the newspaper and having received criticism for her work by the new administration, Waters must have been anxious about the future of the *Bulletin.* She decided to expand the *Bulletin* into a magazine of wider interest rather than focus narrowly on federation matters. Having made an alliance with Current Issue Publishing Company, she moved production of the publication to New York City at the end of 1912.[45] The January 1913 issue revealed a new look and a new name for the *Bulletin,* which became the *General Federation Magazine.* Its front cover no longer carried a different photograph of leaders of the organization each month. Instead the cover would be the same each month, a simpler graphic with the magazine's name. The format of the magazine changed slightly as well. The pages were larger, with three instead of two columns of text, and the articles were longer. The space given for reviews and digests, "giving a comprehensive view of the work of women in the world" through reviews of the great books, was also increased. Waters presented the magazine as the single publication that focused on "the women's movement," noting that there were "innumerable magazines that specialize upon fashions, domestic affairs, [and] dress," but that none "specializes as the *General Federation Magazine* is preparing to do, upon that development that is taking place in the intellectual, industrial, and social status of the feminine half of the race." "Here," she declared, "is the very soul of the 'Woman's Movement,' and if you wish to keep in touch with that, the *General Federation Magazine* will be positively indispensable."[46] Pennybacker and others expressed their approval of the changes, and the tensions seemed to ease.[47]

Tensions, however, did not ease for long and Pennybacker was quickly drawn into another dispute with Waters. Struggling to make a profit from the magazine, Waters formed business relationships with potential investors who created further problems for Pennybacker's administration. The *General Federation Magazine*'s connection with businessman Milton E. Jones, in particular, caused Pennybacker considerable consternation. Associating himself with Waters by promising financial backing, Jones appears to have mismanaged several aspects of the business. In the spring of 1913, Jones visited a competing magazine, *American Clubwoman,* and accused the publisher, Mrs. Valesh, of infringing on the *General Federation Magazine*'s rights by claiming to be an official organ of the GFWC when soliciting advertising. Waters had recently made the same complaint to Pennybacker and gotten little response. In fact, Pennybacker seemed to use the threat of competition to pressure Waters to produce her magazine on time. Confronted by Jones, however, Valesh responded by suing Jones and his associate for slander and threatening to do the same against the federation if they did not offer an official apology for a letter written by board member Laura Holmes Reilley to the state federation presidents, reminding them that the *American Clubwoman* was not the GFWC official organ and encouraging them to patronize Waters's magazine. Pennybacker, again concerned about the public image of the federation, advised, "We must be just to all; we must preserve the Federation from a sensation."[48]

Even if Pennybacker could maintain control over what was printed about the federation in its own official organ, she and her board could not control what other magazines printed, although they could and sometimes did try to do so. In early 1913, for example, when the *Women's*

Journal printed an article claiming "the officers have succeeded in smothering the formal endorsement of suffrage and are proud of their victory," former president Eva Perry Moore, with Pennybacker's blessing, wrote asking for a correction.[49]

LADIES' HOME JOURNAL

In the fall of 1912, Pennybacker was invited to Philadelphia to visit the offices of Edward Bok, editor of the *Ladies' Home Journal.* Bok wished to propose a regular feature about the women's clubs in the *Journal.* Pennybacker worried about negotiating the arrangement successfully. Bok had printed Grover Cleveland's anti-women's club articles several years earlier and continued his editorial hostility toward women's clubs and the issue of women's suffrage. The federation women were well aware of his position and reciprocated the hostility, as Mrs. Grace Julian Clarke, Pennybacker's press committee chair, revealed in a letter to Pennybacker. She wrote: "I hope the Ladies' Home Journal matter will work out all right. I do not see that publication often, and then I usually grow so wrathful over some inanity that it does me no good."[50] The federation women distrusted Bok's motives, but saw the possibility of Bok softening on the issue of women's clubs in an article by Edith Rickert that was published in the October 1912 issue of the *Ladies' Home Journal.* This article was received positively by leading clubwomen and prompted former GFWC president, Eva Perry Moore, to write to Pennybacker, "I think it is an opening for Mr. Bok to take back all that he ever did."[51]

A proponent of club work, Rickert was responsible for arranging the meeting between Pennybacker and Bok in Philadelphia. In September, Rickert sent Pennybacker an outline of her plan. The proposed woman's club department in the *Ladies' Home Journal,* she wrote, would serve two purposes. First, it would provide a "clearinghouse of information" about clubs' activities and methods. Secondly, it would act as "a stimulus to *Journal* readers who are not club women to take up club work."[52] Pennybacker and other leaders of the GFWC saw the *Journal* department as a great opportunity to expand and promote the GFWC by presenting their point of view to a larger public consisting of mainstream, conservative women. The clubwomen, however, continued to doubt that Bok would grant the federation editorial control, despite Rickert's proposal that a federation woman would serve as editor and "have the last word" on the contents of the article.[53] Mary I. Wood, who headed the federation's Bureau of Information, wrote that she suspected Bok "did not intend to play fair" and "would never have come around. . . . if it were not for the fact that it was in some way injuring his business."[54]

Despite her worries about the meeting, Pennybacker was able to negotiate an agreement with editor Bok, giving the federation editorial control over articles about women's clubs that would be published in the *Ladies' Home Journal.* A new department, "What the Women's Clubs Are Doing," was to be a monthly feature in the *Ladies' Home Journal.* The articles would be "under the personal conduct and editorship of the President and Board of Directors of the General Federation." To write the articles, Pennybacker sought a clubwoman who was knowledgeable about federation activities and could portray the federation in an inspiring fashion. After considering several names, Pennybacker selected Mary I. Wood. Wood, one of Pennybacker's trusted allies, had the knowledge of federation activities to do the job. She had worked with Pennybacker in 1905 and 1906 to establish the GFWC Information Bureau, was current chair of that bureau, and recently had authored a history of the GFWC.

Wood expressed to Pennybacker her satisfaction at being able to counter Bok in his own magazine, as well as her doubts about his willingness to let her do so. "I am afraid," she wrote Pennybacker, "that the thing that tempts me to undertake it is largely to get even with Mr. Bok, by attempting to show up through his own columns that the General Federation, which he has decried at such length, is really a vital force in the civilization of today." Still she continued, if Bok were willing to pay $150 per month for the articles and "to allow our material to go in as written," it would be a victory.[55] The clubwomen's concerns about control over the content of the *Ladies' Home Journal* articles were well-founded. In fact, that same year, Wood would complain to Pennybacker that Bok limited the topics that could appear in the *Journal:* "I had quite a day with Mr. Bok and, while he will not let me write just what I want to in the page, I did have the satisfaction of saying to him a few things regarding the club movement which I do not think he had ever heard before." Bok wished to limit the articles to "nothing but the merest statement of what women's clubs have done," but Wood was intent on expanding coverage: "Of course we shall begin that way but I am still hoping that he will let me work into something a little different later on."[56] Despite the disagreement with Bok over the content of the articles, Wood's contributions appeared in the magazine for the next several years. Pennybacker herself contributed complementary articles on topics that related to those submitted by Wood. Whereas Wood would focus on describing the activities and concrete accomplishments of the GFWC and individual member clubs, Pennybacker's articles focused on inspiration and promotion of the spirit of club work. Eventually Pennybacker and Bok developed a friendship. In 1914, Pennybacker invited Bok to attend a GWFC biennial and to making a brief address to those in attendance. Bok attended and later expressed views more favorable to the women's club movement.

Although most of the leading clubwomen congratulated Pennybacker on the *Ladies' Home Journal* agreement, Harriet Waters, managing editor of the *General Federation Bulletin,* resisted the venture on the grounds that it would dilute the importance of the information presented in the *Bulletin* and give the impression that a second official organ had been created (under the contract between them, the *Bulletin* was to be the only official organ). Initially, she refused to run advertisements for the *Journal* articles in the *Bulletin,* writing Pennybacker, "You are putting the *Bulletin* in the position of advertising the *Ladies' Home Journal* to its own detriment."[57] Eventually, however, Waters acquiesced, and the February 1913 *General Federation Magazine* advertised the creation of a "new official woman's club department" in the *Ladies' Home Journal.*

CREATING AND CONTROLLING THE FEDERATION'S PUBLIC IMAGE

After struggling to ensure control over content about the GFWC in magazines like the *General Federation Magazine* and the *Ladies' Home Journal,* how did Pennybacker and the GFWC use these publications to further their causes? Largely, the issue of whether or not the federation should endorse suffrage for women was set aside in favor of creating an image of unity. Pennybacker's administration did everything in its power to distance the organization from overt action on behalf of suffrage. The *Bulletin*'s July 1912 "Official Report of the Biennial" which also announced Pennybacker's election as president, reiterated what was to be the federation's stance on suffrage throughout Pennybacker's first term in office: endorsing suffrage would be too divisive. If the federation were to endorse suffrage, the argument went, it would alienate its anti-suffrage members and cause them to leave the organization "as the strongest of antis," whereas "if they stay in and are educated toward citizenship. . . . they will be among your most conscientious voters."[58] In an effort to expand and unite the organization, the federation attempted to create an image of itself that was inclusive of both the highly progressive and the more conservative woman. In the case of suffrage, questions of women's proper sphere were not the only issue at stake. Suffrage for women was opposed not only by those concerned about the proper place of women, but, in southern states, by those concerned about the political power of the black women's vote. Anti-suffragists argued against allowing women to vote on the grounds that black women would also be allowed to vote. This sentiment was seen as highly problematic in areas of the country where blacks outnumbered whites. Some arguments linked the "true womanhood" ideology to overt racism in opposing suffrage.[59] A typical diatribe claimed that suffrage would force white women to "elbow their way through gangs of Negro women."[60] The black women's vote was an issue within the GFWC, particularly among southern clubs, and Pennybacker, with her Virginian roots and Texas home, was attuned to that sentiment. One newspaper account of the 1912 GFWC election specifically attributed Pennybacker's stance on suffrage to concerns about southern reaction to black women receiving franchise and the "racial disturbances" that might ensue.[61] Another newspaper account of the biennial notes that the resolution for the endorsement of equal suffrage died "under the ominous shadow cast by the black woman of the South."[62]

With the suffrage issue, in particular, threatening to create a rift from within and creating increased resistance from without, Pennybacker and the GFWC had to negotiate carefully their positions on this key question. Pennybacker and her administration addressed the issue by reframing the debate. They shifted focus from political issues to their stated goals to expand and unify the General Federation, and to educate its members. At the same time, however, they discussed federation participation in terms of preparation for citizenship, which they assumed would come. During her 1912 candidacy for president of the GFWC, Pennybacker focused on extending club membership to those women who were unaware of or uninterested in club work. "My greatest aim," she wrote, "is to strengthen that bond which holds up together, the tender bond of sympathy. I want this bond to extend to all classes of women. I do not mean by this that only what we call the rich or upper class may be joined in our work with the poor or lower class, but I mean that this bond shall go beyond that and bring into our sympathies those timid women—they are a large class—that some of us do not consider we should know, those women who now have no interest in our work. All womanhood must work together."[63] Pennybacker and her administration argued that keeping the more conservative woman in the organization was necessary, so that she could be "educated," and thus converted to a pro-suffrage stance. Grace Julian Clarke, who called women's clubs "the most far reaching and at the same time conservative force now at work," restated the importance of education, placing special emphasis on women learning to organize and work together, something which they had not done on a large scale at any time in history. She argued that the federation was "doing a wonderful work in educating the great mass of its membership to a certain civic consciousness hitherto practically unknown in our sex," made veiled reference to the racial concerns of southern women, and pled that the progress the federation was making in "teaching women to work together, and to work disinterestedly" not be jeopardized "by the injection of any issue that would arouse antagonism or altercation."[64] The clubwomen could claim to be conservative in that they supported cherished American ideals of democracy, family, and virtue. Yet they redefined some of what they claimed to be conserving, negotiated existing ideologies of womanhood to expand their influence in the public sphere, organized on a large scale, and promoted a largely progressive agenda.

Part of expanding and empowering the federation included countering the kinds of criticism aimed at both clubwomen and suffragists by antagonists like former president Grover Cleveland in his *Ladies' Home Journal* article. If the "antis" would portray clubwomen as unmotherly, dissatisfied threats to the social order, and perversions of God's will, the clubwomen would counter with images of themselves as mothers fulfilling their divine roles. In this way the clubwomen used existing ideologies to expand their sphere of influence. Descriptions of the federation's leaders published in the *Bulletin* asserted both their womanly characteristics and their leadership ability. In a tribute to past president Sara Platt Decker, who had died shortly after the 1912 Biennial, Pennybacker described her predecessor as being "so clear, so sane, so womanly, so powerful, so full of love and sympathy for humanity!"[65] Similarly, a *General Federation Bulletin* article that introduced Pennybacker as the new president of the organization depicted her as a "home-loving woman," who "believes that the higher inspirations come from home life." The article continued at some length about her deceased husband and her children.[66] While promoting Pennybacker's womanly virtues, however, the same article also referred to Pennybacker's "far-reaching and tremendous power" and compared her favorably to (male) politicians. "No governor of a state is charged with greater responsibilities, nor has within his power the performance of more vital services than that which are embraced within the limits of action of the president of the National Federation of Women's Clubs."[67] It continued by noting that the federation has a "greater grasp of the real needs and aspirations of the masses of citizenship than the political parties which are dominated by men."[68] As if answering doubts about women's ability to lead, subsequent articles noted the administration's competence as leaders: "These women are exceedingly business-like. The President has every detail of Federation work properly pigeon-holed in her well-ordered brain."[69]

Federation leaders would attribute their desire and ability to assume leadership in public roles to their responsibilities as mothers. Grace Julian Clarke's 1913 article in the *General Federation Magazine* called clubwomen's public works "not unwomanly" but rather "divinely Motherly," and attributed clubwomen's "study of educational methods and needs, of industrial conditions, of civic questions" to their love for the child, "the citizen of to-morrow." [70] Playing on notions of the "true woman's" divine calling, Pennybacker implied to *Journal* readers that, rather than perverting God's will, as Cleveland had argued, promoting the club's work was itself "true religion":

> Let us call for volunteers to carry the gospel of the General Federation work to every individual club at least once a year. I would not hesitate to ask these women to offer their services in the highest missionary spirit, for verily the message they will bring is oftentimes of a religious nature. If you could hear as I have heard stories of how sick babies had been saved, of how women to whom every door was closed have had their lives made full of hope and courage; of how those hungering in spirit have been comforted and refreshed, you would not feel that I have overstated the matter when I claim that club work is true religion.[71]

Although Pennybacker and members of her administration stopped short of arguing that woman's public role included the vote, not all contributors to the *Bulletin* did. The August 1912 *Bulletin,* in addition to featuring Pennybacker's first "President's Message," also included an article by Madeline Breckinridge entitled "A Mother's Sphere." At the same time that Pennybacker's message paid tribute to recently deceased past-president Sarah Platt Decker and asked for endowment donations in her name,[72] Breckinridge, who would go on to serve as president of the Kentucky Equal Rights Association and vice president of the National American Woman's Suffrage Association, turned Cleveland's type of woman's sphere argument inside out.[73]

Breckinridge's article accepted the domestic sphere premise that a mother's primary responsibility was to ensure the proper upbringing, education, and health of her children. However, since children live in the public as well as the private realm, a mother's duty to protect her children extends her proper sphere of action into the public. Women's duty as mothers requires them to ensure that schools and cities are free from physical or moral contagion, for, as Breckinridge queried, "What does it profit a mother to have performed her duty within the limited sphere that used to be considered hers within the four walls of her own home if the child has gone out from that home into conditions to which he has succumbed?"[74] To participate in the "great public business on which. . . . private life in the present day absolutely depends," Breckinridge concluded, women need the vote.[75]

In accepting the woman's domestic role, Pennybacker and others were faced with the challenge to prove that club work did not detract from domestic responsibilities. Pennybacker was particularly attuned to the criticism that club work detracted from women's ability to fulfill their duties in the home. In their *Ladies' Home Journal* articles, Pennybacker and Wood exhorted women not to forget their duties to their homes, but rather to organize themselves so that they could fulfill these duties as well as their club work. Pennybacker recounts how she advised a friend to plan for the day so that she wouldn't "wander from what should have been [her] main interest until it was accomplished: the ordering of things in [her] household so that each member of the family might be made comfortable."[76] Having realized that a woman's failure to organize her efforts so that she could complete both her household duties and her club work would erode any support she might find for her club work, Pennybacker advised women not to complain to their husbands about their club duties, giving as an example a woman who finds herself "on the verge of tears" being advised by her husband to "resign from the club" as she "had plenty to do at home and in a social way."[77]

The focus on women's being businesslike became a large part of the federation's education campaign. Pennybacker commented in one of her *Ladies' Home Journal* articles, "Our critics and some of our friends claim that we club women are lacking in business methods," indicating that the club women faced skepticism about their ability as administrators and leaders.[78] A letter to Pennybacker from a *Ladies' Home Journal* editor demonstrates the biases the clubwomen faced. Upon receiving letters of introduction mistakenly sent him by Pennybacker's assistant, he writes: "Oh, dear, dear! Mrs. Pennybacker!. . . . To think that the President of the Federation of Women's Clubs should have made such an essentially feminine error!"[79] Pennybacker countered this criticism by advising women to adopt businesslike strategies, not only in planning at home, but in their club work as well.[80] The importance of organization was twofold. First, the women needed to learn to be organized so that they learned to work together in a large organization. Second, they needed to be organized in order to prove to themselves and their critics that they were capable leaders and administrators. Pennybacker realized that organization required focused efforts. She urged state federations and individual clubs to select only a few causes to advocate and to concentrate their efforts and power on a few issues rather than to dilute them among many.

Pennybacker and the clubwomen of her time often have been criticized for the federation's late endorsement of suffrage.[81] This criticism fails to acknowledge the federation's strategy for advancing its causes, suffrage among them. This strategy was to focus on increasing the support for and expanding the organization. Pennybacker's administration sought these goals by setting aside the contentious issue of suffrage during her first administration, instead focusing on publicizing the organization in order to build wide support and interest. Subverting the opposition's "true woman" arguments, even in antagonistic publications like the *Ladies' Home Journal,* and training members to become organized and businesslike, Pennybacker and her administration oversaw an organization that grew rapidly during her first term and by the end of her second term had doubled in size.[82] The importance of this strategy should be recognized, for even while denying overt politics "the nature and structure of the federated club movement itself taught women to think and act politically, ultimately enabling many to envision themselves as voters."[83] In the "vast public space" provided by the federation, women "found the opportunity to practice in their own network much that men did in political parties."[84] Additionally they gained wide public support for possibility of women's participation in the public sphere. Blair perhaps overstates when she writes that "by 1914 men were no longer frightened that civic work by clubwomen meant the demise of marriage, family, and the home," but she documents a wide acceptance of women's club and civic work among the general public that can, in part, be attributed to Pennybacker's strategy.[85]

Pennybacker managed to quell debate on suffrage for most of her first term as GFWC president. The issue did not, however, go away. In 1913, while visiting Washington, D.C., for the presidential inauguration, Pennybacker and other federation leaders viewed the suffrage procession that took place under the auspices of the National American Woman Suffrage Association and the suffrage societies of the District of Columbia. The parade, complete with floats, bands, and thousands of suffrage supporters, was disrupted by an unruly mob of drunken men. Clubwomen viewed the spectacle with both amusement and disproval, finding the tactics undignified. Grace Julian Clarke derided the actions of the protesters in a rather motherly manner that may have belied generational differences: "I hope no one was seriously injured, and that no one had pneumonua [*sic*] as a result of exposure; but it seems to me those women who appeared with bare arms and necks were very foolish, to say the least, and did not reflect credit on the sex's common sense."[86] The parade, however, represented the growing strength of suffrage supporters. As her first term to a close, Pennybacker and her supporters realized that the issue would reemerge at the upcoming biennial. Helen Varick Boswell of the GFWC's political science committee noted great interest in the issue among women across the country: "A large number of Southern clubs are included in those making inquiries, and asking what they should read to inform themselves on Woman Suffrage."[87] To make matters worse, the biennial was to be held in Chicago, and the women of Illinois had just won suffrage in that state. Pennybacker's supporters heard that the clubwomen of Chicago would oppose Pennybacker's reelection based on her suffrage stance and instead forward ardent suffragist Mrs. George Bass. Board member Grace Julian Clarke warned Pennybacker that the suffrage question was going to be "the ghost that will not down until we endorse the movement," but noted that since few expected the GFWC to actively engage in promoting suffrage, once the endorsement was made they could "go on our peaceful way once more I believe." Clubwomen advocating for endorsement, she believed, looked primarily for the GFWC to say "we wish their cause well, in as much as its success would undoubtedly help forward all the objects for which we are working."[88] Pennybacker was at a loss as to how to handle the issue, writing a fellow clubwoman, "I too have been thinking much on the Suffrage question, and I have been praying that someone wiser than I would suggest a solution. I have purposely made a point of placing Mrs. Catt on the program to show that this administration wishes to be perfectly fair."[89] Recognizing that even southern women were "rapidly increasing in Suffrage interest," Pennybacker decided to follow the advice of Illinois clubwoman Mrs. Francis D. Everett, who recommended having a rather noncommittal resolution favorable to suffrage introduced to the assembly before more strongly worded resolutions could be introduced. That way, suggested Everett, "the people who come intending to fight may realize they have nothing to do."[90] Pennybacker followed through on the plan; the resolution in support of suffrage was passed, and she retained the presidency of the organization.

Despite the majority of clubwomen's support for suffrage, however, a vocal minority, including Pennybacker's friend and advisor Mary Terrell, vigorously protested the resolution. The president of the TFWC at the time, Florence Fall, wrote Pennybacker that Terrell and many others were unhappy over the GFWC's endorsement of suffrage. Fall reported, "I think I managed it well, it had to be."[91] In Georgia, a member of the United Daughters of the Confederacy called her a "traitor to the South" in local papers.[92] Pennybacker reassured one protestor as follows: "May I ask that you read the resolution once more. You will then see that we did nothing but endorse the principle of equal suffrage. No State Federation or individual Club will have any pressure what ever brought to bear to work for Suffrage."[93] Indeed, after supporting the suffrage resolution in 1914, Pennybacker proceeded to ignore or actively quash further attempts to enjoin the GFWC to the suffrage cause.

Pennybacker's position disappointed not just some anti-suffragist clubwomen. Suffrage supporters were also dismayed by it. Mrs. Josiah Evans Cowles, a member of Pennybacker's executive board, received a letter expressing Texas suffrage supporters' great dismay with Pennybacker's refusal to fully support the cause. The letter accused Pennybacker of being a weak supporter of suffrage, noting that she refused to join the suffrage league in Austin and further noting that

> altho there was a bill before the legislature this winter asking that the question of suffrage for women be submitted to a vote by the people—Mrs. Pennybacker did nothing to further the cause—nor mentioned it in any of her public utterances—while women from the prominent cities all over the state were here working in the interest of the bill. . . . Furthermore—She spoke before a large audience in the University auditorium, Economics week, and took special pains to urge the passage of the bill for compulsory education—but did not mention the bill favoring suffrage. Neither has she mentioned it in various letters written to the clubs and published in the Austin Papers—and other state papers. In fact it has always been considered in the South that her attitude toward suffrage for women has been that of an anti—and that policy only led her to favor it at her re-election as Pres. of the National Federation of Clubs. . . . I cannot think that Mrs. Pennybacker would deny the statements made regarding her refusal to join the suffrage league in Austin, or her silence in public concerning the question (except when directly questioned). It is a matter of regret to any women in Texas, and of indignation to many more, considering

the stand she took before the federated clubs at the time of her re-election.[94]

This letter, unsigned, represented views shared by a number of Texas suffrage workers. Elizabeth Herndon Potter, a suffrage leader from Tyler, Texas, was particularly bitter about Pennybacker's stance on suffrage (and could have been the author of the letter).

Pennybacker's stance on suffrage may have angered those who strongly supported or opposed women's suffrage. Nevertheless, this stance, as noted by clubwoman Eva Perry Moore, allowed Pennybacker to keep southern state federations from splitting from the General Federation and creating their own federation at a time when southern women were perceived as softening on the suffrage issue. Pennybacker and her supporters believed working with more progressive women would help change southern women's attitudes better than remaining isolated. Furthermore, by keeping the federation unified, Pennybacker could counter claims that women could not or would not work together. Demonstrating women's ability to work in concert allowed Pennybacker to hold the federation together as it continued to work for many other progressive causes.

SUPPORTING PROGRESSIVE CAUSES

Promoting the GFWC and expanding its influence by increasing membership and funds consumed most of Pennybacker's energy during her presidency. Still, during her presidency, the organization continued to work for social and political reform by advocating for specific progressive causes. In many cases Pennybacker's role in supporting these causes was indirect. As GFWC president, she guided policy and oversaw the actions of her committee chairs. Generally, the committee chairs determined issues of importance, developed a strategy for addressing them, and then kept Pennybacker informed of their work and its results. In some cases, Pennybacker expressed ambivalence toward the initiatives undertaken by her chairs, as she did in January 1914 when a resolution advocating dress reform came before the federation. Pennybacker did not believe the issue to be one of pressing importance, but recognized that support was high among members and that the resolution could come before the delegates to the biennial that year. Pennybacker urged individual clubwomen to concentrate their energy and other resources on focused campaigns supporting issues of particular importance. Too often, she believed, clubwomen wasted their efforts by spreading them over too broad a range of projects. Following her own advice, Pennybacker concentrated her own efforts on a small number of issues during her terms as president.

In her first term as GFWC president, Pennybacker delivered speeches across the country titled "Some Dangers that Threaten the American Home" and "Club Ethics." The latter speech detailed what Pennybacker believed to be women's responsibilities as clubwomen and explained the relationship between individual clubs, city and state federations, and the General Federation. Pennybacker frequently faced the need to explain to clubwomen the benefits of joining the General Federation and this speech likely presented that message. The former speech likely emphasized the importance of work being done by homemakers.[95] Although the text of the speech is not available, Pennybacker detailed what she viewed as threats to the American home in a letter from around that time: "The American home is not in danger, on account of the big interest outside, attracting the woman away from the home. In my opinion the greatest danger lies in the fact that hundreds and thousands of women do not place a proper value upon the dignity and the importance of their profession as home makers. . . . Could the women of America realize concretely as well as abstractly that the business of being a woman and the profession of home making have no superior, they would go at their work in a different spirit. I have come to the conclusion that one reason for this unfortunate state of affairs arises from the fact, that as a nation we have not given and have not demanded scientific training for this all important profession of home making."[96]

Pennybacker's mention of scientific training for the profession of home making is a reference to the efforts of some progressive women activists to have home economics considered a legitimate scientific, educational, and professional discipline. Pennybacker's GFWC presidency coincided with national developments in the vocational education movement. The promotion of homemaking as a vocation included an attempt by federated clubwomen to have training in traditionally female lines of (frequently unpaid) work supported by federal funds allocated for vocational education. In fact, during the first months of Pennybacker's GFWC presidency, the "special work" of the federation's legislative committee was "concentrated upon an effort in cooperation with the committee on Vocational Training and Guidance, to give the strongest possible endorsement to the Page bill providing for vocational training in order to leave no doubt that this measure which made possible Federal aid for vocational training for girls as well as boys was strongly desired by the women of the country."[97] This legislation, known as the Page-Wilson bill, failed in 1913, but the issue was revived with the appointment of a national commission to investigate the subject and to make recommendations to Congress in June 1914. The commission's findings were synthesized in the proposed Smith-Hughes legislation, and "the subsequent floor debates over program definitions and funding. . . . provided a forum for open discussion between people with conflicting perspectives on appropriate vocational programs for women."[98]

The debates that arose from the commission's work placed the GFWC directly in the middle of a debate over the role of women in the United States. While the women of trade unions, represented by the National Women's Trade Union League, argued that girls should receive the same vocational training opportunities as their male peers, the GFWC pushed for home economics to be included in the definition of vocational training. However, the federation missed opportunities to influence what would be included in the bill due to disagreement among its representatives regarding what should be included. A Miss Johnson, who was representing the federation at hearings on the bill, stressed keeping home economics out of industry, and her objections were keeping the bill in committee. In addition, the federation failed to endorse the bill or rally support for it among its members. The chairman of the federation's vocational training committee wrote Pennybacker requesting that Johnson be replaced as GFWC representative and that the federation support the bill even though it wasn't exactly what Miss Johnson had desired.[99] The inclusion of home economics in the bill ensured that the future of vocational education would be sex-differentiated, with young women encouraged to adopt traditional roles in the private sphere and outside the commercial and industrial workplaces. As Jane Bernard Powers notes, "It served as an indicator that the ideal the woman's place was in the home was still a fundamental premise and social organizer for a large group of men and women."[100]

Pennybacker's stance on home economics training for young women supported women's work in the home and placed her firmly in the camp of the domestic feminists, those who believed that "women's true vocation was homemaking but that twentieth century homemaking extended into the neighborhood schools and municipal and federal government."[101] She promoted the idea that homemaking was the most important avocation to which young women could aspire, and she supported education in home economics in part because she identified young wives' lack of knowledge about finance, housekeeping, and nutrition as causes of marital difficulties, and argued that it was unfair to young men and women to have women ignorant in maintaining a household marrying and becoming parasites feeding upon their husband's labor. Despite this strong support for women's role in the home, Pennybacker supported a range of educational and professional options for young women. She realized that, in reality, many women were required to work outside of the home for a number of reasons, including not marrying, or being widowed or separated from one's spouse. For this reason, she advocated that girls should be trained in a paid profession. In fact her arguments for girls being trained for work outside the home originated in her writings for the *Texas School Journal,* and predate her arguments for vocational training in home economics.[102]

In addition to lobbying to have funds for traditionally female work included in the Smith-Hughes legislation, Pennybacker encouraged clubwomen to lobby hard within the states to try to procure federal funds for farmwomen through the Smith-Lever legislation. The Smith-Lever Act, enacted in 1914, established the Cooperative Extension Service to provide "useful and practical information on subjects relating to agriculture, uses of solar energy with respect to agriculture, home economics, and rural energy," through instruction and demonstrations aimed primarily at farmers. Funds were distributed by the states in conjunction with state agricultural colleges. Pennybacker wanted state federations to work within their own states to ensure equal funding for issues of interest to women, and she requested that the *Ladies' Home Journal*'s Bok give editorial space supporting this position.[103] In speeches on the topic, Pennybacker argued that the work of farmwomen was as important as that of men and deserved as much attention. She advocated for college-educated home economists to train rural women in home economics just as rural men were being instructed in agriculture and animal husbandry. "The club women of Texas. . . . are a unit in believing that the rural woman is entitled to the same scientific training, the same careful investigation and consideration of her problems as is given the rural man. They believe the Smith-Lever bill stands for equal opportunities for both."[104] In Texas, the agricultural college administered the funds and allocated only twenty-four percent to farmwomen. Pennybacker and other Texas woman leaders argued that Texas A&M was unqualified to administer the women's programs and requested that the College of Industrial Arts (the women's college created with TFWC support) be allowed to administer the funds. However, their arguments were unsuccessful and the College of Industrial Arts was not allowed to administer these programs.[105]

THE FEDERAL CHILDREN'S BUREAU

Another aspect of promoting traditional women's interests was the federation's support for the federal Children's Bureau.[106] By 1912 the federation had already successfully supported the establishment of a federal Children's Bureau, which President William Howard Taft created. At the urging of clubwomen, Taft placed Julia Lathrop, a Vassar graduate, clubwoman, and Hull House veteran, at the head of the bureau, making her the only female head of a sub-department of the federal government. In 1913, when Lathrop's position was sought by the widow of a democratic congressman, Pennybacker instructed clubwomen to intervene. Pennybacker appealed to the leaders of the GFWC to write to Woodrow Wilson's Secretary of Labor, William B. Wilson, on Lathrop's behalf, "As you know we, of the General Federation of Women's Clubs, asked the creation of the Children's Bureau. As you also know, when President Taft consulted with our officers in regard to the proper woman to become the chief of the Bureau Mrs. Phillip N. Moore and her co-workers hartily [*sic*] recommended Miss Julia Lathrop of Chicago."[107] Pennybacker argued that Lathrop's professional and academic credentials qualified her for the position. Other women, however, argued for the widow, Mrs. Robert Wyckliffe, on the grounds that she possessed the most important qualification for the position—she was the mother of young children herself. Pennybacker, however, supported Lathrop on her professional and educational merits. Pennybacker likely wanted to maintain federation influence within this department. She did not want the position to become a part of a political spoils system which would exclude the GFWC from influence. Additionally, she desired that the position be one of respect and importance: "The very fact that she is the only woman at the head of even a sub-department of the U. S. government makes us all the more anxious that she be given a fair trial," she wrote another clubwoman.[108]

Thanks in part to the efforts of the GFWC, Lathrop retained her position. The GFWC continued to work closely with the Children's Bureau during Pennybacker's presidency to support such initiatives as the promotion of breastfeeding, milk stations with refrigerated milk in cities, baby clinics, visiting nurses, prenatal care, instruction of mothers, Little Mother Leagues for babysitters, education campaigns aimed at the destruction of flies, and, less prominently, addressing housing conditions and birth registrations.[109] In 1914, when the House Committee on Appropriations recommended cutting the bureau's budget, the GFWC successfully asked Congress to better fund the bureau.[110]

In 1915 Pennybacker worked with Lathrop and the Children's Bureau to organize a national Baby Week Campaign. Both the GFWC and the National Congress of Mothers had been planning such campaigns, and Lathrop suggested coordinating efforts. She also proposed including the Bureau of Education and the Agriculture Department, and other organizations soon joined, including the Association of College Alumnae, the Association of Farm Women, the Association for the Study and Prevention of Infant Mortality, and the National Committee for the Prevention of Blindness.[111] As was the case whenever the federation cooperated with organizations, Pennybacker was concerned that the federation be credited with originating the idea, and Lathrop assured her it would be.[112] The campaign sought to get the "whole Nation thinking, from March 4th to March 11th, upon the subject of improved conditions for babies."[113] According to bureau press releases, five thousand clubs planned to conduct a full week's campaign. Fifty thousand press releases were sent out, and federation leaders promoted the issue with every federated club in the country. In addition, clubwomen were encouraged to conduct community campaigns involving as many other organizations as possible. Mary I. Wood noted the strength of the campaign when she wrote that in addition to a half million clubwomen, "the campaign is going outside the clubwomen and is going into the schools, into the churches, into the newspapers of every locality . . . you will already multiply that half-million many times over."[114] Baby Week activities differed in different locales and included short campaigns of one or two days as well as full-week campaigns. Simpler activities included exercises in public schools, rallies, informal meetings, and "baby Sundays" on which pastors spoke on baby-related issues. More elaborate campaigns included "advertising, baby Sabbath, little mothers day, milk station day, nursery and demonstration day with baby campaign, Outing day with excursions for mothers and babies."[115] Newspapers were encouraged to print articles on the proper care of babies, especially during summertime when rates of disease and death increased. Women were encouraged to see the baby campaigns as projects that would continue beyond the formal Baby Week activities.

The Baby Week campaigns were among Pennybacker's most developed ideas during her presidency, but they were not her only focus. Another issue Pennybacker promoted strongly was the teacherage. In 1914 Pennybacker urged clubwomen to establish teacherages or school manses, private living quarters for teachers at rural school buildings (at the time it was common for teachers to board with other families). One benefit of the school manse, according to Pennybacker, was the ability to attract and retain quality teachers by providing them a home of their own and eliminating difficult boarding situations. More importantly, however, the plan allowed the schoolteacher to become a domesticating civic and cultural force in the community, opening up new inroads for the federation: "By giving the teacher a home where he might become a dominant force in the community life, we would be giving every department in our Federation a new avenue for reaching the people," Pennybacker explained to her audience.[116] Although individual clubs sometimes sponsored a school manse for their town, this idea never became as widespread as Pennybacker would have liked.

Another focus of Pennybacker's administrations was General Federation cooperation with the National Education Association on social hygiene education. Representatives from the GFWC served on the School Patron's Committee of the NEA, a new committee founded in 1912 or 1913. They worked for social hygiene education, vocational education, and improvement of rural schools.[117] The GFWC, the Patron's Department of the NEA, and the U.S. commissioner of education, Philander Claxton, determined to work cooperatively, although the GFWC was antagonized by what its leaders felt was obstructionism on the part of the Congress of Mothers: "It will block greatly needed work for schools rather than let any other organization have it (or rather have the 'credit')."[118]

In addition to these other causes, during Pennybacker's administrations the federation invoked its educational role regarding the issue of peace. In 1913, Pennybacker represented the GFWC at a national conference on peace. At this conference, her speech was titled "The Outlook for Peace Throughout the World."[119] Others who attended the conference included Andrew Carnegie, William Jennings Bryan, and Stanford University president David Starr Jordan.[120] The conference generated publicity for Pennybacker and the peace cause. A newspaper editorial cartoon entitled "Hurrying the Hatch" pictured Pennybacker, Carnegie, Jordan, Bryan, and Mrs. Richard Bartholdt as lamps incubating an egg that represented international peace.[121] By 1914 the war in Europe distressed federation leaders considerably, yet they could imagine no political action on the part of clubwomen that would bring about peace.

Running from 1914 to 1916, Pennybacker's second term as GFWC president coincided with the escalation of hostilities in Europe. Like many in the nation at the time, members of the federation were ambivalent about the war. Some were concerned about the plight of European civilians affected by the fighting and suggested the federation contribute to aid efforts. Most supported the national policy of U.S. neutrality. Pennybacker pleaded with members of her executive board for ideas about action the federation could take that might help to effect peace, but they could devise no workable plan.[122] Unable to act directly to prevent war and unwilling to endorse political action they believed futile, federation leaders settled for supporting relief and educational efforts. A federation press bulletin reported of clubwomen: "They are knitting socks and mufflers, collecting money and sending supplies. They are doing these things because they belong to the Mother Sex that suffers when any of the children of earth are oppressed or in pain."[123] The federation also encouraged clubwomen to "focus attention on this subject in all its phases" and encouraged a range of educational activities: "We find clubs all over the country placing special emphasis on Peace, on ways and means of preserving for all time to come friendly relations with other nations and how to convince the rest of mankind to join in an alliance that shall do away forever with the possibility of another international slaughter."[124] Pennybacker exhorted clubwomen to "saturate [them]selves with the horrors of war" and to study its alternatives, particularly proposals for nations to work together diplomatically to end war.[125] Federation leaders encouraged cooperation between clubs and school authorities in the observation of Peace Day on May 18 and suggested that every club should present a program on "some phase of Peace and Arbitration for the people of the Twentieth Century."[126] The federation officially supported U.S. neutrality with regard to the war in Europe. In April 1915, Pennybacker solicited antiwar statements from six prominent women intending to compile their answers into "an ideal protest against war to be sent by the women of the General Federation to the world at large." Whether or not this message was ever broadcast by the federation is unclear.[127] Despite this strong opposition to the war in Europe, however, once the United States entered the war, Pennybacker believed she had a patriotic duty to support these efforts. She was not alone in this belief. Many progressives believed that U.S. entry into the European war was the only way to bring about a lasting, worldwide peace.[128]

ACCOMPLISHMENTS OF THE PENNYBACKER ADMINISTRATION

Pennybacker's second term as GFWC president ended in the spring of 1916. Her attempts to promote peace clearly proved unsuccessful as the United States entered the war just months later. Despite this disappointment, however, her administration had accomplished many of its goals. The federation grew to more than six hundred clubs and two million members during her term, and now had an endowment of $100,000 to support its future leaders.[129] The reorganized departments led by efficient chairwomen were better able to connect with individual clubs and to promote the GFWC agenda.[130] Through the connection she forged with the *Ladies' Home Journal* and increased interest in women's clubs by the press, Pennybacker was able to carry her message to a wider audience than ever before, though she was disappointed never to have been able to establish for the federation an independent official organ to disseminate information to members.[131] Furthermore, Pennybacker had successfully fought what she believed to be commercial exploitation of the GFWC as well as challenges to its social and political clout, as, for example, when federation action kept Julia Lathrop in her position at the Children's Bureau. Despite the nation's entry into war, Pennybacker did not give up on peace. In fact, although she would spend most of the rest of the decade supporting U.S. war efforts, she would devote the rest of her life to seeking a means to ensure a lasting peace.

Chapter Six

1916–1920

World War and Women's Suffrage

PENNYBACKER'S TERM AS GFWC PRESIDENT ended in the summer of 1916. In the ensuing years, no longer representing the GFWC as its president, Pennybacker felt less restrained and was more able and willing to engage in outwardly political struggles. Having attained national prominence leading the GFWC early in the decade, in the later teens Pennybacker used her recognition and public appeal to urge women toward her own progressive vision.

Although she had planned to spend time relaxing after her years of work and travel, at the end of her GFWC presidency she found herself as busy as ever. One activity that filled her time was the presidency of the Chautauqua Women's Club. She accepted this position almost immediately after leaving the GFWC presidency and became a trustee for the Chautauqua Institute as well. Most women's clubs' seasons ran through the fall and winter but left the summer for a break. By contrast, the season of the Chautauqua Women's Club ran throughout the summer months. Women from across the country who stayed at Chautauqua, New York, for at least a part of the summer season comprised the membership of this group.[1] The presidency of the Chautauqua Women's Club required (and enabled) Pennybacker to spend summer months in Chautauqua managing club events. In addition, she devoted time to the institute during other times of the year in order to arrange speakers for following summer. Pennybacker's strength as an organizer and her national acclaim enabled her to double the membership of the Chautauqua Women's Club from 583 to 1,150 during the first year of her presidency.[2] By selling life memberships for $100 each, she also increased the club's funds. In addition to her Chautauqua work, Pennybacker undertook an effort to have her Texas history textbook readopted in

Texas in 1919. Given her other obligations at the time, she could not spend the time needed on the textbook adoption process. However, she did engage Helen Knox to promote the book to influential people within the state. As she had in the past, Pennybacker also contacted clubwomen in Texas to assist this cause. Nevertheless, her effort failed. Her discussions with Helen Knox indicate that the textbook adoption process was highly politicized and Pennybacker did not have the means to compete for adoption against larger publishing concerns.[3]

Even as Pennybacker devoted her energy during this time to her work with Chautauqua and the promotion of her textbook, two larger defining struggles occupied much of her time during the years 1916 to 1920. The first was the struggle for women's suffrage in the United States. After a series of setbacks in the earlier part of the century, the suffrage movement was regenerated, as advocates changed strategies and recruited new members. Pennybacker had deferred participation with suffrage organizations during her GFWC presidency in order to keep the organization from being either co-opted by suffrage concerns or rent by political and ideological differences on the subject. With her GFWC responsibilities lifted, Pennybacker felt free to ally with the suffrage forces. At the same time, a second struggle, the war in Europe which had begun in 1914, continued. In the latter part of 1916, U.S. involvement began to seem inevitable. Although Pennybacker had pressed peace work during her GFWC presidency, initiating a peace crusade among federated clubwomen, like many women leaders of the time she determined to support the country's war efforts from the home front. That her sons Percy and Bonner both enlisted in the U.S. military may have influenced the emphasis of her wartime work at home.[4] Like those of many women at the time, Pennybacker's war efforts focused on support of the country's soldiers. By January of 1917, Pennybacker had taken on important public roles in both the suffrage movement and in the domestic war work.

PENNYBACKER JOINS THE WOMAN SUFFRAGE MOVEMENT

Although Pennybacker had alienated some in the suffrage movement, particularly in her home state of Texas, her wide renown among women across the United States made her a desirable figure to suffrage organizations. The National American Woman Suffrage Association (NAWSA), which had attempted to recruit her during her presidency, now redoubled its efforts.[5] NAWSA leaders had spent the early years of the twentieth century recasting the organization's image and strategies in ways that would make Pennybacker a particularly attractive associate to them at this time.

In the late nineteenth century, NAWSA leaders had professed broadly democratic, egalitarian ideals based in the suffrage movement's origins in the abolition movement. Female abolitionists "employed a broadly drawn theory of natural rights in their argument for the vote."[6] Anti-suffragists used suffrage supporters' challenges to multiple social and cultural institutions and practices to portray suffragists as dangerous radicals. Historian Sara Graham notes: "Suffragism in the early nineteen hundreds was burdened with an image arising from its history that was in many respects a hindrance to further progress. Advocacy of divorce reform, experimental dress, and feminist interpretations of the Bible had given nineteenth-century suffragists a reputation for radicalism that was exploited by their enemies to dissuade more conventional women from participating in the movement."[7] Anti-suffragists, frequently women of wealth with connections to industries opposed to women's suffrage, advanced arguments that pitted the nineteenth-century ideal woman against the suffrage ideal. They "cast their adversaries in the role of fanatical, masculinized extremists," manipulated "traditional symbols of motherhood and womanly virtue" in order to "[taint] the suffrage movement with the stigma of a reform against nature" and "portrayed the suffrage movement as a threat to individuals, to the family, and to society as a whole."[8] In the South, arguments focused on the threat posed by the black woman's vote, but highlighted as well the perceived destruction of the patriarchal family. "Society, even civilization itself, would crumble into chaos if women broke away from the family and established 'individualism.'"[9] Demonizing suffrage supporters permitted the anti-suffrage forces to argue, with some accuracy, that the country's women did not wish to have suffrage conferred upon them.

REINVENTING THE WOMAN'S SUFFRAGE MOVEMENT

The Massachusetts suffrage referendum of 1895 was a turning point in the suffrage struggle. It changed the tactics of suffrage supporters for the next several decades. Pressured by both suffrage and anti-suffrage supporters, and seeking to determine where public opinion lay, the Massachusetts legislature declared a referendum on woman suffrage in which both men and women would be allowed to vote. The political battle in this state pitted suffrage advocates against wealthier, better-funded anti-suffragists who argued that low turnout among women would demonstrate that Massachusetts women did not want the vote.

Referendum results demonstrated that many women had in fact abstained from going to the ballot box, and males voted resoundingly against women's suffrage. Despite the women's favoring suffrage by 22,204 to 861, the anti-suffragists claimed victory.[10] Anti-suffrage advocates would use the Massachusetts referendum results for years to come to argue women's indifference to the subject.

The 1895 defeat in Massachusetts sobered early-twentieth-century suffragists. They faced the apparent weakness of their position and set to work changing public opinion. They sought ways to counter anti-suffrage images that suffragists were radical, unfeminine, and socialist-leaning threats to the established social order. At times, also, they sacrificed the most progressive and democratic aspects of their stand to avoid charges of radicalism. Suffrage leaders during this time presented a "reinterpreted, sanitized version of the past coupled with a sincere celebration of the heroism of pioneer suffragists," and "forged a link between the heroic age of confrontational politics and a new organizational approach to reform."[11] Graham understands the first decade and a half of the twentieth century, a period frequently portrayed as a relatively inactive period in the history of the suffrage movement, as a period of renewal. "So significant were these years of regeneration that the period might more appropriately be called "the suffrage renaissance."[12]

One important way in which NAWSA leaders responded to anti-suffrage depictions of suffragists was to target "society women." NAWSA leaders found that when elite women gathered to discuss or to promote suffrage, the press responded favorably. Another advantage of targeting elite women was the increased ease of fundraising. Wealthy women had money at their disposal to support the cause and could donate large sums more freely than most other women. These elite women also had social and political connections that could help advance the movement even when they themselves participated little in the day-to-day activities of the movement. Clubwomen were particularly attractive to suffrage leaders. Already organized around progressive ideas and civic activism, women's clubs were perceived as fertile ground for suffrage activists. "By concentrating their efforts on prosperous though conservative women, suffragists sought to take advantage of the awakened interest in public affairs manifested by the GFWC and other women's organizations."[13] Pennybacker and other leaders of the women's club movement recognized the desirability of women's clubs to those in the suffrage movement and resisted what they saw as efforts by suffragists to co-opt club agendas.[14] As president of the Texas Federation of Women's Clubs and

General Federation of Women's Clubs, Pennybacker had resisted suffragist incursions into club territory.

NAWSA leaders in the early years of the century also put much energy into recruiting new members for the organization. Despite numerous defeats in their efforts to pass suffrage amendments in various states, NAWSA experienced tremendous growth in membership during the first years of the century's second decade. Membership rose from 26,400 in 1908 to 171,000 in 1912. During these same years, the organization created a "full-fledged press bureau with a publicity budget of more than $3,000."[15] When Carrie Chapman Catt regained the NAWSA presidency in December 1915, "the association boasted a total membership of over two million, with forty-four state auxiliaries and a yearly budget of more than $110,000."[16] Catt, like Pennybacker, was a gifted organizer with "statesmanlike vision" that enabled her to devise a plan and enable its implementation.[17] Catt's strategy would be more political and less idealistic than that of her predecessor, Anna Howard Shaw, who was a powerful speaker, but a weak organizer.[18] Catt insisted that, as president, she must be able to pick her own board, and she selected women of means who could afford to attend meetings. Catt's "first priority was the recruitment of politically astute activists to serve as her advisers."[19] Pennybacker fit into Catt's strategy nicely, and by January 1917 Pennybacker had agreed to head NAWSA's Child Welfare Committee. Although Pennybacker, by her own admission, did little for child welfare in this position, Catt would offer Pennybacker a still more important role a few months later.[20] That March, Catt formed the Leslie Woman Suffrage Commission with funds willed to her by Mrs. Frank Leslie, the wife and heir of publisher Frank Leslie. After protracted and expensive legal battles with Leslie's family, Catt received just over half a million dollars to fund the new organization.[21] On March 29, 1917, in New York City, Catt met with other incorporators of the commission, all of whom were major figures in the suffrage struggle. They included Alice Stone Blackwell, Margaret Dreier Robins, and Harriet Taylor Upton, as well as Miss Mary Garrett Hay acting as proxy for Mrs. Mabel H. Churchill. At a meeting the next day, these individuals chose a board of directors that included Pennybacker for a position as trustee.[22]

In some ways Pennybacker typified the type of society woman Catt was courting. Pennybacker was financially self-sufficient and refined. Catt's motives for wanting Pennybacker, however, extended beyond her desire to recruit society women. Catt particularly sought a southerner for the trustee position, but believed that many of the most qualified candidates for the post already were serving as state presidents. To select any one of them over the others would create dissention. In a situation that recalls Pennybacker's having been selected over higher-ranking TFWC members as a dark-horse candidate for that organization's presidential nomination, Catt selected Pennybacker specifically based on the fact that Pennybacker was somewhat an outsider in suffrage circles. Pennybacker's appointment was unlikely to spark discord among state organizations, particularly in the South. In addition, Pennybacker's perceived conservatism and understanding of southern attitudes and concerns regarding suffrage brought her the trust of and influence among southern women. Writing Pennybacker about her selection, Catt explained, "We wish to appeal to other elements than those already engaged within our association."[23] Given NAWSA's difficulties in the South, Catt hoped that Pennybacker's name and support could foster support for the movement in that section of the country and could calm some of the strife between NAWSA's majority and its southern minority with regard to support for a federal suffrage amendment. Pennybacker's appointment, then, represented a growing conservatism among NAWSA leaders. With women like Pennybacker on board, NAWSA tactics would become less militant and more focused on working within the political system.

The Leslie Commission was formed to further the cause of woman suffrage chiefly through the "establishment and maintenance" of a Bureau of Suffrage Education. Under the direction of this group, "literature may be printed and distributed; a suffrage paper or papers may be published press work performed, advertising placed, or any other form of educational activity conducted."[24] One of the first acts of the Leslie Commission was to purchase Alice Stone Blackwell's *Woman's Journal* and to rename it the *Woman Citizen.*[25] For Pennybacker, this line of work would have been familiar, mirroring as it did issues surrounding public image and publicity that the GFWC had faced during her terms as president. Despite that experience, however, Pennybacker was not central to the daily administration of the new commission. She left the day-to-day management responsibilities to others, including Catt; Rose Young, director of the Leslie Bureau of Suffrage Education; Maude Wood Park, chair of the Congressional Committee; and journalist Ida Husted Harper.[26] When she solicited Pennybacker for the position, Catt requested only that she attend one meeting a year, with expenses to be paid by the commission.[27] Pennybacker appears to have fulfilled her obligation, but attended few of the meetings of the Leslie Commission board of directors.[28] She participated mainly through correspondence with board members and by lending her influence where necessary or helpful. She received minutes of the meetings and was in frequent contact with Catt and other board members. In addition, she supported suffrage efforts in her home state of Texas.

Despite Catt's strategic reasons for appointing Pennybacker to the Leslie Commission, her appointment to such prestigious roles within the movement displeased some of its dedicated long-term workers, particularly in Texas. Suffragist Elizabeth Herndon Potter of Tyler, Texas, became incensed that Catt had chosen Pennybacker over the many who had worked and sacrificed for the suffrage movement for years. She wrote Texas Equal Suffrage Association (TESA) president Minnie Fisher Cunningham to express her frustration with Catt's selection of Pennybacker.[29] Cunningham, in turn, expressed her disgust with Catt's selection of Pennybacker to former TESA president Eleanor Brackenridge, writing: "I suppose it is mean of me, but I simply cannot bear, when I know that you and the women like you 'took the curse off' of Suffrage in public opinion in Texas back in the days when she wouldn't help a particle."[30] Cunningham saw Pennybacker in a position to "reap the reward of the marvelous growth of public sentiment that there has been in the state this past year."[31] Brackenridge had been active in the Texas women's suffrage movement for years, having helped reestablish TESA in 1912, and having served as president from 1912 to 1914. The rivalry between Brackenridge and Pennybacker was longstanding: Pennybacker had defeated Brackenridge for the presidency of the Texas Federation of Women's Clubs in 1901. Brackenridge's loss at that time likely was related to her strong political positions, particularly her support for suffrage.[32] The long-term suffrage workers considered Pennybacker to be a lukewarm latecomer, riding on the coattails of the more dedicated workers.[33]

Despite the lingering hard feelings among leaders in the Texas suffrage movement, Pennybacker worked with the Texas Equal Suffrage Association in addition to her work with NAWSA at the national level. As much as they may have resented her lack of involvement in previous years, like national leaders, Texas suffragists had also hoped for Pennybacker's support at the end of her General Federation presidency. Austin suffragist Jane Yelvington McCallum, for example, noted in her journal of October 1916 that she had contacted Pennybacker regarding her participation with the Texas Equal Suffrage Association. Pennybacker had indicated to her that, with her GFWC term complete, she was ready to become more involved in the suffrage struggle. McCallum hoped that Pennybacker would accept a TESA committee chair that fall. When she received no response to her subsequent letter to Pennybacker, McCallum assumed that she was unable to serve. McCallum recognized that Pennybacker's frequent absences from Texas made it particularly difficult for her to actively be involved in the suffrage fight there.[34] Nevertheless, McCallum and Pennybacker met several times during the following month, and Pennybacker committed to "make several speeches here in the district [,] one here during session of Legislature, and to accept chairman of a committee (to be created) on *Outlook*."[35] By January 1917, Pennybacker was an active TESA supporter. That month she attended a meeting at Austin's Driskill Hotel at which she spoke before a crowd of more than 150 guests, including some of the city's most prominent citizens. McCallum recorded that the program was "said by dozens to be one of the cleverest ever held here."[36] Pennybacker certainly had the national connections that could only help the Texas suffrage movement. Early on, Pennybacker committed to contact Carrie Chapman Catt on behalf of TESA to request that she make a trip to Texas, and later she was instrumental in attracting support and funds to the state from the national association.

THE SOUTHERN PROBLEM

As a southerner with a reputation among clubwomen as being relatively conservative, Pennybacker was brought into the movement, at least in part, to help mend a rift that had developed between NAWSA leadership and some of the southern state suffrage associations. NAWSA's difficulties in the South involved the white South disenfranchisement of blacks, a condition which white southern suffragists such as Louisiana's Kate Gordon and Kentucky's Laura Clay sought to maintain. Although NAWSA leaders, disappointed by setbacks in key states in the early part of the century's second decade, had decided to focus their energies on a federal suffrage amendment, Gordon and Clay and other southern suffragists, as well as southern anti-suffragists, opposed NAWSA's efforts. In fact, they actively worked to undermine these initiatives. The suffrage amendment to the U.S. Constitution, as presented to Congress, contained a clause that enabled the federal government to enforce its provisions. Because disfranchisement of black voters in the South "depended on nonintervention by federal authorities," many southerners opposed any federal suffrage amendment.[37] Southern suffragists instead supported a states' rights stance and a strategy that focused on women's obtaining suffrage through amendments to individual state constitutions rather than a federal constitutional amendment. By 1911, having been passed over for NAWSA leadership positions under Anna Howard

Shaw, both Gordon and Clay had left the NAWSA board. In 1913 Gordon, with Clay's consent, founded the Southern States Women's Suffrage Conference which would focus on gaining suffrage by means of state amendments and which would oppose NAWSA efforts toward a federal suffrage amendment.[38] Pennybacker was likely brought in as a strong southern voice in favor of the federal amendment.

Pennybacker fulfilled the role expected of her by NAWSA leaders. She worked to convince women of the South to support the federal suffrage amendment. In speeches and in print across the South, Pennybacker argued that support for a federal suffrage amendment was in line with traditional southern values. In her speech "As a Southerner and a Democrat," Pennybacker specifically presented her argument with reference to her southern heritage. She noted her descent from the earliest European Americans to arrive in the South. Addressing the anti-suffragists' argument that the federal amendment impinged on states' rights, Pennybacker noted that while southerners valued states' rights, they also recognized the importance of federal action and would support economically and morally beneficial federal laws. Pennybacker avoided explicit reference to southern concerns that a federal amendment would put their state voting laws under federal control and eliminate the various barriers to the vote that the South had raised against blacks and the uneducated poor. Without mentioning the racial issues that underlay much of the states' rights argument, Pennybacker pointed out that the federal amendment granted the vote to no one, but merely prevented gender as a basis for denying the vote. She emphasized that poll taxes and other limits to voting rights would still stand. Furthermore, Pennybacker argued that Democratic Party support for suffrage was crucial to the future of the party. Predominantly Republican states had granted women suffrage in greater numbers than had Democratic states, thus increasing the percentage of voters likely to vote Republican. Pennybacker roused concerns that the largely Democratic South would be greatly disadvantaged if its women were not allowed access to the ballot. Finally, since it seemed inevitable that women would soon gain suffrage, Democrats should court their votes, beginning by supporting their right to have them.[39]

Whether suffragists' arguments that the federal amendment would not affect the disfranchisement of southern blacks were made of expediency or conviction is a matter of contention. For her part, Pennybacker seems not to have made the overtly racist comments of the type that fellow southern suffragist Kate Gordon did regarding the black vote.[40] Nevertheless, that Pennybacker supported the disfranchisement of black voters is likely. As TFWC president early in the century, she led that organization to press for stricter enforcement of her own state's poll-tax laws, a means by which blacks were disenfranchised. As a delegate representing the TFWC and later as president, she supported and aided the enactment of racial exclusion in the GFWC, and she never challenged the segregationist policies advocated by other southern women who corresponded with her. All evidence points to her suffrage arguments having been made of conviction.

WOMEN AND THE WORLD WAR

By 1917, just as Pennybacker increased her involvement in its activities, the suffrage movement in the United States was gaining considerable momentum. Still, suffragists continued to struggle to have suffrage legislation introduced and passed. In 1916, Catt had introduced her "Winning Plan" which advocated for suffrage at both the state and federal levels, but which in practice focused heavily on the federal amendment. The Front Door Lobby, a group of NAWSA suffragists, pressured legislators in Washington, D.C., to support a federal suffrage amendment.[41] The U.S. entry into World War I, however, led Congress to curtail debate on all non-emergency issues, an action that slowed NAWSA lobbying efforts. Nevertheless, NAWSA leaders found ways to use the war to garner needed public support for suffrage across the country. To the dismay of pacifist suffragists, NAWSA channeled its energies into patriotic service and support of the country's war efforts. Across the nation, NAWSA suffragists threw their energies into promotion of food conservation, provision of appropriate environments for soldiers, and the sale of war bonds. The war work provided positive publicity for suffrage leaders and quelled accusations that suffragists were unpatriotic, anti-American pacifists.[42] "Patriotic service served the woman suffrage movement well . . . Census taking and other government-sponsored jobs gave the suffragists the official government sanction they had long coveted."[43]

War work efforts by women in the country included work in many of the progressive causes that they had advocated across the past decade, recast to demonstrate the usefulness of such reforms to the government's war efforts. Judith McArthur notes, for example, "The federal government's cooperation—and in some cases, pressure—helped raise the status of home economics and home demonstration programs, implement child welfare reforms, bring on prohibition, and eliminate vice districts. . . . war gave organized women a new ally in the federal government and new opportunities, through service on government war commissions to pursue public work and progressive objectives."[44] Pennybacker was deeply involved in these efforts. During the summer of 1917, she "was engaged with" the Education Program for Patriotic Service at Chautauqua and served as special agent for the Department of Agriculture.[45] She also held the position of general chairman of the Texas Division of the Army Food Service. In this latter capacity, Pennybacker spoke to women across the state, encouraging them to plant gardens, learn to can, and forego wheat, meat, and sugar. In April 1917 she presided over the statewide meeting of the Texas Division of the Army Food Service in Dallas. Just two years prior to the Dallas meeting, Clarence Ousley, director of the state Agricultural Extension Service, had refused GFWC president Pennybacker's call for Smith-Lever funds to be split equally between typically male and typically female lines of work in order that home economics demonstration work in the state could be funded. At the April 1917 meeting, however, Ousley proposed deploying volunteer demonstration agents to teach home economics, particularly canning and food conservation, to the women of Texas. His support of the women's work indicates how the war helped further causes that clubwomen, including Pennybacker, had been promoting for years.[46]

In addition to her statewide position with the Texas Division of the Army Food Service, Pennybacker accepted positions that were nationwide in scope. As McArthur and Smith note, Progressive Era reformers had long sought to suppress the sex trade, merging "the Victorian moral imperative to rescue and reform prostitutes with the new physician-led social hygiene movement."[47] Now, with so many young men enlisted in the armed services, middle-class women across the country became concerned about the conditions under which they lived. Cantonments often were surrounded by red-light districts, and venereal disease infection among enlisted men was high. Secretary of War Newton D. Baker set out to "ensure that the new training camps did not pose a threat to the recruits' health or morals."[48] Under Baker, the newly formed Commission on Training Camp Activities facilitated the creation of the War Camp Community Service (WCCS) "to encourage communities to open social clubs and sponsor special events for soldiers."[49] In the fall of 1918, Pennybacker accepted the position of special representative of the National War Camp Community Service in the girl's division of the YMCA War Camp Community Service. As special representative, Pennybacker was "to present the purpose and work of the War Camp Community Service to the public; to enlist supporters and workers; to deal with relationships with organizations in girls' work; finally if time permit it, to guide the development of girls' community service in one specific district of the country."[50] This position provided high rank and a handsome salary. Pennybacker reported only to the director of the Department of Girls' Work and earned $5,000 annually, plus expenses.[51] In conjunction with her work with the War Camp Community Service, Pennybacker reached out to Mary Black Terrell. A report from the United War Work Campaign indicated that Texas had done little for the African American serviceman. In what seems to be a shift of attitude for Pennybacker, who had declined to work cooperatively with African American clubwomen in the past, Pennybacker invited Terrell, a prominent African American clubwoman and activist, to discuss what could be done.[52]

Pennybacker also used her position as president of the Chautauqua Women's Club to further the causes of suffrage as well as women's war work and peace. In the summer of 1918, under Pennybacker's direction, the Chautauqua summer program sponsored a National Service School for women. Knox notes that the school offered courses in "reconstruction for disabled soldiers, in dietetics, in Braille."[53] In 1918 Pennybacker became a member of the National Committee of the League to Enforce Peace.[54] In this role and as president of the Chautauqua Women's Club, she corresponded with Bertha Tomlinson of the League to Enforce Peace for recommendations for speakers. At Tomlinson's advice, she invited longtime suffragist and peace activist Anna Howard Shaw to Chautauqua that year.[55] The League to Enforce Peace, despite its dovish name, strongly supported American efforts in World War I. League documents stated that its purposes included emphasis on "the high purpose of the war" and opposed a "premature and German-made peace." Additionally, the league was dedicated to taking "an active part in Win-The-War Activities."[56] The objectives of the league dovetailed neatly with the projects Pennybacker supported during these years. That Pennybacker brought League to Enforce Peace speakers to Chautauqua is but one example of how she used her many organizational connections to bring together people and organizations in support of common goals.

In her lectures across the country, Pennybacker frequently addressed a topic titled "What the Country Asks Today of Its Young Women."[57] Her speech reflected concerns about morals and social hygiene that the war had brought to the forefront of cultural debate. She aimed her lectures particularly at the many young women drawn to the cities and industrial centers for work during the war. Without their usual social networks, Pennybacker believed the girls to be likely to "lower their standards" with regard to their own behavior, particularly their sexual behavior. Pennybacker believed the uncertainty of war meant that "the protective barrier of formal convention was too often discarded as meaningless in the face of dread apprehension of what might happen tomorrow."[58] In her lectures, Pennybacker exhorted girls to remain healthy by consuming a proper diet and getting enough rest. In keeping with the social hygiene aspect of the WCCS, Pennybacker also exhorted girls to be "true to their ideals."[59] Revisiting late-nineteenth-century arguments about women's role as moral guardians, Pennybacker also argued that girls influenced the moral standards of the men around them and were thus responsible for the personal purity of the soldiers overseas. For this reason they needed to control their own behavior carefully. Pennybacker reminded audiences interested in the needs of young enlisted men to be concerned about the needs of young women, noting that they too required social support and appropriate places to socialize.[60]

In Texas particularly, conditions around military bases and training camps were a concern. Texans in Congress were adept at bringing military "plums" in the form of training camps and military installations to the state, but with the camps came attendant social problems.[61] In July of 1917, Texas women's organizations allied to form an anti-vice committee. The purpose of the committee was to eliminate red-light districts near military bases in the state. Minnie Fisher Cunningham chaired the committee, but Pennybacker assisted in related work, and claimed credit for suggesting the creation of the committee to Cunningham.[62] In a letter to Mrs. Eltweed Pomeroy, Pennybacker wrote, "At the conference she [Cunningham] and I held in Austin, I told her I would like to see the Suffrage Association call a meeting of the heads of state organizations of women to form an Anti-Vice Committee."[63] Pennybacker claims to have suggested to Cunningham that the heads of every state organization of women be represented on the executive committee and that Cunningham be its chair. Pennybacker advocated that clubwomen assist in establishing YWCA hostess houses on or near military bases, in order to provide chaperoned, wholesome activities for the enlisted men, and she addressed what she understood to be women's wartime responsibilities general.[64] Despite the fact that the War Camp Community Service worked cooperatively with women's clubs on a variety of projects, tensions between the two groups became clear. Pennybacker was an obvious choice to be called upon to smooth over the contending positions. In January of 1919, for example, clubwoman Ida B. Saunders wrote Pennybacker to complain that the War Camp Community Service had used the clubwomen's services to establish a canteen, and subsequently excluded them from helping to operate it once it had opened. Saunders expressed to Pennybacker that clubwomen were hesitant to work with the WCCS and preferred to work alone in order to get credit for their work.[65]

The budget for the Anti-Vice Committee was small and demands on the organization were great from its inception.[66] Cunningham reported to Pennybacker the first month that she could do "five times that much work. . . . just meeting the demands of the people for information" had the funds been available.[67] With so few funds, the work taxed the resources of the women's associations, particularly those of TESA. In August of 1917, Cunningham reported that the TESA was in debt by $1,500–$2,000 for expenses related to the anti-vice work, and that appeals to Texas Anti-Vice Committee members had failed to generate contributions.[68] Pennybacker committed to raising $500 to help reduce the debt, and over the next months she convinced wealthy friends and colleagues to donate to the cause. In July of the next year, Pennybacker sent TESA treasurer Edith Hinkle League checks she had collected from clubwomen to apply to the debt.[69] Clubwomen also needed funds to support their war work. The GFWC and TEWC attempted to raise funds for the establishment of canteens domestically and for a furlough house in France.[70] The Texas federation also collected money to support its local efforts to establish canteens for soldiers in cantonment and aviation towns in Texas, as well as to contribute to GFWC efforts. Leaders pleaded with Pennybacker to attend district meetings because of her great ability to "make the appeal" and convince clubwomen to donate to the various causes.[71]

Helen Knox, who managed Pennybacker's lecture tours, touted her ability to rouse an audience to patriotic action. "Her addresses are, therefore, arousing a spirit of patriotism that will make a definite contribution towards the resources of our Country in the conduct of the war," Knox wrote to prospective audiences.[72] Speeches Pennybacker delivered to wartime audiences focused on women's role in preparing the country for war. In "The World War and Women," Pennybacker reminded women of their duty to their country during wartime. Upon hearing from the chairman of the exemption board that "ninety percent of the problem" with military exemptions came from women, Pennybacker called upon the "mothers, sisters, and wives" of potential enlistees to respond nobly rather than selfishly.[73] The lecture tours consumed much of Pennybacker's time and she traveled widely. In the month of November 1917, for example, she visited fourteen Texas cities, speaking to clubwomen.[74] She was well paid for this work. She charged

$100 dollars per engagement, but reduced the fee to $75 for multiple engagements in the same geographic area.[75] At times suffrage leaders pleaded for her presence in different parts of the country, and Pennybacker declined. The fees she received for these services likely contributed to her reluctance to cancel speaking dates to provide further assistance to the suffrage cause.

WOMAN'S SUFFRAGE IN TEXAS

Even as American women devoted their energies in support of the country's war efforts, suffragists struggled to keep their single issue before the public. In Texas, TESA president Minnie Fisher Cunningham saw women's wartime civic and patriotic activism as political capital that could be used, as Judith McArthur notes, as "a catalyst for demanding the vote." Writing to Carrie Chapman Catt, Cunningham acknowledged the usefulness of anti-vice campaigns to the suffrage movement and assured Catt that Texas suffragists were "hitching 'Suffrage' to every bit of it."[76] Those who advocated for women's full entry into public life, including suffragists, used women's efforts during the war to support their arguments, and Pennybacker was no exception.

In Texas, the controlling Democratic Party was split on the suffrage issue, and the political situation in 1917 was extremely heated. In particular, a disagreement between Governor James Ferguson and several University of Texas faculty members had reached a boiling point. The governor gained control of the Board of Regents and attempted to purge the university of professors he deemed politically unsupportive of his administration. In June 1917 Ferguson vetoed the legislature's appropriation for the university. Shortly thereafter, Pennybacker sent a circular to friends and colleagues, and requested signatures on an appeal in behalf of the university. Pennybacker's circular reached Cunningham, who at that time was working in the field for suffrage and had not yet joined in any group action on behalf of the university. Cunningham wrote Pennybacker that she felt obliged to speak with the TESA executive board to determine its position on the suffrage association taking action in favor of the university,[77] but that she half wished that Pennybacker had added her name. Later that month, financed by an anonymous donor, Cunningham and other colleagues staged a women's uprising against Ferguson.[78]

In part, the woman's uprising was sparked by university regent George Littlefield's "challenge to womanhood," in which he derided home economics as a field of academic study and women and their work in general. In particular, Littlefield derided the pay and work of University of Texas home economist Mary Gearing, whom clubwomen had helped to place on the faculty. Littlefield reportedly asserted, "No woman in the world is worth $3,000 (Miss Gearing's salary)" and "further proclaimed the Department of Home Economics a farce, stating that his $40.00 cook could do better."[79] The women's uprising, however, was aimed at Ferguson, and undertaken with broad support that included many of the university's faculty members. These Texas women had multiple motives for moving against Ferguson. The governor, who had run on a populist platform, opposed most of the progressive reforms advocated by women activists, including prohibition. Most egregious, however, was that Ferguson was one of the state's chief opponents of women's suffrage. Removing him would open the way for suffragists to begin to make progress in Texas. Helen Knox noted that Cunningham, McCallum, the university's Mary Gearing, and Elizabeth Speer of the Anti-Vice Committee all attended the planning meeting in "a militant frame of mind.[80] With the support of most of the women's organizations in the state, they planned a massive demonstration at which all of them were scheduled to speak. Although Helen Knox kept her informed of events, Pennybacker did not attend the meetings. Instead she remained at Chautauqua for the summer and kept abreast of developments through correspondence with Knox who wrote her how badly she was needed.[81] Struggling to raise funds for TESA and anti-vice activities, "very deeply engrossed in the University situation," and enduring the heat of August in Texas, Cunningham closed her letters to Pennybacker with good wishes that may reveal a bit of resentment regarding the role Pennybacker was playing (or not) in the struggle: "Hoping that you are having a very cool and enjoyable summer in Chautauqua," she wrote Pennybacker from Texas in August 1917.[82]

The campaign against Ferguson succeeded. After the women's meeting, held during the annual Farmer's Institute in Austin during the summer of 1917, many of Ferguson's supporters turned against him. Ferguson resigned in late August amidst numerous charges of corruption and formal impeachment proceedings. Ferguson's removal opened the way for women to demand suffrage. Not only did they no longer face a corrupt and strongly anti-suffrage governor, but, as Minnie Fisher Cunningham noted, "The exposure of so much venality and corruption made it difficult for male politicians to look the suffragists in the eye and tell them that they were not fit to vote."[83] Additionally, the women had demonstrated their political strength to other politicians who "perceived the benefits of supporting woman suffrage either to save their political careers or to enhance the issues they supported."[84] After Ferguson's ouster, Pennybacker supporters petitioned his replacement, Governor William Pettus Hobby, to appoint Pennybacker as a regent of the University of Texas. Despite support from the Texas Federation of Women's Clubs and the Texas State Teachers Association, Hobby did not decide to appoint her to that position.[85]

Ferguson's resignation cleared the way for a number of successes in 1918, a year that would become a watershed one for the suffrage movement in both Texas and nationwide. The federal suffrage amendment came up for vote in the House in January 1918 and in the Senate later that year. In Texas, women worked to gain the right to vote in primary elections, a measure that went before the Texas legislature that spring.[86] Later that year, defying Catt's plans to focus on passing the federal amendment, a "renegade band of San Antonio suffragists" pressed for an amendment that would give Texas women full suffrage in the state.[87] Fighting the suffrage battle on several fronts complicated the work of Texas suffragists, and, in addition to the numerous war-related projects women had taken on, occupied much of their time and energy during 1918.

In January 1918, suffrage leaders across the country mobilized support for the federal amendment. NAWSA sought Pennybacker's influence in Texas for the campaign. On January 4, 1918, Catt pleaded with Pennybacker to influence people to wire Texas members of the House of Representatives because the Texas delegation could prevent passage of the amendment.[88] NAWSA suffragists in Washington, D.C., had found Texas congressmen Martin Dies and Sam Rayburn to be strong anti-suffragists. Dies lectured suffragists on the separate roles of men and women, using the example of "the cockrell [*sic*] who protects his hen" and Rayburn argued for male representation of women as well, telling a widowed Kentucky suffragist who protested that such a model left her with no representation that he would represent her.[89] At the urging of Catt and Texas suffrage leader Minnie Fisher Cunningham, Pennybacker pressed Texas legislators to vote in favor of the federal amendment giving women suffrage. She personally petitioned congressmen (one of whom responded favorably with a note that he had studied her Texas history book as a child) to vote in favor of the suffrage amendment. Additionally, Pennybacker contacted longtime colleagues in high places. R. B. Cousins, who had become president of West Texas State Normal College, and H. F. Estill, who had attended Sam Houston State Normal Institute with the Pennybackers forty years earlier, were enlisted to support the amendment.[90] Mary Woodson of the Texas Women Bankers wrote that her organization had wired Texas legislators Tom Connelly, Daniel Garrett, Marvin Jones and Jeff McLemore, and was sending "a long list of organizations here favoring the amendment, answering the same old question raised that the wom- [*sic*] of Texas do not want suffrage."[91]

Although some Texas legislators supported the amendment, Texas senator Charles Allen Culberson, Democratic minority leader of the Senate, was perceived to be so unshakably anti-suffrage that Woodson and others thought it "a waste of time and money" to send anything to him.[92] Catt, however, recognized that every vote was crucial, and Cunningham wrote Pennybacker an urgent letter saying that national leaders did not regard Senator Culberson as hopeless: "We are leaving no stone unturned—thank Heaven, it will be not so expensive to work on one man as on eighteen," Cunningham wrote Pennybacker on January 18, 1918.[93] In response to these requests for intervention, Pennybacker devised a strategy for reaching Culberson by determining his wife's view on the issue. Working through common acquaintances, she was able to schedule a meeting with Mrs. Culberson to discuss the issue. Through their conversations, Pennybacker determined that Mrs. Culberson was a suffrage supporter with typical southern concerns about race, states' rights, and the voting power of the black woman. As diplomatic as ever when it came to explicitly taking a position on the issue of the role of blacks in society, Pennybacker assured her, "The vote of the Negro woman was no more to be feared than the vote of the Negro man."[94] Pennybacker's contact with Mrs. Culberson, combined with the efforts of University of Texas education professor Caswell Ellis, who directed his arguments at Mr. Culberson, appears to have been successful.[95] Culberson voted in favor of the amendment.

By January 8, 1918, Elizabeth Speer confidently could assure Pennybacker that the situation in Texas with regard to the House vote on the federal amendment was "pretty well in hand." Letters and telegrams were "going by the hundreds daily from every portion of Texas" and due to reach the Texas representatives in Washington "possibly every moment in the day on Wednesday (tomorrow,) in addition to numerous night letters yesterday and more tonight from all points in our great state." Pennybacker had given Cunningham permission to add her name to a telegram sent to legislators "in the name of practically every head of women's organization." Speer wrote Pennybacker, "The women all over Texas are making magnificent efforts, and the signatures of many prominent men previously wedded to 'States Rights' have surprised even Mrs. Cunningham, and she hears is having great weight with our representatives in Washington. The last word from Washington this morning is 'Watch us go over the top,'—meaning Texas, and written by a loyal Texas Suffragist in Washington."[96] The text of the telegram to which Cunningham added Pennybacker's name said much about the rhetoric used to garner support for the amendment in January 1918: "WAITING WATCHING HOPING YOU WILL VOTE FOR SUFFRAGE GIVING AMERICAN WOMEN AT LEAST EQUAL CHANCE IN TEXAS WITH ALIEN ENEMIES WHO VOTE AND SECURE CITIZENSHIP FROM UNITED STATES CONSTITUTION."[97] With the United States at war with Germany, suffrage advocates exploited anti-German sentiment in the state. In this message, Cunningham used the war and hostilities with Germany to argue for women's voting rights based on the fact that Texas's large population of German immigrants could vote after receiving first papers before attaining U.S. citizenship. Native-born Texas women argued that allowing non-citizens to vote while women were forbidden to do so was unjust and dangerous. Other arguments that Texas suffragists forwarded invoked their roles as mothers of servicemen. At one point, Jane McCallum, serving as secretary of the Press and Publication Committee of the Texas Equal Suffrage Association, requested a statement from Pennybacker regarding her views on suffrage. McCallum suggested that Pennybacker include mention of "a disfranchised mother of two disfranchised (because not here in time to pay their poll taxes) soldier sons, as she looks helplessly on the spectacle of aliens who have only declared their intentions of becoming American citizens marching to the polls to pass on laws that are to govern her and her sons."[98] Pennybacker obliged McCallum by providing her a statement that expressed her grief that her sons were out of state and unable to cast their own votes for suffrage. Pennybacker did not include anti-immigrant comments in her statement, but did borrow from U.S. pro-war rhetoric as she referred to soldiers fighting for freedom overseas: "Would that my two soldier sons—for the present, alas disfranchised—could vote, for they, together with the great majority of our army and navy, would register a rising 'Aye' to the call of justice as they have already answered to the call of freedom."[99]

The federal amendment passed the House in January 1918 with the support of six of eighteen Texas representatives.[100] The vote in the Senate was delayed until September of that year. In the meantime, during February, the Texas legislature met in a special session and addressed many of Texas women activists' concerns. The legislature banned bars, brothels, and pool halls around military bases, ratified the national prohibition amendment, and "passed a constitutional amendment for statewide prohibition."[101] In addition, with the specter looming of a Ferguson bid for governor in the upcoming elections, the legislature granted Texas women the right to vote in primary elections, after being convinced by Cunningham that the woman's vote would assist current Governor Hobby and prevent Ferguson from regaining office.[102]

With primary suffrage granted them in the spring of 1918, Texas suffragists faced a new battle. Their old nemesis Ferguson ran for governor that summer, and suffragists recognized that his election would mean the demise of their primary voting rights and their hopes for full suffrage. However, TESA, which had been struggling financially for years, was now indebted by $2,700, and Minnie Fisher Cunningham had used personal property as security for loans. The group had no money left for a battle against Ferguson. When she learned of the situation, Pennybacker wrote Catt an urgent letter, pleading for financial assistance. Help came in the form of $1,000 given to TESA by the Leslie Commission "for the campaign against Ferguson and with the view of maintaining their primary suffrage."[103] Ferguson was defeated, but he would fight against the suffragists again the next year when the federal suffrage amendment went to the states for ratification.

THE WOMEN'S ASSOCIATE DEMOCRATIC NATIONAL COMMITTEE

As the Texas legislature considered allowing women to vote in primary elections, prominent Democrats, including national committeeman William Poindexter of Texas and Elizabeth Bass, chair of the Women's Bureau of the Democratic National Committee, invited Pennybacker to represent Texas on the newly formed Women's Associate Democratic National Committee. Bass explained in the invitation that she was responsible for the "political organization and education of women in the United States" and had been appointed chair of the Advisory Committee of Women. She explained that each member of the advisory committee would become the state chair for Democratic women in her state, "and a part of the organization of the Democratic National Committee," although "in states where women do not yet vote, the position for the present will be purely advisory." Expressing confidence that the Senate would pass the federal suffrage amendment within a few weeks, she noted that "the position of State Chairman of women for the Democratic National Committee will then become one of practical importance and responsibility as ratification of the amendment will doubtless be satisfactorily concluded within a couple of years."[104] Bass hoped that Pennybacker could provide insight into the "interests of women in your state upon which action of the Democratic party is desirable."[105] As was frequently the case, Pennybacker's appointment to this committee irritated some Texas suffragists. Elizabeth Herndon Potter, who had suggested Minnie Fisher Cunningham for the position, and wished to see "a fine & true hard working Suffragist" in the position, was frustrated but unsurprised to see Pennybacker once more selected for a position of prominence.[106] Texas's leading women were suspicious of the party's motives in forming the committee. Cunningham, Potter, and other female leaders also believed the committee's purpose to be the segregation and marginalization of women within the party, and Cunningham had little respect for the Women's Bureau director, Bass, whom she believed to be "undistinguished and ineffective."[107]

Despite the uncertainty about what the function of the women's committee would be, Pennybacker accepted and attended the meeting of the Democratic National Committee as a member of the women's committee in May of 1919.[108] Pennybacker described the meeting in a press article, noting that the women's quarters were sufficiently feminine, "filled with flowers and pictures," and that the men and women were mutually curious about each other.[109] According to Pennybacker's later press accounts, the women especially wanted to know what the term "Associate Committee" really meant, while the men didn't fully understand the women's presence. Pennybacker noted that the men who had already come out in favor of suffrage were particularly confused about the women's presence, implying that even the pro-suffrage men had difficulties conceptualizing a role for women in politics beyond voting. "The attitude of the men," she wrote, "was both interesting and amusing. . . . In spite of all their kindness however, there was prevalent a certain air of 'What in the world do these blessed women want here anyway?' "[110] At first, Pennybacker noted, the women were self-effacing, "saying nothing but playing the watchful game."[111] Later, however, they became more active, impressing the men with their knowledge of political history. Although Pennybacker's report of the meeting does not explicitly indicate women's displeasure with their role as associates, Pennybacker does recount the women taking a humorous jibe at the men. At a women's dinner, the women referred to the six male invitees as "associate members," she noted, "much to the amusement of all the diners."[112] Pennybacker played a particularly active role in the meetings. Early on she called on Representative Cummins of Idaho to clarify the role of the women's committee with respect to the Democratic Party generally. Cummins replied that while the Women's Bureau at Democratic headquarters had been financed by the Democratic National Committee, he hoped that the women would finance their work on their own. Although she doesn't state so directly, Pennybacker's account makes clear that the women intended their role to include influencing policy.

Pennybacker took a first step toward this goal when she used her position on the Democratic National Committee to further the suffrage cause. During the meetings, women speakers echoed what Pennybacker later called their "keynote"—that a Democratic victory in the 1920 elections would depend on the party's ability to attract "new women voters who had made no connection with party lines."[113] She suggested that women voters would be attracted to the party not based on a background, "ethnologically Democratic," but based on the party's ability to "present in vivid fashion certain vital truths that appeal to the moral sense."[114] Specifically she argued that women would be attracted to issues now considered traditionally female, "whatever concerns the welfare of the child, the safety of the home, the peace of the world."[115] As a first step, Pennybacker introduced a resolution that the party encourage the states to call special sessions to ratify the suffrage amendment. She argued that the suffrage issue was crucial to the Democratic Party and that the party should "do all in our power to repair the damage" done by the party's historical opposition to suffrage. The text of her resolution read as follows:

> Whereas the Democratic Party is on record as favoring Woman's Suffrage, and
>
> Whereas it now appears certain that the Federal Suffrage Amendment will pass the United States Senate within the next few days, and
>
> Whereas it is the earnest desire of the Democratic Party that all women vote in the elections of 1920,
>
> Be it resolved, therefore, that the Democratic National Committee urges the calling of special session of the State Legislatures where ever necessary to bring about a speedy ratification of said Federal Amendment.[116]

The committee passed the resolution "without a dissenting vote."[117]

Newspaper reports of the meetings revealed the cultural attitudes toward feminine behavior and women's role in the public sphere that Pennybacker had faced for years. The meetings had involved particularly heated debate on the League of Nations. Under the headline "Women Join the Attack," one article described how Democratic women "excoriated" Republican women who opposed the League of Nations.[118] In response to news reports that she personally had "scored" the party on the issue of suffrage and that the women attending engaged in political storms and coarse behavior, Pennybacker's account of the meetings stressed the women's feminine behavior: "We were never more proud of womanhood than as we listened to our members who, with pleasing voice and manner, spoke sanely, constructively and inspiringly . . . There was such an entire absence of strained voices, of ranting, of theatrical manner, of empty words, words, words; there was such a delightful prevalence of humor without a trace of scolding or scoring as some of the press reported."[119] More complimentary newspapers described Pennybacker herself as "small and dainty, exquisitely feminine yet gifted with a voice of most unusual carrying power," and noted that "Democratic party leaders congratulated themselves on this acquisition to the ranks."[120] Pennybacker relied on traditional nineteenth-century ideals of femininity in her arguments as well, stressing the importance of morals to women: "The party that wants to bring the woman voter into its folds must have behind it a great moral purpose,"[121] she told party leaders. In arguing before the committee in favor of the League of Nations, she stressed the moral imperative behind the league. Newspapers reported that she, along with Montana's J. Bruce Kremer, "praised President Wilson as the greatest statesman since Jefferson, and declared that in the League of Nations covenant alone the Democratic Party had a moral issue with which to sweep the country."[122]

In correspondence before and after the meeting, the Democratic women strategized about ways to increase the appeal of the party to newly enfranchised women. As Pennybacker argued in her speech detailed above, the women believed that attracting female voters was critical to the party's success and could only be accomplished by appealing to women on social and moral issues. Stressing that the suffrage issue was also important, Pennybacker wrote to Elizabeth Bass: "This recent lecture tour has taken me into Oklahoma, Arkansas, Florida, Virginia, Louisiana, and East Texas. With the exception of Arkansas, I am more and more impressed by the fact that the chief trouble is the lack among the rank and file of the women, of a sense of personal responsibility about the suffrage question." She queried Bass, "Is there not some way to get the Democratic leaders,—State, District and County, as well as precinct to pass the word around that the salvation of the Democratic Party demands the support of the rank and file for suffrage?"[123] Pennybacker suggested that the Democratic Party "utilize the teachers in the public schools" to garner support for suffrage by impressing upon them the importance of bringing justice to women. She noted that public school teachers' influence was often overlooked, but, approached in the right way, public school teachers would be eager to participate.[124]

In the latter years of the century's second decade, the women's committee leaders undertook a campaign of "propaganda of political education and information" among women in non-voting states who were about to obtain suffrage. Although they had few funds compared to the thousands of dollars Republicans spent for every campaign, the women reasoned that they could, with little money, develop political education and "at least the beginnings of political organization" among women, in order to bring awareness of the Democratic administration's policies and recent record.[125] Antoinette Funk took control of the newly created Educational Department of the Democratic National Committee. This committee formed its plans to educate newly enfranchised women on the club model, by organizing "the women of the United States into Democratic Women's Political Study Clubs." Funk noted that a large majority of women were "not prepared by previous thought upon political matters to understand the problems that confront them and the issues they must consider in choosing their party." The average woman, she wrote, "shies a little at the word 'politics.' They are afraid of getting mixed up in something they do not understand. But women are accustomed to working in organizations; particularly clubs and education along any useful line makes a strong appeal to them."[126] In June of 1919, Funk asked Pennybacker to recommend women for the educational chair in Texas. After consulting with Carrie Chapman Catt to ensure that there would be no conflicts with suffrage work, Pennybacker promptly recommended Minnie Fisher Cunningham for the position.[127] Clearly Pennybacker did not return the resentment Cunningham and others felt toward her. However, given the prominence Cunningham had attained in the state and nationally, determining how great a compliment Pennybacker's recommendation carried is difficult. Still, in addition to this recommendation, Pennybacker wrote to Miss Rose Young the same month, encouraging her to publish an article paying tribute to Cunningham in the *Woman Citizen*. "I am sure," she wrote Young, "that you and Mrs. Catt realize that Mrs. Cunningham has done more in Texas than any other ten women put together."[128]

Because Texas was a single-party state, once the Texas legislature allowed women to vote in primary elections Texas women considered themselves to have "for practical purposes, almost full suffrage." TESA leaders determined to focus their energy on what Minnie Fisher Cunningham called "our next great task, the passage and ratification of the Federal Amendment." Cunningham invited Pennybacker to serve as a member of the Ratification Committee, "which will ask of our legislators, next January, the immediate ratification of the Federal Suffrage Amendment, which will, we hope, have passed the Senate by then."[129] However, this task was complicated in January 1919 by the Texas legislature's passage of a state suffrage amendment "subject to approval by voter referendum."[130] The amendment was forwarded by what Jane McCallum called "some friends backed by some enemies."[131] McCallum referred to the fact that the amendment was supported by pro-suffrage politicians and women's groups as well as anti-suffrage forces. The referendum was a high-stakes proposition for suffrage supporters and did not suit TESA leaders, who were discreetly supporting Catt's directive to focus on the federal amendment. Fighting for the state amendment would drain resources from the federal battle, yet a loss in the popular vote would give anti-suffragists grounds to argue that suffrage lacked popular support in the state. TESA and NAWSA devoted what resources they could spare to campaign for the amendment. NAWSA contributed $5,000 and sent Cunningham home from Washington, D.C., where she had been working for the federal amendment.[132]

Pennybacker was out of state, and refused to return to Texas to support the campaign.[133] Instead she assisted the efforts from New York, where she was working with the War Camp Community Service. She agreed to join Cunningham's advisory committee, and provided her with a statement for publication. She also wrote Cunningham that NAWSA would be mailing a thousand letters in support of suffrage to Texas women.[134] In addition, she provided a longer statement to Jane McCallum, listing reasons why the men of Texas should support the amendment. In her statement, she used the work women had done in support of the country during the war to argue that the men of Texas should and would vote for women's suffrage as recognition of the role women had played in the war: The Texas man is just, the statement asserted, he feels that "if the government called upon woman in its hour of crisis and she gave her strength, her spirit, her means most generously, then the government should recognize her service by giving her the one thing she lacks to make her a living part in the government of her State—full suffrage."[135] Pennybacker also argued that Texas men should endorse suffrage because women in other Anglo-Saxon countries, Great Britain and Canada, could vote, and because more than half the states had already given women some form of suffrage. Aiming squarely for the pride of Texas men, she challenged them to be leaders in bringing about the inevitable.[136]

However, neither Pennybacker's arguments and efforts nor those of anyone else could convince a majority of Texans to vote for women's full suffrage. Amid suspicions of voting fraud and the opposition of Texas's many immigrants, whom the amendment would have disenfranchised, Texas voters rejected the amendment at the polls in May of 1919. After this setback, TESA devoted all of its resources to efforts to ratify the federal amendment. Although they had many supporters, ratification did not come without a struggle. When Governor Hobby called a special session of the Texas legislature, but failed to introduce the ratification of the federal amendment, Texas suffragists addressed their representatives directly. The amendment moved through the House quickly, but debate in the Senate raged for days, as old foe Ferguson rallied his supporters against ratification. In the end, Caswell Ellis and others had to retrieve anti-suffrage senators from a Pullman car as they tried to "disappear from Austin on the night train" to break quorum. On June 28, 1919, however, the Texas Senate ratified the amendment, thereby making Texas the ninth state in the country to do so and the first in the South.[137]

By the fall of 1919, suffrage leaders were confident that the federal amendment would be ratified by the required majority of states. Still, they continued to work in southern states. Throughout 1918 and 1919, Pennybacker was in great demand as a speaker in support of the federal suffrage amendment, particularly in the South. Nettie Shuler, NAWSA's corresponding secretary, pleaded with Pennybacker that she speak in Oklahoma to mobilize women there to support the amendment. Busy with other engagements, Pennybacker was unable to comply at that time.[138] Later, however, she would travel widely throughout the South at the behest of Carrie Chapman Catt, who asked her to take conferences in the South in the fall of 1919.[139]

Despite strong anti-suffrage sentiment and the futility of attempting to have some southern states ratify the suffrage amendment, some southern women wanted to campaign vigorously in that part of the country. In part this was because the amendment would need the support of some southern states. However, southern female Democrats were also concerned that if some southern states did not ratify the amendment, the Republicans would take credit when it became law and win the loyalty of newly franchised women. Pennybacker's ability to convince women to offer active support, including financial support, was put to use in the campaign. Her trip to Mississippi in November 1919 is an example. As Pennybacker described in a letter to Catt and Shuler after the trip, she was initially discouraged by the women's lack of support for suffrage: "They were leading happy lives, their section of the state was extremely prosperous, and they didn't see any need to worry." By agreement, GFWC president Alice Ames (Mrs. Thomas G.) Winter spoke first, and as they had arranged, "played right into my hands." Pennybacker then presided over a suffrage discussion the next day, at which prominent Mississippi suffragists spoke. Under Pennybacker's leadership, forty women "volunteered to throw themselves heart and soul into the work." They formed a ratification committee and selected a Mrs. Saunders, whom Pennybacker praised as one of the strongest, sanest, most popular women in the United States, as chair. Within minutes, Pennybacker had obtained donations of more than $800, with more coming in the next day. Later in the week, Pennybacker met with Mississippi suffrage leaders to map out a campaign.[140] In her letter to Catt, Pennybacker requested that NAWSA send two organizers to the state. She requested Cunningham and Mrs. Shuler specifically. Whether Pennybacker's work helped or hurt the national efforts in this case is unclear. Despite the initial enthusiasm reported by Pennybacker, Cunningham arrived in the state to find the situation nearly impossible. She expressed a very different view of the Mississippi leadership: "The State President is not a leader but an *incubus* that has to be placated," Cunningham reported to Catt. Cunningham's presence in the state made little difference in the eventual outcome, and drew her from possibly more productive work elsewhere. Despite her best efforts, in early 1920, "after endless speechmaking on the threat to white supremacy and state sovereignty," Mississippi voted against ratification.[141]

THE LEAGUE OF NATIONS

The last years of the decade saw activist women planning ahead. Although the World War ended with the signing of the armistice in November 1918, women continued their war work, shifting focus slightly to include services to support returning veterans as well as those still actively enlisted. In addition, these women fought to have input into the peace process. Days after the signing of the armistice, Carrie Chapman Catt, under the auspices of NAWSA, sent out a letter inviting the heads of the nation's women's organizations to a meeting to discuss the role of women in the peace process. Catt claimed a role for women based on their maternity: "You who know the price that women pay in war, you who know as men cannot know the damage done to posterity by the imprint on motherhood of the horrors, the privations, the grief and the outrages of war, know that womanhood and motherhood should have a voice in the terms that shall end the war," she wrote.[142] Five days later Pennybacker repeated Catt's argument in a letter to President Wilson. Writing as the president and representative of the 1,300 members of the Chautauqua Women's Club, "women from all parts of the country," Pennybacker requested that Wilson "give women adequate representation on the United States Peace Commission." Like Catt, Pennybacker argued that women brought an important perspective to the peace process, and that "in a critical hour we need the wisdom of men and women combined." Pennybacker also argued that the presence of U.S. women on the Peace Commission would set an example of democracy to other nations "in recognizing its Womanhood."[143] In January of the next year, William Howard Taft, president of the League to Enforce Peace, invited Pennybacker to speak at the National League of Peace congresses on a League of Nations that would take place in February 1919. Taft, former GFWC president Eva Perry Moore, and Lawrence Lowell, the president of Harvard University, were among those to speak at this series of conferences. Pennybacker was to speak in favor of a League of Nations.

Pennybacker had been interested in peace since her GFWC presidency. Now, at the war's end, Pennybacker believed that women had a particular duty to mold public opinion in favor of the league. She argued before the Democratic National Committee that Democrats should support the league "as a moral issue with which it could sweep the country."[144] Later that year she added her signature to a written appeal for ratification of the Versailles treaty that was submitted to every member of the Senate in September 1919. Two hundred fifty of those whom the *New York Times* called "leaders in American life" added their names to the petition.[145] Convincing the public of the good of the league would be no small task. The league was a controversial issue that would occupy Pennybacker's time and interest for years into the future.[146]

THE LEAGUE OF WOMEN VOTERS

As the nation looked forward to the end of the war, NAWSA leaders looked forward to women's increased political power as they gained suffrage in states across the country. Even as they gained suffrage, however, leaders recognized that they would continue to struggle to have the political parties address issues of concern to them. At the NAWSA convention of 1919, leaders created a new organization that would promote what they understood to be women's political interests. They named the new organization the National League of Women Voters (NLWV). In her examination of women's organizations and political literacy, Wendy Sharer notes that the purpose of League of Women Voters (LWV) was to "allow women to move beyond the limited scope of political discussion within parties." Sharer notes that the initial organizational plan of the LWV addressed progressive women's political interests "by including committees on the legal status of women, child welfare, women in industry, and U.S. citizenship (a committee that encompassed educational and electoral reform and food supply and demand)."[147] At the NLWV's founding meeting in 1919, Catt asked Julia Lathrop, director of the Federal Children's Bureau, to head the citizenship committee. Lathrop, however, declined. Catt then approached Pennybacker, who was already serving as chair of NAWSA's Child Welfare Committee.

Pennybacker declined Catt's first request that she chair the NLWV's Child Welfare Committee. In part, she was reluctant because she recognized that Catt would have preferred Lathrop in the position. However, in addition to not being the first choice, Pennybacker questioned whether the position was where she could best serve. She had already committed to help Catt in the push to have the federal suffrage amendment ratified. "I thought we were agreed that I could be of more service in trying to help in the Southern States late in the fall," she responded to Catt's requests.[148] Already heavily engaged in other work, Pennybacker simply was not anxious to take on more. Catt, however, kept the pressure on, impressing upon Pennybacker the importance of the Child Welfare Committee particularly with respect to the federal Children's Bureau.

The Children's Bureau had been created with the help of the GFWC in part during Pennybacker's presidency. Now the progressive women responsible for the Children's Bureau were concerned that its power was being diluted. Children's Bureau responsibilities were being diverted to other divisions of the federal government, divisions led by men and less friendly to women's leadership. In a letter to Pennybacker in May of 1919, Catt quoted Mrs. Woolley of the Woman Suffrage Committee of Greater Cincinnati: "What I am frankly afraid of is that now that child welfare has become so 'popular,' it may be virtually taken away from the Children's Bureau by making it a sub-division of the Public

Health Service."[149] Catt, following Woolley, noted that child labor law had been given to the "internal revenue division of the Treasury, with permission to call upon the Children's Bureau." Women were concerned that "there [was] 'no dispensation' to call on [the] children's bureau," and that the bureau was being bypassed. The Children's Bureau was important to progressive women activists in part because it was one small federal program run by females. Catt and Woolley saw the reassignment of responsibilities as a move to take power out of female hands; Catt quoted Woolley's analysis of the situation: "The present Secretary of the Treasury is, according to the Press, a strong anti-suffragist. Both internal revenue and public health fall in his department. Moreover, the Red Cross is now announcing an active child welfare program and its opposition to women in administrative position is well known." Woolley asked the NLWV to "come to the rescue" by supporting the bill which provided for maternity and infant welfare work under the Children's Bureau.[150]

In letters to Pennybacker in the spring of 1919, Catt insisted that the NLWV's child welfare department, "must not be a conservative department."[151] Still, she assured Pennybacker that the work, although important, would be focused and limited: "The committee will have no other official duties than to study the questions and bring to the conference of next year a program suited for legislation." The three main topics which demanded the attention of the new chairman were "1. The abolition of child labor; 2. more attention to education; 3. protection of child morals." Catt noted that the work involved with each of these tasks properly belonged to other NLWV committees: child labor to the industrial committee, education to citizenship committee, and protection of child morals to the social hygiene committee.[152] Another associate assured Pennybacker that "the most important work for the National Chairman of the Committee and the only work of any size for some time will be the preparation of a bulletin, stating the reasons for the committee, its plan of organization and its aims." Further, she proclaimed, developing a program of action for the committee would not entail much labor because NAWSA leadership planned to use "the program formulated by the children's bureau."[153] By August of 1919, Pennybacker was convinced and accepted the position in the new organization.[154] Although her time was heavily invested in her other work, she laid out a plan of action for the committee for the months between November 1919 and March 1920, when, at the fiftieth anniversary meeting of the NAWSA, the NLWV would officially come into being. Pennybacker's plan, which she called "extremely simple, but concrete," called for "an effort to secure hot school lunches for all school-children and teachers" and to monitor children's weight with a report issued to those who were underweight or showing signs of malnutrition.[155]

In the ensuing months, however, the demands of the position grew greater. In February 1920, at its annual conference, NAWSA celebrated its fiftieth anniversary and formally announced the creation of the National League of Women Voters. In conjunction with this conference, Pennybacker hosted a child welfare conference whose speakers included Catt and Florence Kelley.[156] Having invited the heads of multiple organizations doing child welfare work, Pennybacker proposed forming a cooperative of organizations working for women and children's welfare.[157] Additionally, the board of the NLWV invited Pennybacker to attend both the Democratic and Republican national conventions that year to request that the parties add desired legislation to their platforms.[158] In her position as chair of the Child Welfare Committee, Pennybacker argued strongly in favor of the Sheppard-Towner Maternity and Infancy Act. The act would provide funds for educational efforts to prevent mortality in childbirth and the death of infants. With the League of Women Voters, Pennybacker also supported a bill that would introduce physical education into the country's public schools.[159]

By the February NAWSA/NLWV conference in 1920, Pennybacker realized that the scope of the work involved being the chair of the NLWV's Child Welfare Committee was greater than she was prepared to take on. During the national convention, she requested that Maude Wood Park, NLWV president, find a replacement. At Park's request, she agreed to remain the titular head of the committee until after the national political conventions in June, with the understanding that a secretary would take on the active duties of the position.[160] Pennybacker remained in the position officially until August of 1920. Before resigning, she attended the Republican national convention in May. For several weeks thereafter, she traveled with NLWV leaders on speaking engagements throughout western states before attending the Democratic national convention in San Francisco that June. At these conventions she presented planks of interest to the NLWV on child welfare and education.[161] The lecture tour required that she decline an invitation from Baylor University to speak at graduation and receive an honorary degree. Pennybacker had desired a college degree from childhood, and passing up the opportunity to receive even an honorary degree felt like a great sacrifice. "Still," she wrote Baylor's Dr. S. P. Brooks, "when I consider what others have given up for the cause of suffrage,

I know it would be selfish in me not to be willing to do all that the leaders ask."[162]

THE DECADE DRAWS TO A CLOSE

The years between 1916 and 1920 were busy and intense for progressive women. Despite losses in states such as Mississippi, which would not ratify the nineteenth amendment until the 1980s, suffragists gained success in having the federal suffrage amendment ratified in 1920 when the unlikely state of Tennessee ratified it.[163] The end of the war in 1918 and success in passing the suffrage amendment encouraged progressive women with the promise of future success and the formation of new organizations dedicated to furthering their causes. The ensuing decades, however, posed further challenges to women who sought to consolidate and use their new political power to enact the progressive social changes they had sought for years. As the 1920s dawned and Pennybacker entered her sixties, she would continue to play an active role in the struggle to bring progressive ideas into reality.

Chapter Seven

PROMOTING IDEALS OF CITIZENSHIP

"The highest patriotism teaches love for one's own country but also love for other countries."

—PENNYBACKER TO CLARA GUTHRIE D'ARCIS, MAY 5, 1925

THE END OF WORLD WAR I and the granting of suffrage to women in 1920 brought to fruition some of the activities that had occupied Pennybacker during the latter half of the second decade of the century, and transformed other activities. As war work began to wind down and suffrage societies disbanded or shifted focus, Pennybacker, too, shifted focus. Women's work supporting the country's military continued, with a shift in emphasis to include the needs of returning war veterans. Additionally, with the war over, progressive women transferred some of their time and attention to the problem of war in general, as they sought ways to ensure a lasting peace. Finally having achieved success in the battle for suffrage, progressive women could return their focus to the many other social and political issues they had supported before the war and to a lesser extent during the war.

The postwar era brought continued challenges to supporters of social-progressive causes. Despite the major success of women's suffrage nationally, social progressives in the 1920s faced a social and political climate that would complicate their work and limit their expectations and achievements. To the dismay of many progressives, the rhetoric of nationalistic Americanism that had accompanied war preparations continued into the 1920s. This virulent strain of Americanism proclaimed immigrants a threat to American values and to the state itself. The Bolshevik Revolution of 1917 had increased fears of people, ideas, and social movements that were considered foreign, socialist, or otherwise anti-American. In some cases immigrants were attacked and killed by vigilantes in the name of patriotism, and violent clashes between industry and labor continued. Racial tensions, too, had come to the forefront as African Americans migrated north for work in the war industries. Urban race riots, some instigated by working-class whites incensed by perceived competition for jobs by African American newcomers, roiled major cities in the latter years of the second decade of the century. The Ku Klux Klan expanded rapidly as it successfully stoked fears of both African Americans and new immigrant groups.[1] The war years had given the federal government new powers, which it quickly used against groups that opposed government policy. The Espionage Act of 1917 and its amendment, the Sedition Act, were used to suppress free speech and to imprison leaders in the labor and peace movements, and "100 percent Americanism had a firmer grip on the American people than did ideas about continuing social reform."[2] Progressives, who had fought for a strong and active federal government, now saw the power of the state used increasingly against its citizens. "Following a series of dynamite bombs, including one sent to the home of Attorney General A. Mitchell Palmer, the new Justice Department bureau was authorized to round up suspected terrorists and to invade meetings of any presumed radical groups."[3] President Wilson's attention turned to his international peace plans, while federal troops were used to contain and suppress work strikes across the country. Historian Maureen Flanahan notes, "The ruthless suppression of free speech and dissent, the surge of antialien antiradical sentiment, the assignment of the word un-American to anyone who disagreed, and the Red hysteria of 1919 and 1920 all determined that the capacious progressive ideas of citizenship and democracy would be limited in the coming years."[4] Throughout the 1920s, in the face of these challenges, Pennybacker would continue to support the broader vision of citizenship and civic action that had shaped her activities in the past. Ever practical, Pennybacker responded to the repressive atmosphere with a cautious approach, choosing her words and activities with care in order to maintain her public image as a patriotic American and avoid being classified a radical.

Despite the resistance toward social progressivism in the postwar period and the challenges faced by its supporters, Pennybacker's postwar years brought her happy changes in her personal life and continued professional success. Her older son Bonner had returned from military service in France and her younger son had recovered from serious medical problems, possibly service-related, that kept him in a New

Jersey hospital for an extended time after the war. Both boys were back in Texas, providing Pennybacker the opportunity to visit with them. Pennybacker had assisted daughter Ruth in obtaining a position as secretary to Carry Chapman Catt in New York. Her many letters to friends during this time indicate her pleasure in spending time with her sons, and her announcing Ruth's position to friends attests to the fact that Pennybacker was pleased to have Ruth in this position. This was the first time in years that Pennybacker was able to spend much-appreciated time in Austin with her boys, and in January 1920, she noted in a letter to a friend, "We have many delightful evenings in our comfortable library, each of us busy either with writing or with books and no one speaking a word for sometimes an hour."[5]

Although Pennybacker spoke warmly of a renewed, idyllic domestic life, she did not adopt domesticity for long. Instead she remained active in a variety of professional activities and traveled widely during this period. Speaking engagements continued to take her across the country and to provide a substantial portion of her income, as she continued to charge $75–100 per engagement. In early January 1920 she visited Washington, D.C., and New York City for speaking and social engagements. That month she spoke to the Forum Club in New York and at the highly publicized Roosevelt Memorial at Carnegie Hall.[6] Anxieties about immigration and the defining qualities of "American" and Americanism surfaced at the Roosevelt dinner, which was held the first week of the new decade. The dinner, held January 5, 1920, recognized the first anniversary of Theodore Roosevelt's death. The Woman's Roosevelt Memorial Association, which claimed Pennybacker as a member, worked in tandem with the all-male Roosevelt Memorial Association to sponsor the affair, and Pennybacker was featured on a program that included Dr. Nicholas Murray Butler of Columbia University and Col. Arthur Woods (both described as close associates of Roosevelt), and Roosevelt's sister, Mrs. Douglas Robinson. Before a gathering of over two thousand, Pennybacker delivered a speech titled "Colonel Roosevelt, the Father and Citizen," focusing on the connection between domestic and civic life. "No government can flourish. . . . unless it has well-ordered and happy homes," she told the crowd. "Roosevelt has set a fine example as a father and a citizen."[7] As if setting the agenda for Pennybacker's work in the early 1920s, Colonel Woods addressed issues of immigration and American ideals in his speech, "Roosevelt and the Foreign-born Citizen." Roosevelt, he asserted, "believed that the American ideal, that the American life, is true enough, is sound enough, is compelling enough, inviting enough to capture the people of the world as they come to this country looking here to realize the chance of their lives." Woods noted that the few foreign-born accused of "striking at the root of all we believe in" were not representative of all immigrants, and that the country should proceed equally against those of American birth who act against American ideals. Woods also noted the importance of dealing with immigrants by showing true hospitality, "the kind of hospitality that treated them on the same level with others." The speeches, in some sense, were prophetic, defining the issues that would in large measure shape Pennybacker's work in the 1920s and reflecting the stance she would take toward these issues.[8]

If the speeches at the Carnegie Hall memorial countered anxieties with confidence in the power of the American ideal and the American way of life to prevail over perceived challenges, speeches at another Roosevelt memorial the day prior revealed darker fears about the social issues that would occupy Pennybacker and her peers during the twenties. At the earlier memorial, sponsored by the American Defense Society and held at Trinity Church, Rev. Dr. William T. Manning spoke vehemently about pursuing domestic "reds" and against the "cult of internationalism." Manning likened love of one's own country to love of one's own wife, arguing that "those who are trying to destroy loyalty to country are trying also to destroy the home and the marriage tie."[9] Like Pennybacker, Manning linked the strength of the state to the strength of its homes and families, and understood the structure and strength of the state to be related to domestic and gendered social structures within it. Manning's argument, however, both recalled earlier antifeminist arguments that warned that clubwomen's public activism threatened the social fabric and hinted at emerging arguments that women activists were either communist dupes or sympathizers. Such arguments saw gender, economic, social, and political reforms as striking at the basis of American way of life. As the decade continued, female activists, including many of Pennybacker's longtime colleagues and friends, would face accusations of being anti-American.

Pennybacker's New York–Washington trip of early 1920 also took her to the Democratic National Committee meeting and the subsequent Jackson Day Banquet, which provided a forum for Democratic presidential nominee hopefuls to express their views. While Pennybacker did not speak at the banquet, she would have listened to speeches by twelve Democratic contenders.[10] Her trip also afforded her opportunities to meet with senators Henry Cabot Lodge and Gilbert M. Hitchcock as a representative of the League to Enforce Peace. Senators Lodge and Hitchcock were key players in the Senate battle over ratification of the treaty of Versailles, which would have created the League of Nations, a goal of the League to Enforce Peace. Republican Lodge, chairman of the Senate Committee on Foreign Relations, and an antagonist of Wilson, had helped to prevent Senate adoption of the treaty the previous summer by adding reservations that eventually led the Senate to reject the treaty. Hitchcock, the Senate's leading Democrat, had attempted, but failed, to convince Wilson to agree to compromises with Lodge that would create a treaty that the Senate would pass. Undoubtedly Pennybacker urged the senators to find a compromise that would allow the treaty to pass. Her efforts clearly not successful, the treaty ultimately failed a few months later, when, in March, Republicans and Democrats again could not reach agreement.[11] After the visit east in January, Pennybacker returned to Austin. February would take her to San Antonio to speak at a high school commencement and then to Chicago for the National Suffrage Convention and the League of Women Voters convention. There, as chairman of the LWV's Child Welfare Committee, she spoke at the general sessions and "presided at a mammoth conference held in the Gold Room of the Congress Hotel," and later over a dinner of two hundred attendees.[12]

CHAIR OF THE CITIZENSHIP DEPARTMENT OF THE GFWC, 1920–1924

In addition to her numerous speaking engagements and continued involvement working in executive roles with other organizations, in 1920 Pennybacker once again took a formal, national-level, leadership role with the General Federation of Women's Clubs. As previous chapters have indicated, Pennybacker had continued to work within the GFWC as a president of both the Chautauqua Women's Club and the Austin American History Club after her GFWC presidency ended in 1916. She also advised and directed some of the politics of federated clubwomen at the state and national levels. As a past president, she offered subtle behind-the-scenes support and advice to leaders of both the Texas and general federations. In this role, Pennybacker supported Mrs. Thomas Winter's 1920 campaign for the GFWC presidency. Pennybacker, at the time a committee chair for the National League of Women Voters, expected Winter to foster good relations between the GFWC and the NLWV. Additionally, Pennybacker saw in Winter a woman with the ability to deliver "with an intensely practical message, that deep spiritual note that is so necessary to hold the best women fast to any cause."[13] Winter was elected president of the GFWC that spring and promptly appointed Pennybacker to the position she herself had just vacated, that of chair of the General Federation's Department of American Citizenship. The citizenship department was born of the GFWC's reorganization earlier that year and consisted of several divisions: citizenship training, community service, and Americanization. In addition were two committees associated with the department: the Committee on Motion Pictures and the Committee for Friendly Co-operation with the Ex-Service Man. The chair of this department seemed a natural position for Pennybacker, as it related to her longstanding interest in civic issues and offered her the opportunity to promote several of her pet projects. Despite the possibilities the position offered, her work, as always, would be circumscribed by the cultural currents of the time—particularly larger cultural debates about what it meant to be a citizen, to be female, and to be American.

DIVISION OF CITIZENSHIP TRAINING: PREPARING WOMEN FOR CITIZENSHIP

Early in her tenure as chair of the citizenship department, Pennybacker worked with GFWC president Winter to appoint appropriate women to head departmental divisions and committees, to focus the direction of the department, and to prepare materials for distribution. The federation left most legislative work in this area to the League of Women Voters in order to focus its attention on educational and civic activities.[14] Of the Department of American Citizenship's divisions, Citizenship Training absorbed most of Pennybacker's attention and related most directly to the work she had been doing with NAWSA and the National League of Women Voters prior to accepting the citizenship department chair. Pennybacker took charge of the department in the summer of 1920. As chair she first outlined two modest activities she wanted clubwomen to work toward: having at least two clubwomen present in court when immigrants became naturalized citizens and celebrating Citizenship Day on July 4. However, as the first national elections in which women would be allowed to vote approached in the fall of 1920, Pennybacker quickly expanded the list of activities expected of clubwomen to include an intensive drive to prepare women to exercise this newly granted right. Under her leadership, the Department of American Citizenship's Division of Citizenship Training strongly promoted voter preparation and education using methods that closely paralleled those of the League of Women Voters. Specifically, Pennybacker encouraged clubs to take four steps toward the goal of preparing women to vote. Clubs, she argued, should induce women to register to vote, study state and local issues in nonpartisan fashion, study national platforms ("being careful to have both sides of every mooted question presented adequately"), and "demonstrate why it is the duty of every club woman to go to the polls and vote."[15] Perhaps informed by the philosophy of object teaching and recalling the activities of the literary clubs she had presided over as a young woman, Pennybacker urged clubs to "ask some well-known publicist to explain the method of voting" and then hold a mock election. "Have ballots drawn up in the accepted form," she urged. "Stage voting booths, and let the actual voting take place, observing all regulations that must be carried out at the polls in November. When the result has been announced the successful candidates may be presented and a speech demanded."[16]

For Pennybacker, women's exercise of their newly won voting rights would be a test of their civic devotion. She exhorted women to educate themselves on civic issues and go to the polls. "This is the hour in which the womanhood of America is on trial,"[17] she told clubwomen. She traveled the country delivering a lecture entitled "What Can I Do?" which, she noted, "bears particularly on our preparation on voting and yet has a good bit of the human nature about it."[18] Pennybacker urged every club to emphasize citizenship training, her slogan being Every Club a Training Camp for Citizenship. She was cited in newspaper descriptions of her speeches as telling audiences, "If I were king, I'd make every girl fit to become mayor at 18," a comment that provoked teasing by a fellow clubwoman who pointed out that Pennybacker should have said "If I were queen" to signal the growing power of women in politics.[19] In her speeches, voting took on almost religious significance, and she invoked enduring popular views that depicted women as the more moral and spiritual of the sexes.[20] Bemoaning a lack of ritual in national life, Pennybacker argued that women should make voting part of "women's instinctive knowledge toward the Right" (not the political right, but the moral), and accused those women who did not vote of being traitors to their country. Over the years, Pennybacker had called for churches to open on evenings before elections to give voters the opportunity for reflection and to lend a sense of solemnity and importance to the decision being made. In 1924, as GFWC chair, she renewed this call, urging that churches be opened on Election Day for prayer. In 1920, while arranging for speakers for Chautauqua, Pennybacker noted, "We wish to lose no opportunity to impress upon the women the sacredness of the obligation that has come with the privilege of suffrage."[21] The call to spiritualize civic participation was not uncommon among women civic activists at the time. It continued the suffragist strategy of feminizing civic participation, particularly voting, by reforming politics from a rough-and-tumble, masculine, party-based scuffle, operating out of saloons and back rooms, odiferous fish shops, and greengroceries, to "more dignified" activities and locations that would have been more closely associated with middle-class femininity of the day.[22] Also, as historian Wendy Sharer notes in her detailed examination of the League of Women Voters, religious-type rituals, even prayers, were used by the LWV to help cultivate a sense of responsibility for voting.[23]

In addition, speaking to women across the country, urging them to become educated voters, Pennybacker arranged a citizenship school for women at Chautauqua.[24] This project was begun early in 1920 when Pennybacker still held her chair position in the National League of Women Voters and was president of the women's club at Chautauqua. Later that year and for several years to come, as chair of the GFWC citizenship department, she continued to work closely with the NLWV in arranging speakers for the schools. The first year, Pennybacker and Chautauqua president Arthur Bestor struggled to find a date for the schools—the June date suggested by Bestor conflicted with the 1920 Democratic national convention which would be heavily attended by League of Women Voters members. Since Pennybacker and Bestor both hoped to draw large numbers of attendees from the League of Women Voters to the citizenship school, other dates were considered. In the end, a three-week June session presented much the same program as citizenship schools, and Pennybacker arranged a women's week in mid-August on "Woman and Her Life Today."[25] For that program, four sessions a day were devoted to "Questions of Efficiency in Organized Public Service." Topics treated are reflected in the titles of presentations, which included "The History of the Woman's Movement," "Women in the Industrial and Political World," "The Relations of Home Child Welfare and Education to National Efficiency," "Women's Citizenship," "National State and Municipal Government," "The Political Parties," and "Methods of Club Organization, Procedure, Publicity, Money Raising, Club Ethics, etc." GFWC president Winter presented every morning about women's development and responsibilities. For morning and evening lectures, Pennybacker arranged nationally known speakers, many former suffrage activists, to speak on a variety of topics.[26]

Pennybacker thought that maintaining Chautauqua's nonpartisan stance was crucial, particularly as she was trying to demonstrate that women could work together politically and still remain ladylike.[27] She invited speakers who represented a variety of viewpoints: Mrs. Samuel

Semple spoke on women in industry, Mrs. George Bass represented the Democratic Party, Mary Garrett Hay presented the Republican viewpoint, and Texas's Annie Webb Blanton spoke on education. Male speakers, including Dr. Gordon Hayes and Prof. Thomas Moran, the famous landscape artist and conservationist, also spoke. Carrie Chapman Catt had been invited but, to Pennybacker's disappointment, was unable to attend.[28] Pennybacker also brought Mrs. Douglas Robinson and Mrs. John Henry Hammond to Chautauqua for lectures that summer, as they had promised her at the Roosevelt Memorial earlier in the year.[29] In 1921, and for several years thereafter, Pennybacker continued working with Bestor and the NLWV to host weeklong citizenship schools. Results for the 1921 citizenship school indicate that it was well attended, with three hundred women attending the school proper and with speakers in the amphitheater drawing audiences of between seven and eight hundred. "This enrollment compared most favorably with that of the courses in the Summer School," Pennybacker concluded that fall.[30]

Women who attended the Chautauqua citizenship schools participated in a discourse taking place in the culture at large, on the place of women in politics now that they had gained suffrage. One of the central questions in this discourse was whether women would or should form a particularly female voting bloc or align, as men did, with existing party affiliations. Did women, as such, bring specifically feminine issues and values to politics?[31] In a 1921 letter to Pennybacker, Katherine Ludington, a potential Chautauqua lecturer and president of the Connecticut League of Women Voters, summarized the debate over the role of women in politics: "There seem to be two quite different conceptions of woman's place in the electorate. One is that she simply comes in as a unit, without sex bringing in nothing very different from what men had contributed, but merely adding to the number of voters; the other is that women enter the electorate *as women* and have a special woman's contribution to make to our national life."[32] Although Ludington backed out of her Chautauqua engagement that year, her point, that women had policy goals and a political style that differed from that of men, was a common presupposition (and political strategy) for the time. "Women activists and political observers generally perceived male and female political styles as being at odds."[33] These differences in political style were commonly understood to result from women's different motivation for political participation. Women were believed to approach politics from a "disinterested, altruistic" perspective, as they supported causes related to home and family. Their "prime role would be to serves as a moral force, essentially outside the political structure, though not disassociated from it."[34] The question of women's nature and interests was central to arguments about the political goals and strategies for women at the time, particularly with respect to political parties. Because women were understood to be approaching politics from a moral position, the way they would approach political involvement was a matter of debate and concern. A central question was women's relationship to political parties. Some women advocated that women affiliate with political parties. However, women were concerned that the loyalty demanded by the parties might not be rewarded by attention to their own demands and moral imperatives. Others believed women would be better served if they formed their own political organizations or interest-oriented support groups separate from the political parties.[35]

Pennybacker, ever the southern lady, insisted that women not adopt masculine standards of political behavior, largely because it meant giving up women's claim to moral superiority and the persuasive force gained through this claim. Women who adopted competitive, "selfish" masculine standards, according to Pennybacker, risked giving powerful men the wrong impression. In a letter to Rose Young, another potential Chautauqua lecturer, she asserted the importance of women upholding feminine values:

> I have a dream of both of us speaking at Chautauqua on the necessity of women using ethical and absolutely courteous methods in public life. It makes me sick at heart when I think of the impression that some men are getting of woman's part in the political world. The most tragic thing about the people whom you saw, 'the getting all' ideals at the polls at Chicago, is that they are tearing down the good opinion that some men have held and they are poisoning the minds of thousands of other men. Perhaps if we could make a vigorous onslaught in season and out of season we might make some of these people think. I know we could put in the minds of the great masses who are so sane and so fine the necessity for our being gentle women and Christian women in all that we do.[36]

Though she decried women adopting coarse and un-Christian political tactics, Pennybacker's definition of the term "political" had changed from earlier decades when clubwomen assiduously avoided any possibility of their organizational behavior being given that label. Now, Pennybacker argued, political behavior was not only proper, but expected of women. "Won't you use the word 'political' and 'non-political' with more care?" she chided another woman, "In reality, politics is a science of government and every woman should feel her political responsibility."[37] Even as she embraced women's political action, however, Pennybacker distinguished this new definition of "political" from "partisan." Although she herself worked closely with the Democratic Party, in her work with women's organizations she encouraged a nonpartisan, issue-based approach. The debate over women's role highlighted the situation women found themselves in as they gained suffrage—traditional women's roles may have been confining, but women had found ways to exert cultural power through their gendered positions. To give up this power in order to assume the tactics exercised by males in politics could cost more than the women would gain.

By 1922, the two tasks Pennybacker had recommended for the citizenship departments of local clubs across the country in 1920 had expanded to four: (1) Make a survey of members voting at the last general election, reporting findings to the state chair, (2) Hold annually a citizenship school, (3) Have two members present whenever the Naturalization Court admits men and women of foreign birth to United States citizenship, and (4) Begin in January to make plans for celebrating July 4, 1923, as Citizenship Day. Pennybacker reminded women that Citizenship Day was "a permanent contribution that the General Federation is endeavoring to make to our national life" and that the day had received the endorsement of President Harding and of the American Legion.[38] As in earlier years, however, the seemingly simple agenda of the department continued to grow. In addition to these projects, Pennybacker was soon encouraging club leaders to stress the importance of each woman training herself for citizenship duties by forming intelligent opinions, inviting new citizens to American homes, cooperating with ex-servicemen seeking resources and aid, and fighting for better motion pictures.[39]

To determine the percentage of clubwomen voting, Pennybacker herself conducted a survey among federated clubs in the United States. Hundreds responded, with figures ranging from around 50 percent to 100 percent of club members voting.[40] What Pennybacker did with the information is unclear. However, the pressure to report back positive results or to explain poor ones likely encouraged club leaders to urge their women to go to the polls, both to increase the percentage voting and foster the club's public image. This sort of social pressure and competition were strategies Pennybacker had used successfully in the past. As a school principal she encouraged student attendance by pitting the various classes against each other in a competition. Also, as chair of the GFWC's endowment fund, her fundraising campaigns centrally featured reporting state rank with regard to funds raised.

Pennybacker's attempts to initiate citizenship training for women extended beyond the GFWC, as she reached out to form alliances with other organizations and institutions. In addition to encouraging citizenship training among local clubwomen, Pennybacker and the GFWC's Division of Citizenship Training worked with Columbia University faculty and Harcourt Brace and Company to produce a series of books on the political, social, and economic phases of U.S. government.[41] Federation leaders envisioned clubwomen using the books as educational resources in their citizenship training projects, and anticipated the first four volumes of the books being ready by the fall club season of 1921. Topics to be treated by the books included "How the People Rule"; "Newer Devices for Increasing the People's Control"; "Public Opinion and Political Parties"; "Political Institutions and Their Operation"; "Governments and Social Relations"; and" Government and Economic Relations."[42] These efforts were not the success Pennybacker hoped for. Publication of the books was delayed in the summer of 1921, and they were not available to clubwomen as expected.[43]

In another attempt to expand women's education for citizenship, Pennybacker wrote the presidents of all the colleges and universities in Texas to enquire what the institutions were doing to prepare female students for citizenship.[44] Among the questions she asked was what percentage of girls took courses in political science. Whether she was satisfied with the answers, generally, that women were given the same opportunities and requirements as male students to take courses in government and history, is unclear. In any case, Pennybacker focused most of her own energy on educating the mass of women not associated with institutions of higher education by using women's clubs as a forum for such training.

Mississippi's program of work, presented to Pennybacker in October 1922, was representative of the type of work undertaken by clubwomen at state and local levels: Mississippi clubwomen at the state level urged local clubs to study and provide education in the mechanics of voting, including paying the poll tax and registering, to both clubwomen and those not in clubs. Study of how the government functioned at various levels, including the federal, state, county, and city, was also emphasized, as was law enforcement. State-level clubwomen encouraged local clubs to study candidates, including their morals and ability, rather than party lines. Additionally, women were to study pending legislation regarding women and children as well as community laws. Work with public school systems was also on the agenda. Club women were to attempt to get citizenship training curriculum into high schools, place U.S. flags inside and outside of school buildings, offer patriotic pictures and books as prizes to students, and ensure that all students salute the flag and repeat the Pledge of Allegiance. Civic celebrations and work with other organizations were encouraged. Clubs and schools were to observe Constitution Week and Citizenship Day, and clubwomen were encouraged to work with the Hi-Y's, Girl Scouts, and YWCA to further common goals.[45] Despite the efforts of Pennybacker, the GFWC, and other organizations to educate women about exercising the right to vote, public perception was that women lacked interest in voting and failed to show up at the polls. From 1896 into the 1920s, voter turnout in general was in decline, possibly as a result of the dominance of the two major political parties in specific regions of the country, the Democratic Party in the South and Republicans in the North and West. Nancy F. Cott notes that the blame for the drop in turnout fell on "newly eligible women, although dependable data on actual voting behavior were very scarce." By 1924, magazines "bloomed" with assertions that women's suffrage was a failure, assertions countered by suffragists such as Jane Addams and Ida Tarbell who pointed out that women's participation had to be considered within a context of falling overall turnout and that such claims themselves provided a deterrent to women's voting.[46] The eagerness of researchers and the media to declare women indifferent to the vote likely provided some of the urgency to efforts to exhort women to exercise their hard-won citizenship.

CITIZENSHIP DAY—A JULY 4 CELEBRATION

A belief in the importance of celebrating citizenship informed Pennybacker's work in U.S. citizenship as well as that of clubs across the country. During her tenure as GFWC president and earlier, Pennybacker promoted her plans for a Fourth of July celebration that would celebrate citizenship in a dignified manner. In 1915 the plans were published in the *Ladies' Home Journal*. Posited as an alternative to raucous, militaristic celebrations of the Fourth (with fireworks and gunfire), Pennybacker's vision, which she had first written about in 1906, included a ritualized pageant honoring newly naturalized immigrants and U.S.-born youth who had reached voting age. Though she had proposed her ideal citizenship celebration years earlier, chairing the citizenship department allowed Pennybacker to take more direct action toward promoting Citizenship Day to communities across the country.

Originally Pennybacker's Citizenship Day plan was to honor young U.S.-born men who had reached voting age. Over the years she had expanded the concept to include young women and newly naturalized immigrants. However, the ceremonial tone of the affair changed little over the years. Under her leadership, the citizenship department printed plans for sample pageants and distributed them to clubs across the country. Pennybacker's original 1906 proposal for an Election Day celebration of citizenship suggested a day during which, "at an early hour, while the freshness of the summer morn is still felt, the town is astir making ready for a gladsome holiday. School buildings are opened, children come by hundreds laden with flowers. At the sound of martial music a great procession is formed; there are boys and girls, young maidens dressed in white and crowned with garlands. . . . The procession sweeps on until the temple of justice is reached."[47] That early plan proposed a celebration that was highly religious and ritualistic, the ritual serving to highlight the gravity of the moment. Pennybacker believed that "if we genuinely placed such importance upon the entrance into civic life, the day would come when the man on the eve of casting his first vote would feel as did the squire of old on the eve of knighthood; and if he spend that night in fasting and prayer, so much the better."[48] The Citizenship Day plans Pennybacker promoted in the 1920s echoed many of the themes of her earlier proposals. According to Pennybacker's later plans, the day should be dedicated to "a solemn, dignified, beautiful, inspiring welcome to our new citizens, both our native-born children, who during the last twelve months have passed their twenty-first birthday, and the men and women born overseas, who have renounced fealty to the land of their birth and sworn allegiance to the United States of America."[49] Pennybacker's ideas inspired her longtime GFWC colleague, Mrs. Albion Fellows Bacon, to develop a fully scripted Citizenship Day program that the GFWC citizenship department published and distributed upon request to clubs across the country during Pennybacker's term as department chair. The program continued the classical style of Pennybacker's original, adding a choral drama in which Columbia and other symbolic characters, including Liberty, Justice, Opportunity, and History, wore "the simple Grecian costume of white, hair in a soft Grecian knot," and sang their parts. The pageant also included historical tableaux with slides or living pictures of key events in the history of the United States—the landing of the Pilgrims, the signing of the Declaration of Independence, Betsy Ross making the first flag. At one point, American Legion members were to take the stage to participate and be recognized for their service. Then a "minister, magistrate, or other fitting person" was to lead a "responsive reading." The GFWC materials encouraged community leaders in charge of Citizenship Day to "make it a day of consecration to the old ideals of honor, patriotism and courage that have lived always in the pages of our history—a great Citizenship Day for all classes of Americans."[50]

Pennybacker's vision included Citizenship Day celebrations taking place in communities across the country, and she recognized that this required that the plan be widely publicized and promoted. She sought publicity for the plan from a variety of sources. In 1921 she gained some additional publicity for Citizenship Day from the National Education Association. After the organization misquoted Pennybacker in a published interview, she asked that it compensate for the error by publishing an article that she wrote promoting Citizenship Day. Pennybacker was pleased with the compromise, believing that the publication of her article brought wide publicity to the plans.[51] Pennybacker also promoted Citizenship Day by encouraging contests to recognize the communities that organized the best celebrations. In Texas, Pennybacker personally offered prize money for the community that sponsored the best celebration.[52] In 1922, a letter from President Harding provided additional validation and publicity for the idea. Harding wrote: "I am very pleasantly impressed with your program of celebrating the nation's natal day in the dignified, impressive and inspiring fashion which you suggest; making it an occasion on which to welcome to the duties and obligations of citizenship those young men and women who have come into citizenship within the preceding twelve months and to those of foreign birth who have come into full realization of duties and privileges of American citizenship."[53] The GFWC reprinted the letter in pamphlets outlining sample Citizenship Day pageants, and a *New York Times* article about the Citizenship Day movement included Harding's words as well. The *Times* article noted that the Citizenship Day movement, begun in 1921, had resulted in Citizenship Day observations in three hundred communities across the country that year. It also noted that every community was urged to conduct a pageant in 1922.[54] To further promote her ideas, Pennybacker approached the American Legion regarding the possibility of joint work involving Citizenship Day. She went so far as to join the women's auxiliary of the Legion, in part to gain cooperation between the two organizations on this and other issues in 1922, although she disagreed with the Legion's position on immigration.[55] Despite the extra publicity brought by these early efforts, however, a few years later Pennybacker wished for still more widespread publicity for her Citizenship Day idea. She wrote a friend in 1923 that she wished she could "get for my 4th of July Citizenship Day 1/100 of the publicity that I am receiving from the chairmen of the National Women's Committees of the Near East Relief."[56] No evidence indicates that she received much additional support.

In 1921, Pennybacker called for clubwomen to report back to the GFWC news about the types of celebrations that had been held in their communities. Clubwomen reported a wide scope of celebrations that had been undertaken, large-scale and small. Reports indicated that Pennybacker's efforts in having her vision enacted across the country had met with mixed success. At least one clubwoman organizing at a local level noted that immigrants were unsure as to the motives of organizers, but came around. The same correspondent reported that young people weren't necessarily eager to be paraded through town, but participated more frequently if they were in a group with friends. In 1922, based on these reports, Pennybacker determined that too much emphasis had been placed on honoring the naturalized citizen and not enough on the U.S.-born young people who had reached voting age, and she wrote clubwomen across the country urging them to rectify the problem by stressing the role of the native-born new citizen.[57] Reports from some clubwomen also indicated that the activities sponsored in some communities ran counter to Pennybacker's ideal of a dignified celebration. Pennybacker biographer Rebecca Richmond recounts that in at least one instance clubwomen reported hosting a celebration that involved "foot races by fat people, the conventional climbing of a greased pole," and, as a climax to the meeting, a crate of chickens that "would be taken aloft in a balloon and turned loose to flutter and squawk their way back to earth." Pennybacker is reported to have merely scrawled "Entirely too undignified," on the letter before mailing it back to the sender. In 1923 Pennybacker attempted to have the Chautauqua celebration filmed as a model. However, difficulties with the arrangements resulted in a less than successful film. Pennybacker's private secretary of the time believed that, with regard to Citizenship Day, she "never quite succeeded in putting her ideas across."[58]

DIVISION OF AMERICANIZATION

By 1920, the waves of immigration that the United States experienced in earlier decades had subsided somewhat, but the number of immigrants was still about four hundred thousand per year. In 1920, when Pennybacker became chair of the citizenship department, the General Federation recognized that millions of foreign-born individuals lived in the United States, thirteen million in 1920, nearly nine million of whom did not speak English.[59] These numbers convinced the federation that the country claimed as residents many immigrants from past years who had not yet been reached with clubwomen's "friendship and attention."[60] The context for this concern for the immigrant was the widespread, general cultural anxiety over the position of immigrants in the United States at the time. Such anxieties were expressed, for example, by the speakers at the Roosevelt memorials at the opening of the decade as discussed earlier in this chapter. The early twenties saw widespread concerns about the possibility of immigrants bringing anti-American, antidemocratic and anticapitalist sentiments. Congress "was ready to pass a restriction bill that capped immigration," targeting in particular immigrants from eastern and southern Europe.[61] GFWC leaders, like many Americans of the time, viewed immigrant populations as potentially destructive. However, the GFWC understood the threat to originate not in the immigrants but in the living conditions they faced upon arrival in the United States, and the organization's stance had been in alignment with that of John Dewey, as well as Jane Addams, Frances Kellor, Lillian Wald, Florence Kelley, and other settlement house workers. Addams, in particular, had been highly influential in the GFWC for years.[62] Clubwomen recognized that for many of these immigrants, life in the United States consisted of cramped apartments, unsanitary streets, and low pay and difficult working conditions in factories and sweatshops. Typically, progressive clubwomen eschewed socialism and any movement perceived as radical. Instead they understood their political mission "as creating social cohesion through responsible political actions" that maintained a capitalist system that "allowed for unequal class divisions but also permitted reforms protecting society from the worst hazards of unregulated capitalism."[63] In its pamphlet on its Americanization Program, the GFWC noted that in the immigrant's "isolation and ignorance and disappointment" there was a "fruitful nesting place for all the hurtful microbes that attack society."[64]

Clubwomen sought to integrate new immigrants into U.S. culture and to counteract the effects of "isolation and ignorance" through outreach programs, what they called "neighborhood Americanization."[65] Pennybacker and the federation promoted an agenda aimed at involving immigrants with the U.S.-born community, making them feel welcome, and showcasing "the American home." The ideal American home, according to GFWC literature, was run democratically, "with justice to all, and no special privileges to any." The home was filled with a "spirit of love" and of "human friendship," clothing and food were simple and wholesome, and the ambitions of the home were "worthy," not financial or social. Like the Citizenship Day celebration, this policy toward immigrants was a continuation of plans Pennybacker promoted during her GFWC presidency. Pennybacker and the federated clubwomen wanted to demonstrate neighborliness and to form personal connections. They also wanted to ensure that newcomers understood and adopted their ideals of what it meant to be American. "Liberty, love of humanity without distinction of race or creed, fair play and equal opportunities for all," were the explicit ideals, but historian Gayle Gullett notes that individualism and de-emphasis on ethnic group cooperation as well as disdain for poor living conditions were implicitly included in clubwomen's American ideals.[66] The emphasis on equality within the home reveals, as well, clubwomen's perceptions of the role of the male in presumably patriarchal immigrant households, and suggests both the importance to clubwomen of maintaining the new freedoms and equality they had achieved over the past decades as well as their perception of an immigrant threat to these gains.

While they targeted both male and female immigrants, the clubwomen argued that the woman immigrant's situation was potentially more isolating than that of the male immigrant, and thus the GFWC gave special attention to the needs of the female immigrant. Addressing the perceived needs of the female immigrant would also be the most effective means of spreading what they clubwoman understood as the values of American home life. "A woman may be content to continue living according the standards of her native country, or she may be anxious to learn the ways of her adopted country; she may be lonely and discouraged or humiliated by the necessity of having to depend upon her children for an interpretation of the new life," noted a citizenship department publication. "In any case," it continued, "she needs personal contact with American women and American homes if she is to catch the vision of American ideals and we need personal contact with her to develop the broad-mindedness that begets understanding."[67] In 1920, shortly after becoming chair of the GFWC department of citizenship, Pennybacker laid out her plans for a national strategy for clubwomen to Americanize immigrants. She requested that each club in the federation "undertake two concrete tasks" discussed earlier. The first was to have at least two clubwomen present every time the court conferred citizenship upon the foreign-born, the second to devote July 4 to celebrating the newly gained citizenship. This was not the only work the federation encouraged during Pennybacker's tenure. The passing of the Cable Act made women's citizenship less dependent on that of their husbands, and federation women recognized that immigrant women would be applying for citizenship on their own behalf rather than gaining it indirectly through their husbands as they did under the older laws based on coverture. They encouraged clubs to offer citizenship classes especially for immigrant women, attending to their needs with respect to scheduling and format.[68]

As chair of the citizenship department, Pennybacker set the tone and agenda for the GFWC's interaction with immigrants. To her credit, she was a scrupulous advocate of positive, respectful interactions with immigrants, at times in the face of the strongly expressed racism and anti-immigration sentiments of some clubwomen and allied organizations. In an era of immense national resentment and fear of immigrants, not all clubwomen across the country shared her tolerance. For example, Mrs. E. B. Page, chair of Americanization of the North Dakota Federation of Women's Clubs, openly expressed a vein of eugenics-based anti-immigrant sentiment that ran throughout the country at the time: "If we continue to allow this horde of undesirable aliens to enter our country, it will only be a few years until they inter-marry with our own people, thereby lowering the mentality, ideals and health of our own race permanently, for it is a scientific fact, universally known and accepted that the germ plasm upon which heredity rests is the most stable, persistent and permanent form of matter known."[69] Not surprisingly, Mrs. Page called on Pennybacker to support restrictions, if not a complete ban, on immigration. By contrast, Pennybacker, representing the federation, noted that the federation did not support a freeze on immigration. To counter the latent (and active) anti-immigrant and racist sentiments of clubwomen and others, she consistently urged clubwomen across the country to not just tolerate, but to appreciate, the cultural "gifts" the foreign-born brought with them. Newspaper accounts of a Pennybacker lecture in South Dakota indicate she argued that women in particular should honor cultural traditions. "Our aliens bring rich gifts," Pennybacker told her audience. "We turn them away with a hostile look and a cheap nickname for each nationality. We make them citizens with as little ceremony as if we were selling potatoes. We take away their pride of race, and when the pride of race dies, the man dies." Instead, Pennybacker argued, "All traditions should be clung to by women in particular, as it is through the women of the land that the beauty of the home becomes beauty of the state. If you are an American, or if you are of some other country, keep whatever you have, throw no memories away—accumulate."[70] Pennybacker promoted interaction with immigrants as a duty for clubwomen on par with other civic duties, such as voting. She promoted a course of study for clubwomen which included duty toward foreign-born people as well as economics, history, and government. Federation literature reminded clubwomen that they needed to respect, study, and celebrate the cultures of immigrants in their communities. Clubwomen were encouraged to learn as much as possible about immigrant groups and to arrange cultural days with exhibits of the food, crafts, and handiwork of various immigrant groups. Although historians would later see in these exhibits "Americanization rituals" by which American officials became gatekeepers accepting only "gifts" deemed suitable for American life, in context, Pennybacker's calls for welcoming immigrants can be understood as standing against waves of hostility from many parts of mainstream American culture.[71]

Pennybacker's international travels likely shaped some of her views of immigrants as well as her determined appreciation for other cultures. Despite widespread anti-German sentiments in the United States during the World War I and after, Pennybacker remembered Germans as a cultured, peaceful people. She took great pains to demonstrate the hospitality she promoted by extending courtesies to foreigners others may have ostracized, inviting a German delegation to sit with her at an International Council of Women meeting, for example. And although she joined the women's auxiliary of American Legion in order to foster joint work between that organization and the federated women's clubs, when asked by the Legion to help promote an anti-immigration essay contest, Pennybacker denied GFWC support, noting that "the resolutions adopted in [the GFWC] Convention assembly in no way agree with the position the American Legion has taken."[72]

COMMUNITY SERVICE DIVISION AND FRIENDLY CO-OPERATION WITH THE EX-SERVICE MAN

Of the citizenship department's three divisions, Citizenship Training, Americanization, and Community Service, the Community Service Division seems to have required the least of Pennybacker's attention, perhaps because the activities that fell within its domain were those with which clubwomen had several decades of experience. This division oversaw clubwomen's activities in civic housekeeping, and was an umbrella for such traditional clubwoman concerns as civic beautification and sanitation. Literature from this division encouraged clubwomen to research conditions in their own communities with regard to sanitation, beautification, holiday celebrations, community recreation and events, and the ethnic makeup of the population. The division focused on encouraging clubwomen to form alliances with individuals and groups within the community to effect desired changes. Clubwomen were advised to contact mayors, washwomen, teachers, churches, labor unions, men's organizations, women's organizations, foreign groups, old and young.[73] The Plant Another Tree movement, for example, was among the division's activities.

While many of the ideas and strategies of this division were not new to clubwomen, in the postwar years the Community Service Division did host a new committee, Friendly Co-operation with the Ex-Service Man, which, like the Community Service Division itself, was chaired by Mrs. George Plummer. The work clubwomen did to support the nation's war efforts in the latter years of the century's second decade transformed in the early 1920s, as clubwomen focused their efforts on assisting returning war veterans. The new committee required a plan of action, and Plummer communicated with Pennybacker about what this should be. Plummer proposed that the committee engage in "team work with the Red Cross or Legion in caring for our wounded men," "team work with other organizations or leadership in Armistice Day programs and other patriotic observances," and the establishment of hostess houses or employment centers. As with Americanization, clubwomen focused on the need for personalized care. The committee urged clubwomen to visit hospitals and help make connections between patients there and "someone back home," determining that the first service under this new branch of federation work would be to "let us see to it that not one Ex-Service Man is out of employment or in want of warm friendship."[74] The Military and Naval Insurance Act of 1917, shaped in part by Julia Lathrop of the Children's Bureau, provided compensation for servicemen affected by service-related injuries or disease, but clubwomen sought to provide still more support.[75] Psychologically impaired servicemen were of particular concern, and Plummer urged clubwomen to continue to advocate for the ex-servicemen in Washington, though again she stressed personal contact: "No government machinery can be made to adjust many of these cases; it needs a strong, patient, sympathetic friend."[76] Plummer wrote Pennybacker criticizing the care veterans received in some states and, in a GFWC bulletin, noted that many ex-servicemen could be cured with proper treatment, but often didn't get it. Plummer expressed concerns as well about vocational education provided to returning war veterans. In many cases, she argued, such training did not prepare the men for "remunerative positions."[77] For Pennybacker and many other clubwomen who had sons serve in the war, this was a personal as well as civic issue. Pennybacker attributed her son Percy's diabetes to the poor diet he received during his National Guard service, and his health was of constant concern to her in the postwar years.[78] She did her part to support legislation aiding the ex-servicemen.

In 1922 Pennybacker wrote her senators asking them to appropriate at least $90,000 for hostess houses included in an army appropriation bill, noting that the GFWC was "instrumental in establishing these hostess houses" and that "the army officials are now strong in their approval."[79] Beyond this, however, she seems to have been content to leave the work of the division in the competent hands of Mrs. Plummer.

COMMITTEE ON MOTION PICTURES

Pennybacker's confidence in the chair of the citizenship department's only other committee, the Committee on Motion Pictures, was not as sure as that she held for Mrs. Plummer of the Friendly Co-operation with Ex-Service Man committee. The Committee on Motion Pictures addressed clubwomen's concerns that the newly emerging film entertainment industry was promoting films with immoral messages and countering their attempts to reform society. The committee's aim was "to make motion pictures a vital factor in up building the nation's life."[80] Clubwomen were not alone in their concerns. As the film industry became big business in the second and third decades of the century, many of what historian John Chambers calls "custodians of culture"—including educators, clergy, writers, and publishers—were concerned by the content of films, and feared that graphic depictions of crime and sexuality would corrupt young people and subvert middle-class values. Localities across the country enacted licensing for theaters and formed censorship commissions which banned objectionable scenes.[81] As with so many issues the clubwomen addressed in the 1920s, the context for clubwomen's concerns included fears about social change and international tensions. In some cases, such concerns devolved into racist paranoia. For example, upset by the film *Foolish Wives* and its principle character, "a German of the vilest type," clubwoman Katherine Scott Finn of Michigan, whose two sons served overseas, wrote Pennybacker of her hatred for all things German and expressed fears that Germans were using film to undermine American morale, morals, and domestic ideals: "Such a picture causes divorces among young women who should be making homes contentedly and raising families if America is to live and not be overcome finally by the descendants of the rabble that is constantly being let loose in this country through immigration." Finn continued with an anti-Semitic harangue, "Our American women are feasting on the salacious, insidious, licentious pictures that a parcel of filthy-minded Jew producers are releasing . . . The Jews have no use for Christianity."[82] She called for the federation to support "a good strong law against beastly pictures" and argued that a strategy that involved working with exhibitors and filmmakers to improve the quality of films could not work because the Germans and Jews who ran the industry sought to destroy American society.[83]

Typically Pennybacker did not respond to such tirades directly. Like the Committee for Friendly Co-operation with the Ex-Service Man, the Committee on Motion Pictures was newly formed, and Pennybacker oversaw the committee chair's efforts to effect a plan of work. With Mrs. Woodallen Chapman as chair, the Committee on Motion Pictures shaped a moderate policy and addressed concerns about films in nonracial terms. Instead of working with lawmakers to promote censorship laws, the organization worked with film producers to encourage production of morally uplifting films consistent with the federation's views of proper behavior and social relations. The committee adopted a plan that emphasized promoting movies with educational or social value, and condemning immorality in film. Pennybacker understood that Mrs. Woodallen Chapman's role as committee chair would be to "wage an active campaign to bring about a closer and more sympathetic relation between woman's clubs and local picture producers" and to "issue monthly bulletins in which films that you could commend would be listed."[84] To Pennybacker's dismay, however, Woodallen Chapman did not put these plans into action. Instead, she sent out film recommendations from the Indiana Indorsers of Photoplays, and put her efforts into developing some sort of educational film, probably regarding suffrage. Frustrated, Pennybacker threatened to insert a card in the *General Federation News* retracting what she had said Woodallen Chapman would do.

With its millions of members, many of them prominent in their communities, the federation garnered the attention of the film industry, particularly in a time of growing censorship. Will Hays, president of the Motion Picture Producers and Distributors of America, an organization formed by the industry to monitor itself (and to ward off state attempts at censorship) spoke at the GFWC biennial in 1922. The title of his talk was "Upbuilding the Nation's Life through Motion Pictures."[85] Under pressure from progressive reformers, as well as conservatives, to create films that promoted middle-class values and censor those that did not, Hays argued that though people in the industry might desire high standards in film, "certain objectionable pictures" had met public demand and done well in terms of box-office receipts. Rather than advocate government censorship, the GFWC Committee on Motion Pictures sought to change public demand and demonstrate that pictures with uplifting messages could be commercially successful.[86] The committee took the position that women needed to educate themselves and the public about films. Clubwomen were encouraged to appoint members to view and report on films showing in their locales so that filmgoers could avoid films with negative messages: "Clubwomen have the opportunity to create and maintain a demand for the best type of picture, thus inspiring its production and exhibition in increasing numbers," Woodallen Chapman wrote.[87] Pennybacker herself declined to publicly criticize at least one film objected to by a clubwoman for its divisiveness. In 1923 fellow Texan Marie E. Finnegan wrote Pennybacker asking for action against *The Birth of a Nation,* a film she argued aroused "bitter feeling against the North and niggers."[88] Pennybacker suggested that Finnegan write the theater in which the film was shown, as well as producer Griffith's headquarters, to "frame a strong dignified protest." Pennybacker claimed that "this will have far more weight than for me to make a protest," but whether she believed she lacked power of position enough to influence the issue or whether she again sought to avoid the most inflammatory issues is unclear.[89]

Film producers, for their part, understood clubwomen to be a large constituency, and at least one attempted to produce and market films specifically geared toward women's organizations. The Pyramid Film Company proposed a national film weekly covering topics of interest to organized women throughout the country.[90] However, Woodallen Chapman opposed the plan in a letter to Pennybacker, on the grounds that it would not be feasible financially and would compromise the clubwomen's movement for improving motion pictures.[91] The GFWC does not seem to have formed an alliance with Pyramid. Although unconvinced of the feasibility of weekly films promoting club interests, clubwomen believed in the educational value of film and promoted film as an educational tool. The committee urged clubwomen to work at a local level to learn the attitudes of local school officials and to work with them to allow schools to "have the benefit of this form of visual instruction."[92] Woodallen Chapman also suggested the committee should find films appropriate for clubs wanting to put on special programs for children.[93] Pennybacker attempted to work with Hays to have a film on citizenship produced, and although Hays agreed to help find a producer, he didn't follow through.[94] Similarly, Pennybacker's attempt to have to have a Chautauqua Citizenship Day pageant filmed (as discussed earlier) led to disappointment when there were problems with production. The federation, at least during Pennybacker's tenure as chair of the citizenship department, failed to successfully utilize film technology to successfully promote its educational and civic causes.

Chapter Eight

A CITIZEN OF THE NATION AND THE WORLD

THE WORLD WAR had demonstrated to progressive women the importance of working not only at the local and national levels, but internationally as well. They understood the social issues they were addressing to be influenced by international events. This was certainly Pennybacker's perspective. During the 1920s and into the 1930s, the range of activities and organizations Pennybacker was associated with was incredibly broad. As a well-known public figure, she was sought after by many organizations, often less for the skills she could contribute than for the publicity and goodwill associated with her name. Although, as noted earlier, Pennybacker worked extensively with the General Federation during the 1920s and into the 1930s, she did not work exclusively with the GFWC. She also maintained affiliations with numerous other civic and politically related organizations. Pennybacker was, for example, an honorary member of the National Committee on American Japanese Relations. This organization, formed around 1921, worked against legislation that discriminated against the Japanese in the United States. A letter Pennybacker received as a member of the organization noted its success in convincing the courts to rectify "the injustices that had been imposed on the Japanese by the Legislature: and thereby justify the many declarations of confidence in America's sense of justice and humanity made by leading Japanese."[1] While Pennybacker does not appear to have been an active member of the organization, her honorary membership lent her name and prestige to the cause and made a clear statement as to her position regarding the treatment of immigrants of various races in America. She served as well on the board of the National Mayflower Councils, an organization dedicated to planning "the celebration of the Pilgrim Tercentenary" and the committee of National Physical

Education Service of the Playground and Recreation Association of America, an organization promoting universal physical education for male and female students.[2] Pennybacker was also a member of the National Committee of 100 for Enforcement of Law and Obedience to the Constitution. Pennybacker spoke at one or more of the organization's public meetings of women to discuss the organization's work, though the extent of her connection with this organization, likely prohibition-related, is unclear.[3] In 1921 she joined the American Academy of Political and Social Sciences upon invitation by the president of that organization.[4] She remained, as well, a member of the League for Peace as discussed in the previous chapter.

Pennybacker also remained a visible public figure in Texas during these years, despite spending so much of her time out of the state. In Austin she served as chair of the Church Service League of the Episcopal Church.[5] The league "co-ordinated church services in the parishes to meet parish, community, diocesan and national needs."[6] Her work put her in close contact with Bishop Quentin Quin and his wife. In 1920 she spoke at her alma mater, Sam Houston Normal Institute at the graduation ceremonies celebrating the fortieth anniversary of the school. The invitation to do so made Pennybacker the first woman to speak at commencement in the forty years of the school's existence.[7] She repeated this honor in 1926, after corresponding with members of a student organization named in her honor, the Pennybacker Club.[8]

Pennybacker also worked within the Texas Federation of Women's Clubs during this period and promoted the interests of Texas women within the General Federation. In addition to serving as president of the Chautauqua Women's Club in New York, she held the presidency of Austin's American History Club for a time and was a member of the Austin Open Forum.[9] In 1922 she worked behind the scenes to influence the election of Texas's Florence Floore, a TFWC president, to an executive position within the GFWC.[10] Although Floore was not elected to the position Pennybacker desired for her, she was elected treasurer, a position Pennybacker herself had held years earlier. Despite the fact that the women regarded the position as a difficult one, it could still be a steppingstone to higher office, an objective that Pennybacker held for Floore.[11] Floore, in turn, used what political power the Texas federation had to support Pennybacker's candidacy for regent of the University of Texas.[12] In a letter to Governor Hobby, Floore noted that at the 1917 Annual Convention in Waco, the Texas Federation of Women's Clubs determined to "use its best efforts to have women placed on the boards of all schools supported wholly or partially by the state."[13] Texas clubwomen also suggested that the governor appoint Pennybacker to the board of directors of the North Texas State Normal School in Denton.[14] Although neither of these efforts was successful, in 1921 new governor Pat Neff appointed Pennybacker to a committee to survey higher education in Texas. In addition to promoting Pennybacker as a candidate for a state appointment, some clubwomen suggested her "for high office in the state of Texas." Pennybacker declined to run for office, stating that she "had no political ambitions."[15] Instead she chose to focus on her civic mission: "There is no elective office within the gift of the people for which I would be a candidate. If God had given me a mission I believe that mission consists in preaching the gospel of civic righteousness as it is revealed to me."[16] Despite her lack of interest in holding political office, Pennybacker continued to be active in the politics of Texas. She wrote legislators advocating the establishment of a new women's prison administered by an all-female board and to support moving the girls' training school to the site then occupied by the Gainesville prison.[17] She also supported the Smith-Fess Act, which created federally funded programs for disabled people and advocated strenuously in Texas for the Sheppard-Towner Maternity and Infancy Act, which provided federal funds for infant and maternal care.[18] The act, considered one of few legislative success stories for the women's movement in the 1920s, became law in 1921. The act created programs for "prenatal and child health clinics, information on nutrition and hygiene, midwife training, and visiting nurses for pregnant women and new mothers," and was administered by the federal Children's Bureau, still headed by Julia Lathrop, whom Pennybacker had struggled to keep in her position during the second decade of the century.[19]

The Sheppard-Towner Bill was a key issue for progressive women, and the struggle to get the bill adopted as law was particularly contentious. Opponents, including many former anti-suffragists, decried it as socialistic, and women's support for the bill quickly became fodder in attacks by right-wing red-baiters.[20] Carrie Chapman Catt and the National League of Women Voters advocated vigorously for the bill, but in the process offended many of the more conservative clubwomen Pennybacker was attempting to reach through more measured argument. Catt created considerable consternation among clubwomen when her articles sharply criticizing Republican Party loyalists who had acted against the Sheppard-Towner bill appeared in the *Woman Citizen*.[21] Like many clubwomen, Pennybacker was upset by Catt's actions and believed that her harsh criticism of the Republican women was counterproductive. Still, she remained supportive of Catt. Despite some protest by other clubwomen, Pennybacker invited Catt to speak on behalf of the citizenship department at the GFWC 1922 Biennial.[22]

AN INTERNATIONAL PERSPECTIVE

Although Pennybacker worked extensively on citizenship issues within the United States during the 1920s, this period also saw her broaden her focus from national to international work. With the World War over, Pennybacker joined in war relief efforts. The most visible of these was the Near East Relief Fund, organized to provide support for war orphans in Greece. Pennybacker served as chair of the Women's Near East Committee in the early 1920s, gaining national publicity she sought for her Citizenship Day efforts.[23] In this position she primarily worked with publicity efforts. The Near East Relief raised money through donations from individuals and through various fundraisers, including tin cup dinners, and "Golden Rule Sundays." The tin cup dinners were benefit dinners at which donors met and ate typical orphanage meals using orphanage-style tin dinnerware. Golden Rule Sundays were a more widespread and private effort in which families were encouraged to eat a simple Sunday dinner, again something comparable to what would be served in the orphanages of the Near East, rather than a typical American Sunday dinner. The savings were then donated to the Relief Fund.[24] In her role with the Near East Relief Fund, Pennybacker worked with the leaders of national women's organizations helping to coordinate the fundraising and publicity efforts.[25] Pennybacker's articles urging women to contribute to the Relief Fund were widely published in popular women's magazines, including the *Ladies Home Journal, Vogue, Good Housekeeping,* the *Delineator* and other Buttrick publications, *Our World,* and *Review of Reviews.* In addition, editorial material in the name of the women's committee was sent to 240 editors of select daily papers, and her illustrated story, a three-column article entitled "Seeks Fairy Godmothers for Near East Orphans" was carried in one thousand newspapers.[26] Pennybacker became one of the first women appointed to the Near East Relief Fund board of directors after leaders of the women's committee petitioned the national committee to appoint female members to this board.[27] Pennybacker, Miss Mary E. Woolley, and another GFWC past president, Mrs. Philip N. Moore, were elected the first female members of the corporation and trustees of the Near East Relief Fund in 1923.[28] Carrie Chapman Catt was also suggested for chair of the main board of directors, but did not serve in that capacity.[29] Catt did serve as chair of the Women's Emergency Committee of the Near East Relief

Fund.[30] In addition to the joint work on the Near East Relief Fund, Pennybacker cooperated with Catt on other war reconstruction efforts. Both supported efforts to restore the Catholic University of Louvain in Belgium, which had been destroyed in the war, and they served together on the women's committee of the National Committee of the United States for the Restoration of the University of the Louvain. For a time, Pennybacker served as chair of this committee.[31]

Pennybacker also continued her work with Catt and the Leslie Commission into the 1920s. Though the nation's women had been granted suffrage with the passing of the Nineteenth Amendment, the commission prepared for possible legal or political challenges to the new law. In addition, it continued to fund the *Woman Citizen,* despite constant concerns over the amount of money needed to do so. With the domestic suffrage battle for the most part over, the commission turned its focus internationally, and Catt and the board helped fund suffrage efforts in other countries. Pennybacker urged Catt to support work toward suffrage for women in Switzerland, a country to which she traveled frequently during the 1920s. Pennybacker believed that U.S. women could help the efforts of Swiss women in conjunction with their support for the League of Nations. She believed the league could be used to influence public opinion in favor of women's suffrage in Switzerland as well as other countries: "More than once in Geneva, the thought came to me that the whole cause of suffrage might be helped if some of our best trained women went over, during various sessions of the Assembly and the Council of the League of Nations, and watched proceedings, bearing in mind the best ways and means of getting the League to assist in the backward countries. I am using the term *backward* as applying to suffrage. Some may say the League has no authority in such matters but you and I know that public opinion is an irresistible power and public opinion has been created in more than one country by the work of the League."[32] The Leslie Commission contributed funds to suffrage efforts in countries as widespread as Switzerland, Japan, Hungary, France, and India, as well as to the International Woman's Suffrage Alliance. Additionally, the commission compiled and distributed information on the history of the suffrage movement in the United States. Pennybacker remained on the board until the Leslie Commission disbanded in 1929.[33]

Pennybacker continued her work in the broader women's movement into the 1920s, but challenges to the movement and her moderate stances and concern for public image limited her involvement in significant ways. One of the greatest challenges faced by progressive women in the 1920s was forwarding the cause of international peace. Progressive women's organizations in the twenties viewed modern war as a threat to the social programs and domestic policies they sought to advance. These women argued that women, having been historically excluded from "nation states' war making councils," could devise more objective, innovative measures for maintaining peace and settling disputes among nations. The late teens and early twenties saw the advent of a widespread women's peace movement, spurred both by the war (and its end) and women's hope of using their newly won suffrage to advance their agendas. In 1921 the National Women's Party (NWP) mobilized existing women's groups to form the Women's Committee for World Disarmament, which organized mass meetings on the topic of peace in sixteen states, declared Easter Sunday in 1921 to be "Disarmament Day," and planned a disarmament week for May 1921. The same year, in a move perceived to be strongly influenced by female opinion on the issue of peace, President Warren Harding called the Washington Disarmament Conference. Although no women were selected as delegates to this conference, four prominent clubwomen, including the GFWC's Mrs. Winter, served on the advisory board. The peace movement's successes provoked swift backlash, however, as conservative, pro-military individuals and organizations reacted to the publicity generated by the peace movement and efforts by the House Naval Affairs Committee to cut naval personal by nearly half. Big navy advocates, including chambers of commerce, the American Legion, and the International Association of Machinists, whose members' employment depended on military appropriations, fought back with their own publicity campaign. The pro-navy groups created a national Navy Day in October 1922, while other pro-military groups attacked the women's peace movement directly. John D. Weeks, Harding's secretary of war, sponsored conservative, anti-suffrage speakers who derided "silly pacifists" caught up in "the enthusiasm of newly conferred suffrage."[34] Weeks was a former senator from Massachusetts who had lost his bid for reelection in part due to the Massachusetts Woman Suffrage Association, at the time led by Lucia Ames Mead, a prominent peace activist and leader in the Women's International League for Peace and Freedom (WILPF). WILPF faced especially harsh and inaccurate criticism by military advocates. Amos A. Fries of the Chemical Warfare Service incorrectly accused WILPF of requiring an oath of wartime noncooperation. Fries also attacked the National Council for the Prevention of War in 1922, issuing the gendered warning that "Uncle Sam will wake up one morning to discover that long-haired men and short haired women have enthroned themselves in the place where patriotic intelligence once prevailed."[35] The organization, Fries argued, promoted communism. In 1923 and 1924, the infamous Spider Web Chart, created by Fries's Chemical Warfare Service circulated among the American Defense Society and J. Edgar Hoover's Federal Bureau of Investigation. The chart tied the "Socialist-Pacifist movement in America" to international socialism and named "all the major and less than major women's organizations" with ties to the peace movement, including the GFWC, Women's Joint Congressional Committee, the League of Women Voters, and the National Council of Women (NCW). The chart also identified twenty-nine individuals, including longtime Pennybacker colleagues Zona Gale, Lucia Ames Mead and Maude Wood Park.[36] Although the chart was ordered destroyed by Weeks, the accusations lingered and resurfaced over the next years. In 1924 the American Defense Society's R. M. Whitney, who worked closely with the FBI, published a book, *Reds in America,* which included a chapter on the use of women's organizations to spread communist ideologies. Whitney mentioned Carrie Chapman Catt, the NLWV and WILPF specifically.[37]

The negative publicity hurt women's peace organizations. In December 1922 the two largest constituent organizations of the National Council for the Prevention of War—the National Congress of Parents and Teachers and the GFWC—withdrew their affiliations. By 1922 and 1923, women peace activists, including some clubwomen, rued the inroads militarists were making in the GFWC.[38] The National Council of Women, an organization with which Pennybacker was involved, also was rent by the internal rifts and external pressures. A longstanding coalition of existing women's organizations, including the Daughters of the American Revolution (DAR), the GFWC, and "almost every other women's organization," the National Council was a branch of the larger International Council of Women (ICW) which dated back to the late 1880s. The National Council had supported suffrage, the League of Nations, and the World Court, as well as numerous progressive causes.[39] Although considered conservative (a necessity due to the wide range of constituent groups), the national and international councils were attacked particularly for their peace work. In the midst of this turmoil, Pennybacker served as the chair of the citizenship committee of the National Council of Women in the mid-1920s.[40] In 1925 she reported the work of her committee to the organization, noting that "all organizations represented in the Council of Women of the United States of America have concentrated their efforts on impressing upon women the necessity of forming an intelligent, individual opinion as to public matters. . . . of attending precinct meetings and primaries thus helping to establish policies and to secure desirable candidates. . . . of casting an intelligent, conscientious vote."[41] She understood the tasks of the committee to be educational and noted that they were being carried out "by means of schools of citizenship, institutes for training in citizenship, and other forms of organized effort."[42]

In her position as chair of the citizenship department of the National Council of Women, Pennybacker was included in attacks against progressive women. Pennybacker was pressured by outside interests to purge the organization of women with possible communist leanings. In 1924 Harland Lund of the Institute of Government wrote Pennybacker that "the Attorney-General of the United States in his annual report states that there are 427 propaganda organizations in our country spending millions monthly to mislead our people." Lund continued, noting that "several patriotic organizations" had affirmed "that the churches and women's organizations are the special prey of these propagandists" and were "assisting Socialism to bring about their 'Bloodless Revolution' in the name of Pacifism and Child Welfare."[43] Lund demanded that Pennybacker introduce a resolution that the National Council of Women appoint a committee to investigate the subject of communist propaganda within the organization. Pennybacker resisted such demands and did not introduce this resolution. However, the social and political climate led her to warn other women activists to take measures to avoid accusations that they were unpatriotic, communist dupes. For example, in May 1925, Pennybacker urged Madame Clara Guthrie d'Arcis of the World Union of Women for International Concord to revise her organization's print materials, which promoted an international perspective, in order to "see to it that no person may feel that in any way you are even indirectly pledging that every one of us should not love his own country."[44] Pennybacker was alarmed by a specific line in d'Arcis' materials that read "We must be true patriots in the deepest interpretation of the word—not Nationalists." Seeing the potential for this remark to be misconstrued, Pennybacker warned d'Arcis that by urging women not to be nationalists, d'Arcis may "have given a loophole to those who which to make trouble," and she urged her to alter the statement: "Would not your gospel be more clearly pledged if you perhaps omitted those two words and had the last sentence to read something like this: We must remember that true patriotism teaches love for ones own country but also love for other countries." "The highest patriotism," she continued, "teaches love for ones own country but also love for other countries: the highest patriotism is both nationally and internationally minded: The the [*sic*] humanity of all patriotism is making the land of our birth lovable and beloved above all others."[45]

In 1924 Pennybacker was appointed a National Council of Women delegate to a meeting of the International Congress of Women which was to take place in the United States in May 1925. The months prior to this meeting were full of turmoil for the international organization as its constituent organizations feuded among themselves. At the insistence of the DAR and other super-patriotic women's organizations, WILPF withdrew from the council. The leadership of the DAR also insisted that no "radical" or "pacifist" addresses be allowed. NCW leadership capitulated, excluding "all radical approaches to ending war."[46] At this meeting Pennybacker presided over the international council's Pan-American evening. Despite the council's rejection of WILPF, Carrie Chapman Catt was her most prominent speaker. Neither the antiwar nor the ultra-patriotic women were satisfied with the meeting: the ultra-patriots saw "the pacifist menace everywhere," while the peace activists saw their views stifled, particularly when NCW leaders destroyed antiwar pamphlets published by members of the Women's Peace Society and the Women's Peace Union. Racial antagonisms surfaced as well when black members walked out in protest of segregated seating arrangements. Despite the rifts among the U.S. council's member organizations, the ICW successfully passed moderate resolutions calling for member organizations to work toward bringing all nations into the League of Nations and World Court, and endorsed gradual multilateral disarmament without U.S. support.[47] Nevertheless, the meeting received negative press reports, for which Pennybacker chastised the press, indicating that she believed adversaries to be behind the stories. "Propaganda was at work on both sides of the ocean against it, which is only another proof of how foes work day and night under cover," she wrote. "No one could sith [*sic*] through the programs, see the delegates from forty different countries conferring on vital topics, without realizing that this was a great opportunity for international understanding."[48] Around this time, prominent NCW members suggested to Pennybacker that she take the presidency of the U.S. National Council of Women. They hoped that she could provide much-needed leadership and stability to the badly divided organization.[49] Perhaps recognizing the difficulties the position would entail, Pennybacker declined. "It would be neither wise nor profitable for me to consider the presidency," she wrote council leaders in 1926.[50] Later that year Pennybacker was involved with planning for a meeting of the National Council of Women. The planning process demonstrated changing views on race. A colleague wrote Pennybacker that Mary McCloud Bethune ("president of the Colored Women") and Mary Terrell refused to accept racially segregated hotels or social functions. In sharp contrast to the Ruffin incident two decades earlier, and perhaps in response to the walkout in 1925, white clubwomen not only admitted African American women to the organization, they acknowledged their concerns. Southern locations were excluded and the women considered going to Detroit.[51]

Despite being involved with a wide range of nationally and internationally oriented activities during the 1920s and 1930s, Pennybacker focused a considerable amount of effort on just two causes: supporting the League of Nations and World Court, and continuing the Chautauqua Women's Club. Pennybacker's interest in the proposed League of Nations began during her GFWC presidency when, in response to the war in Europe, she determined that the establishment and maintenance of peace should be an issue of concern and concerted study by clubwomen. As noted earlier, in the latter years of the second decade of the century she joined the League to Enforce Peace, an organization that supported the formation of a World Court and League of Nations, but also supported U.S. efforts in the World War. During this period Pennybacker advocated within the Democratic Party for U.S. participation in the League of Nations, arguing in 1920 that the peace was an important moral issue and one that the party should endorse for both moral and political reasons. Although she herself worked within the Democratic Party to garner support for the league, she also vigorously promoted the League of Nations as a nonpartisan issue. In 1922 she added her name to a list of 112 sponsors of the League of Nations Non-Partisan Association.[52] Taking a nonpartisan stance, she spoke and wrote in favor of the League of Nations throughout the decade. In an interview published by the *International Interpreter* in 1924, she argued that international responsibility should be a nonpartisan issue.[53] The same year she presented the same message to the GFWC, submitting a resolution in support of an International Court of Justice. The federation adopted the resolution unanimously after hearing her speak.[54] In January 1925 Pennybacker attended the Conference on the Cause and Cure of War, a seven-day session organized by leaders of nine women's organizations, including the GFWC. She had been involved in organizing the conference, along with Carrie Chapman Catt and Mrs. Thomas Winter.[55] In particular, Pennybacker helped to raise funds to support the gathering.[56] In August 1925, despite being ill, she made the first of several trips to Geneva where she spent five weeks attending the Council and Assembly of the League of Nations.[57] She traveled there as a special correspondent for the *Dallas Morning News, Galveston News,* and the *Woman Citizen.*[58] Upon returning home, she lectured widely throughout the country on the topic titled “What I Heard, What I Saw, What I Felt, at Geneva.”[59] She returned to Geneva repeatedly in the following years, in all attending five annual meetings of the League of Nations. After each trip, she returned to the United States to advocate public support for the organization.[60]

Although she worked with numerous organizations on the issue of world peace, Pennybacker declined to join WILPF, even though the organization, founded in 1915, claimed her colleagues Jane Addams and Carrie Chapman Catt among its founding members. As noted above, WILPF members were among those most vilified by red-baiters in the United States, and many found their names on the Spider Web Chart. When asked to join in 1921, Pennybacker declined, explaining that she did “not know enough about the plans and the real accomplishments of the International League for Peace and Freedom, to give the unqualified endorsement that you desire.”[61] Likely, she felt more comfortable with organizations that took a more conservative approach to peace.

SAVING CHAUTAUQUA

In addition to her work advocating for the League of Nations, Pennybacker continued in her position as president of the Chautauqua Women's Club throughout the last decades of her life. During the 1920s and 1930s she used her position there to speak to women about issues of importance to her. She placed special emphasis on the World Court and League of Nations. During this time, Pennybacker befriended Eleanor Roosevelt, wife of Franklin D. Roosevelt, with whom she corresponded regularly into the 1930s. Roosevelt and Pennybacker shared interests in many progressive causes as well as an allegiance to the Democratic Party and to the Chautauqua Institute, and Eleanor Roosevelt viewed Pennybacker, twenty-three years her senior, as a mentor.[62] Pennybacker's relationship with Eleanor Roosevelt provided the Roosevelts with important contacts, connections, and information needed for Franklin's political career. At the same time, Pennybacker used the Roosevelts' support to advance her work in support of both Chautauqua and the World Court and League of Nations. Eleanor Roosevelt spoke at Chautauqua frequently during the 1920s and 1930s, often in response to invitations (and pleas) by Pennybacker. In 1927, for example, when Franklin Roosevelt could not appear, Eleanor agreed to speak, on a topic titled “The Civic Responsibilities of Women.”[63] In 1928 Eleanor assisted Pennybacker in identifying appropriate speakers for Chautauqua. She also agreed to appear on the program, but had to cancel when her children's nanny left for a new position.[64] In January 1929, with Franklin Roosevelt the newly elected governor of New York, Eleanor invited the members of the Chautauqua Women's Club to a luncheon at the governor's mansion.[65] That summer both she and Franklin appeared on the Chautauqua program.[66]

The Depression hit both Pennybacker and Chautauqua hard. Pennybacker had to foreclose on several farm properties for which she had served as mortgagor. In addition, she was increasingly asked to reduce her speaking fees as the organizations for which she spoke faced their own financial problems.[67] Chautauqua, too, struggled, and Pennybacker again invited Eleanor Roosevelt, repeating pleas that Roosevelt speak despite initial refusals.[68] Roosevelt finally agreed to speak, on a topic titled "Some Dangers that Threaten the American Home Today."[69] In 1931 Pennybacker arranged for Eleanor Roosevelt to visit Texas to deliver a lecture at Pennybacker's alma mater, Sam Houston State Teacher's College (formerly Sam Houston Normal Institute).[70] The same year Eleanor again invited the women of Chautauqua to visit her, this time at a reception in her home in New York.[71] At that time the Roosevelts were planning Franklin's run for the presidency, and Pennybacker reported to Eleanor on public sentiment across the United States. In one letter to Eleanor, Pennybacker reported that Texas's Tom Connelly supported Franklin for president, and gave Eleanor the names of several prominent female Roosevelt supporters. In addition, she thanked Eleanor for securing her a "fortunate seat for the great Democratic dinner in New York."[72]

In 1932, as Franklin's campaign accelerated, Pennybacker continued to provide support from the field, sending Eleanor the names of women on the Democratic National Committee who were Roosevelt supporters.[73] Pennybacker also sought to advise the Roosevelts on Franklin's stance toward the World Court and League of Nations. In the spring of 1932 she reported to Eleanor her success in having several major Texas newspapers and roughly eighty smaller ones editorialize on or otherwise publicize attempts to have the United States join the World Court. Pennybacker also critiqued Franklin's decision to question the effectiveness of the League of Nations in the middle of the campaign to have the United States enter the World Court. She requested that Eleanor convince Franklin to cease his criticism of the League of Nations and to speak in favor of the World Court.[74]

At Pennybacker's request, Eleanor Roosevelt again appeared at Chautauqua in 1932, lecturing on the role that big business had played in the economic depression.[75] Her talk stressed the "The Spiritual Values of the Depression," as it was titled, and she advocated that Americans care for their neighbors in times of need.[76] The next year Pennybacker again pled for Eleanor's support, as the financial situation at Chautauqua had become "critical."[77] Roosevelt spoke that year on the role of women in history, arguing that women had provided the impetus for most of human progress.[78] In 1934, with Chautauqua in receivership, Pennybacker reported to Eleanor that the Women's Club had seen an increase in membership from 1,334 the previous year to 1,650. "I realize fully how much of this increased membership we owe to you, dear friend," Pennybacker wrote to Roosevelt.[79] Eleanor's support for Pennybacker and Chautauqua continued as the Depression dragged on. That year Eleanor had again entertained the members of the Chautauqua Women's Club, this time at a White House luncheon.[80] In 1935, with the Depression still crippling Chautauqua financially, Pennybacker helped to keep the organization afloat by arranging with Eleanor to have Franklin Roosevelt speak there in 1936.[81] The same year Pennybacker made plans for Eleanor Roosevelt to speak at Sam Houston State Teacher's College and the University of Texas.[82] Pennybacker, at this time in her seventies, had the honor of introducing her at both events.

"A BIG PLACE FOR HERSELF IN THE HEARTS OF SO MANY WOMEN"

Although the 1930s brought considerable hardship to the nation and posed continued challenges to Pennybacker personally, the last decade of her life also brought her recognition and honor. In March of 1930, for example, she was invited as an honorary guest to a celebration of the tenth anniversary of the League of Women Voters in Louisville, Kentucky. Although she was able to attend some sessions of this celebration, her busy lecture schedule prevented her from attending the entire session.[83] In 1932 she attended a party celebrating Carrie Chapman Catt's seventy-third birthday. Catt had learned of the surprise party in advance and revealed to the press the names of two of the guests. One of these was her "old friend" Anna Pennybacker; the other was Ruth Morgan, vice-chair of the Cause and Cure of War Committee.[84] The year prior, in Austin, Texas, friends gathered for a large celebration of Pennybacker's own seventieth birthday. So many attended that they exhausted the capacity of the Austin Country Club. In addition to the many who attended, prominent friends and colleagues sent acknowledgments from around the world: Eleanor Roosevelt sent a tribute that called Pennybacker "the greatest inspiration to all young women because of her indomitable courage and energy."[85] Roosevelt noted Pennybacker's many accomplishments and asserted that she "made such a big place for herself in the hearts of so many women, that no one can know her without feeling she has contributed something to the cause of all women throughout the world."[86] Lord and Lady Aberdeen, with whom Pennybacker worked on international peace efforts, sent their congratulations from Scotland. Clubwomen from across the state and the nation sent messages as well, including Texas's Florence Floore, Mrs. Henry B. Fall, and TFWC president Mrs. R. F. Lindsay. Past GFWC presidents Alice Ames Winter and Mary E. Sherman also sent words of appreciation.

By this time in her life Pennybacker was considered one of Texas's "first citizens."[87] Those who spoke or wrote in Pennybacker's honor at her birthday celebration emphasized her dynamic personality, her public service, and especially her role in creating a role for women in the public sphere. Fellow educator R. E. Vinson wrote: "Mrs. Pennybacker has been the type of woman in her generation, whose force of character, ability to see and meet the problems of her day, have convinced the world that woman has a constructive part to play in public affairs."[88] Similarly, Mrs. Thomas Winter noted, "Mrs. Pennybacker has served to raise the level of American womanhood to her own standards of wise public service."[89] Pennybacker herself addressed the friends and colleagues assembled at the celebration requesting that they "ask for me that my 70th year may be the best of my life, that I may be able to accomplish some lasting good, something worthy of all this."[90] Pennybacker would, in fact, continue to support the causes in which she believed over the next years. She remained able to address an assembly, as she did, for example, in 1935 at the annual dinner for the TFWC.[91] Similarly, in 1936 she presented a speech of welcome to Eleanor Roosevelt when she visited Sam Houston State Teacher's College. Pennybacker also continued to serve as the president of the Chautauqua Women's Club, a position she held until her death.

On February 4, 1938, Pennybacker died in her Austin home after a long illness.[92] The recognition bestowed upon her at her birthday celebration several years earlier was repeated. Pennybacker was remembered widely in Texas and among clubwomen in particular. Her death was announced in other parts of the nation as well. The *New York Times,* for example, ran a short article announcing her passing.[93] At a tribute to her life and accomplishments held at the Chautauqua Institute, her close friend Chautauqua president Arthur Bestor remembered her inner vitality. "Real personalities so live that the institutions with which they have been identified are able to go on with enthusiasm and effectiveness," Bestor asserted. "Mrs. Pennybacker lived a full, rich and influential life and every one of the organizations to which she gave herself goes on with vitality and enthusiasm as if she were still living."[94] Pennybacker did not live to see the demise of the League of Nations, and she would have been sorely disappointed at the onset of yet another world war. Nevertheless, despite these setbacks, nearly seventy years after her death many of the institutions which she supported throughout her lifetime continue: the public schools of Bryan and Tyler, Texas; Texas Women's University, the Texas Federation of Women's Clubs and the General Federation of Women's Clubs; the League of Women Voters; and the Chautauqua Institute are but a few examples.

As she had throughout her life, Pennybacker spent the 1920s and 1930s promoting causes in which she believed strongly. Her focus during these years was on citizenship, and her conception of that term included not just one's duty to one's own country but one's duty to the world. She worked tirelessly on behalf of many causes and organizations related to citizenship during these decades. As she had most of her life, she avoided extreme positions and consistently took a moderate approach, supporting, for example, the League for Peace and the United Nations Non-Partisan Association, but avoiding connection with organizations perceived as more radical, such as the Women's International League for Peace and Freedom. Pennybacker remained a reformer, not a revolutionary. This stance complemented her belief in the power of public opinion. She believed that educating public opinion was the key to effecting change, particularly in a democracy. She protected her reputation as a moderate in part to ensure that she would retain her power to deliver a message to her audience. She recognized that if she were vilified as an extremist by more conservative thinkers and activists, her ability to convey her message would be affected. Through her speeches and articles as well as the educational activities she organized through women's clubs and Chautauqua, Pennybacker attempted to persuade the American public, particularly American women, in favor of the progressive causes she supported.

EPILOGUE

"THE BIOGRAPHICAL PROJECT IS AN ILLUSION," writes Norman Denzin, "for any coherence that a life has is imposed by the larger culture, by the researcher, and by the subject's belief that his or her life should have coherence.[1] In this view, biography is at best a fiction and at worst a delusion, an exercise based on a misguided belief that the discrete events that make up a life possess an inherent meaning and coherence. Still, a consideration of the way individuals and the larger culture find coherence and meaning is a worthy undertaking. Anna Pennybacker had her own ways of making meaning of her work and her life in thoughtful and conscious ways. In particular, Pennybacker understood her work to cohere around particular concepts and roles. Most prominent among these was her conception of citizenship. Pennybacker's ideals of citizenship shaped the roles she chose for herself. She understood herself to have held three occupations: teaching, lecturing, and organizing.[2] In all of these she worked to embody her ideals of citizenship. Her ideas, however, weren't hers alone. Her individual ideals, her actions, and her ability to be efficacious were rooted in the broader cultural movements of her times. Biography, Barbara Finkelstein tells us, enables us to "explore intersections between human agency and social structure."[3] Anna Pennybacker was both a product of her times and an active organizer and creator of them.

Pennybacker was one of a great first wave of middle-class women who were provided their educations in normal colleges, and, like many women reformers of her day, began her public work as a teacher.[4] As a teacher Pennybacker believed that the purpose of education was to prepare students for citizenship. In so thinking, she shared the belief of her contemporary, John Dewey, that democracy required education and that education could be organized in democratic fashion.[5] Pennybacker also understood education and action to be inextricably linked. Young women who attended normal colleges were expected to put their education to use in the service of their larger communities.[6] This principle shaped Pennybacker's understanding of the purpose of education—to shape and inspire action. People, she believed, were motivated to act when they were inspired, and inspiration required operating on what Pennybacker believed to be the "spiritual plane"—the realm of highest ideals. Education should provide facts for the intellect, but should not overlook the affective. As a classroom teacher and as a mentor to other teachers through her educational articles and institute leadership, she stressed the importance of history. Especially was she interested in biographies of accomplished people. She believed in studying their lives as exemplars. She told stories of historical figures overcoming great obstacles, almost always leaving out facts that would tarnish the reputations of heroes. She herself seems to have been inspired by the stories she read or told of the lives of great statesmen or literary figures. It is not hard to see her using these stories to shape her own. In keeping with her focus on practicing democracy, Pennybacker stressed the social aspects of education. She arranged activities in her classroom that required students to cooperate, and encouraged a community atmosphere. Similarly, she encouraged young teachers to join teacher associations and to attend summer normal institutes at which they could form social and professional bonds with other teachers. She understood that building a strong educational system in her state would require teachers to work together. She and Percy were active in the Texas State Teachers Association, themselves helping to shape the profession.

Pennybacker envisioned the practice of education broadly. She was ever an advocate of formal, often publicly supported, educational institutions, yet she also helped to develop other venues for education, as her work with the Chautauqua Institute, women's clubs, and the media demonstrates. Again, the purpose of all of these forms of education was, for Pennybacker, to inform and inspire civic action. Although she understood herself to have multiple occupations, she did not understand these occupations to be discrete. In all of her roles she was an educator. In expanding her circle of influence from a school classroom to statewide stature, to national and international recognition, biographer Rebecca Richmond notes, "Mrs. Pennybacker was primarily a teacher, passionately so. She had enlarged her Texas schoolroom."[7]

As she moved from teaching to club work and activism, Pennybacker retained her belief in the power of education and a vision of education that incorporated social interaction toward civic goals. Like Carrie Chapman Catt, another former teacher, Pennybacker understood that social activism involved educating a constituency.[8] Pennybacker shared the view of fellow clubwoman Grace Julian Clarke, who called women's study clubs "the school in which women learn how to think together, to differ from one another without giving or taking offense, and to work together for altruistic ends."[9] For her, "organizing," the name she gave to her activism within women's clubs and other organizations, was an educative activity predicated most heavily on inspiration. Organizing and lecturing were her means of inspiring her audience to civic action.

CONTRIBUTIONS AND CONTRADICTIONS

Summarizing the significance of Anna J. H. Pennybacker's work is made difficult by the wide range of activities in which she was involved, and the fact that in all of her activities she worked not alone but as a member and leader of organizations. She belonged to a class of women who, in her era, worked collectively for social change. Although she promoted many ideas and causes, some of which she fought to have recognized as her own, determining whether or not she originated the ideas is impossible. Similarly, she worked diligently for the causes she supported, but did so in collaboration with many others. In many instances, to directly correlate the results of the work with Pennybacker's individual efforts would be overstepping. Still, as the previous chapters have shown, Pennybacker contributed to growth of many of the most innovative and important ideas, movements, and social institutions of her time. As educators, she and her husband Percy Pennybacker helped to develop school systems in the towns in which they lived and worked to increase support for public schools in the state of Texas. They held leadership roles within the Texas State Teachers Association as well as other organizations promoting education. As an education writer and teacher educator, Anna Pennybacker promoted progressive, student-centered approaches to classroom instruction even before John Dewey became well-known as the father of progressive education in the United States. As a textbook author, she introduced a mythic Texas to generations of young Texans, inspiring in some a lasting love of history and of the state. Later, as president of the Texas Federation of Women's Clubs, Pennybacker supported initiatives to increase funding for public schools and lobbied the state legislature to support increased opportunities for women in higher education.

As a leader in the General Federation of Women's Clubs, she strengthened that organization by increasing its membership and raising an endowment fund to support future efforts. While helping to create opportunities for women in the public sphere, she advocated funding and programs to support women's work in the private sphere, attempting to ensure that equal funds were allocated for programs serving women as for those that served men. Success was sometimes elusive as, for example, in the case of spending under the Smith-Lever Act. In that case, her efforts to equalize spending for men and women were never completely successful. However, many of the other ideas and movements Pennybacker supported have become commonplace, if not uncontested. The League of Women Voters endures, and most American women today expect that they will not be denied an education based on their gender, that they will engage in paid work, and that they will be permitted to cast their ballots at the polls. In addition, many of the progressive institutions and practices for which she advocated, public schools and libraries, safe food laws, and mothers' pensions (now Social Security), have become well established.

Some of Pennybacker's ideas and causes never gained wide popular support despite her efforts, and today seem particularly old-fashioned. Independence Day continues to be observed with raucous celebrations rather than the solemn ceremonies Pennybacker suggested during her lifetime. Similarly, her rhetoric about the solemnity of the vote seems overblown. Teacherages, established in few communities during Pennybacker's lifetime, did not become widely popular. Those that were constructed were often undesirable and of poor quality, and the movement collapsed with the onset of the Depression.[10] Pennybacker's citizenship schools prepared hundreds of women for the vote, but women's indifference, as indicated by voting patterns across the nation, was resistant to education efforts.[11] Her plans for the Americanization of immigrants likely showed similarly limited results. Historian Gayle Gullett notes that such education efforts generated scant interest in the communities to which they were directed.[12]

Still other of the ideas, activities, and institutions Pennybacker promoted achieved some success in their time, but did not endure and have fallen out of fashion in more recent times. Home economics, or scientific housekeeping, has lost favor in recent years, and even in Pennybacker's years may have been less appealing to young women than preparing for paid work outside the home.[13] Pennybacker's conception of history would be easily critiqued by contemporary social scientists and critical theorists. Her Texas history textbook is highly ethnocentric and biased by today's standards. Similarly, her concerns about the intermingling of the races, typical of her time and region, have also lost much of the power they once had. In retrospect they make a woman of broad interests and concerns seem small-minded. Pennybacker's views on race were among her least progressive, but reflect a failure of vision common to many progressives of her day. Throughout her lifetime, however, Pennybacker slowly changed her attitudes regarding race. Whereas in the early 1900s she supported segregation and rebuffed northern women's attempts to form alliances between black and white women, by the 1920s, she worked with prominent black women in the National Council of Women. It cannot be said that she was ever an advocate for black causes. But seeing the direction the women around her were taking, particularly in the National Council of Women, she was at least wise enough not to resist. Given her leadership role in keeping black women out of the GFWC in the preceding decades, this constitutes significant, albeit not sufficient, change. Her racial animosity toward blacks did not extend to other races, and she can be credited with resisting intolerance toward immigrants and promoting an appreciation for diverse cultures. At the same time, she promoted views of citizenship and American democracy that were highly grounded in her own ethnic, racial, gender, and class background, and that have been called patronizing and coercive by recent historians.[14]

Progressivism was a multifaceted, sometimes contradictory movement, so much so that historians sometimes refer to "progressivisms."[15] It could be at once sharply radical and deeply conservative. Historian Michael McGerr calls progressivism a "radical movement," not in the sense of economic or political radicalism, but rather in its sweeping demand for social transformation and the audacity of the middle class to demand that other classes adopt its values.[16] Maureen Flanagan argues that progressives were not revolutionaries but "reformers and regulators" who "never set out to change the structure of American society."[17] Like so many of her contemporaries, Pennybacker was both radical and conservative. Pennybacker addressed civic action, and women's clubs especially, with radical fervor, seeing in them new possibilities for women to effect social change on a scale that they never had before. Throughout her life she worked for causes that were sometimes portrayed as deeply threatening to American social, political, and economic structures. Opponents of women's clubs and anti-suffragists declared that giving women the vote would ruin the country by destroying its foundation: the patriarchal family. Social welfare programs for which she advocated were labeled socialist, and women peace activists were portrayed as communist sympathizers by pro-militarists. Even so, Pennybacker herself was often accused of being overly conservative. She was certainly not progressive enough by the standards of some of the progressive women with whom she worked. Jane Addams, trying to open the General Federation to black women must have been frustrated by Pennybacker's opposition at the GFWC biennial convention of 1902. Longtime suffrage supporters questioned her commitment to that cause and resented her late, less than fervent support.

Because Pennybacker worked to expand opportunities for women in her time, but never overtly rebelled against the strictures of southern womanhood, she could reach audiences that may not have placed their faith in more radical women. Her approach was not dramatic or confrontational. She and her associates found, for example, the actions of the suffragists who marched on Washington, D.C., in 1913, to be unwise and counterproductive. Pennybacker, by contrast, used social expectations of femininity to her advantage. She maintained the manners of a southern lady in many respects. Her exceptional ability to address an audience powerfully, yet still be perceived as feminine, likely helped to change public opinion about the desirability of women adopting such public roles. Her perceived conservatism permitted her to reach audiences more radical women could not and deflected accusations that her progressive ideas were radical. At the 1893 World's Fair in Chicago, Sue Huffman Brady, Anna Pennybacker's former SHNI classmate, gave a presentation titled "Changing Ideals in Southern Womanhood." Sylvia Hunt notes that Brady's speech "indicates that some middle-class southern women had an interest in expanding women's rights and contributed leaders to the effort."[18] Like Brady, Pennybacker both urged the expansion of women's rights and opportunities, and emphasized the importance of their work in the domestic sphere. Demanding equal money and attention for women's traditional work was both radical and conservative—conservative in the sense that she did not challenge women's roles as mothers and housekeepers, radical in that she expected these roles to expand and to be valued and supported in ways they never had been before.

Although she did not use the term herself, Pennybacker unquestionably worked to further what today would be called "feminist" issues. In an era when the dominant ideology divided the world into separate public and private spheres, and relegated women to the private, Pennybacker ardently promoted women's entry into civic life. Pennybacker's view of women in civic life was as follows: "We should be broken-hearted if our sons could not say, 'I'd swear by my mother's religion, and she'd die for it'; but we crave that they may also affirm, 'Mother's ideas about public questions are sane; she reasons, she knows, as well as feels, and I'd put her argument against anyones.' "[19] In so thinking, Pennybacker was one of a number of women historian Margaret Smith Crocco and others call "civic women."[20] Denied access to male-dominated civil institutions, these women developed alternative routes to "express their citizenship and participate in civic life."[21] In many ways Pennybacker exemplifies this conception of the civic woman. Pennybacker not only lived her own version of how to be a responsible citizen, she worked tirelessly to inspire other women to do the same. "Call me a citizen," she once instructed a reporter. "The term citizen is comprehensive of every thing I have tried to do and be."[22]

NOTES

INTRODUCTION

1. Marjorie Spruill Wheeler, *New Women of the New South: The Leaders of the Woman Suffrage Movement in the Southern States* (New York: Oxford University Press, 1993).

2. Maureen A. Flanagan, *America Reformed: Progressivism, 1890s–1920s* (New York: Oxford University Press, 2007), vi–vii; Michael E. McGerr, *A Fierce Discontent: The Rise and Fall of the Progressive Movement in America* (New York: Free Press, 2003).

3. Helen Knox, *Mrs. Percy V. Pennybacker: An Appreciation* (New York: Fleming H. Revell, 1916), 67–70.

4. *Handbook of Texas Online*, ed. R. Tyler. (Austin: Texas State Historical Association, 1999) s.v. "Texas Federation of Women's Clubs," http://www.tshaonline.org/handbook/online/articles/view/TT/vnt1.html (accessed June 7, 2009).

5. Nancy Hoffman, *Woman's "True" Profession: Voices from the History of Teaching* (New York: Feminist Press and McGraw Hill, 1981), xv.

6. Nancy F. Cott, *The Grounding of Modern Feminism* (New Haven: Yale University Press, 1987).

7. Ibid.

8. Judith Harlan, *Feminism: A Reference Handbook* (Santa Barbara: ABC-Clio, 1998), 1.

9. Ann Mies Knupfer, "If You Can't Push, Pull; If You Can't Pull, Please Get Out of the Way: The Phyllis Wheatley Club and Home in Chicago, 1896 to 1920," *Journal of Negro History* 82, no. 2 (1997): 221–31.

10. Louise Michelle Newman, *White Women's Rights: The Racial Origins of Feminism in the United States* (New York: Oxford University Press, 1999); Judith McArthur, *Creating the New Woman: The Rise of Southern Women's Progressive Culture in Texas, 1893–1918* (Urbana: University of Illinois Press, 1998).

11. Sandra Harsanger, *Organized Womanhood: Cultural Politics in the Pacific Northwest, 1840–1920* (Norman: University of Oklahoma Press, 1997), 23.

12. Barbara Ryan, *The Women's Movement: References and Resources* (New York: G. K. Hall, 1996), 79–80.

13. Ryan, *The Women's Movement.*

14. Laurel Thatcher Ulrich, *Well-Behaved Women Seldom Make History* (New York: Random House, 2007).

CHAPTER 1

1. Caroline E. Janney, "To Honor Her Noble Sons: The Ladies Memorial Association of Petersburg, 1866–1912," in *Virginia's Civil War*, eds. Peter Wallenstein and Bertram Wyatt-Brown (Charlottesville: University of Virginia Press, 2005), 257.

2. Cole C. Kingseed, *The American Civil War.* (Westport, Ct.: Greenwood Press, 2004), xvii, 13.

3. Helen Knox, *Mrs. Percy V. Pennybacker,* 16–17; Rebecca Richmond, *A Woman of Texas: Mrs. Percy V. Pennybacker* (San Antonio: Naylor, 1941), 128.

4. Knox, *Mrs. Percy V. Pennybacker;* Linda Hardwicke, "The Rev. Benjamin Hardwicke: A Biography by Linda Hardwicke," Corpus Christi Public Libraries, http://www.library.ci.corpus-christi.tx.us/oldbayview/hardwickejbbiobyhardwicke.htm.

5. "Hardwicke, J. B., D. D," *The Baptist Encyclopaedia. A Dictionary of the Doctrines, Ordinances, Usages, Confessions of Faith, Sufferings, Labors, and Successes and the General History of the Baptist Denomination in All Lands.,* ed. William Cathcart. (Philadelphia: Louis H. Everts, 1883).

6. Ibid.

7. Knox, *Mrs. Percy V. Pennybacker,* 19.

8. Richmond, *A Woman of Texas,* 3.

9. Ibid.

10. Ibid.

11. United Daughters of the Confederacy J. E. B. Stuart Chapter, *War Days in Fayetteville, North Carolina: Reminiscences of 1861 to 1865* (n.p.: Judge Printing, 1910).

12. James I. Robertson, *Civil War Virginia: Battleground for a Nation* (Charlottesville: University Press of Virginia, 1991).

13. Richmond, *A Woman of Texas.*

14. Knox, *Mrs. Percy V. Pennybacker,* 21; "Hardwicke, J. B., D. D."

15. Richmond, *A Woman of Texas,* 6.

16. Robertson, *Civil War Virginia.*

17. United Daughters of the Confederacy J. E. B. Stuart Chapter, *War Days in Fayetteville, North Carolina,* 5.

18. Richmond, *A Woman of Texas,* 22–23.

19. United Daughters of the Confederacy J. E. B. Stuart Chapter, *War Days in Fayetteville.*

20. Richmond, *A Woman of Texas,* 7.

21. Knox, *Mrs. Percy V. Pennybacker,* 38.

22. Ibid., 27.

23. Richmond, *A Woman of Texas,* 9.

24. Ibid., 10–11.

25. Ibid.

26. Ibid.

27. Ibid.

28. Ibid., 18.

29. Lucy Sims Clark, letter regarding Anna Hardwicke as a young woman, 1915, box 2M84, Pennybacker Papers.

30. Richmond, *A Woman of Texas,* 11.

31. Anna J. H. Pennybacker, letter to the editor, *Happy Home Magazine,* 1876, clipping in scrapbook, box 2M84, Pennybacker Papers.

32. Ibid.

33. "Invitation," 1878, newspaper clipping in scrapbook, box 2M84, Pennybacker Papers.

34. Ibid.

35. "A Bower of Beauty," 1878, newspaper clipping in scrapbook, box 2M84, Pennybacker Papers.

36. Richmond, *A Woman of Texas,* 11.

37. Clark, letter regarding Anna Hardwicke as a young woman, 1915.

38. "Academy of Science. An Interesting Meeting and Election of Officers," [1879], newspaper clipping, box 2M84, Pennybacker Papers.

39. Frederick Eby, *The Development of Education in Texas* (New York: MacMillan, 1925).

40. Ibid.; Richmond, *A Woman of Texas,* 34.

41. Richmond, *A Woman of Texas,* 37.

42. *Handbook of Texas Online,* ed. R. Tyler (Austin: Texas State Historical Association, 1999) s.v. "Sam Houston State University," http://www.tshaonline.org/handbook/online/articles/view/SS/kcs2.html (accessed June 7, 2009).

43. Knox, *Mrs. Percy V. Pennybacker.*

44. June Welch, *The Colleges of Texas* (Dallas: GLA Press, 1981).

45. Anna J. H. Pennybacker, "My Experiences at the Sam Houston Normal Institute in 1879–80," with a letter dated 10 August 1904, box 2M84, Pennybacker Papers.

46. Newspaper clipping describing graduation ceremonies at the Sam Houston State Normal College, 1880, box 2M84, Pennybacker Papers; Pennybacker, "My Experiences at the Sam Houston Normal Institute," Pennybacker Papers; newspaper clipping describing graduation ceremonies at the Sam Houston State Normal College, 1880, box 2M84, Pennybacker Papers.

47. Pennybacker, "My "Experiences at the Sam Houston Normal Institute," Pennybacker Papers.

48. I. R. Dean, "The Normal Method," *Texas School Journal* 1, no. 6 (1883): 101.

49. Anna Pennybacker's articles were published regularly in the *Texas School Journal* during the 1880s and 1890s. For an example, see her series, "Letters to a Young Teacher," which began in January 1890 and ran monthly for roughly a year. Anna J. H. Pennybacker, "Letters to a Young Teacher No. 1," *Texas School Journal* 8, no. 1 (1890): 4–6.

50. Mary Ley and Mike Bryan, eds. *Journey from Ignorant Ridge: Stories and Pictures of Texas Schools in the 1800s* (Austin: Texas Congress of Parents and Teachers, 1976).

51. Newspaper clipping describing graduation ceremonies at the Sam Houston State Normal College, 1880, box 2M84, Pennybacker Papers.

52. Christine A. Ogren, *The American State Normal School: An Instrument of Great Good* (New York: Palgrave Macmillan, 2005), 16l.

53. Knox, *Mrs. Percy V. Pennybacker.*

54. Anna J. H. Pennybacker, "My Experiences at the Sam Houston Normal Institute," Pennybacker Papers.

55. Ogren, *The American State Normal School,* 160.

56. Ibid.,161.

57. Ibid.

58. Ibid., 167.

59. Ibid.

60. Richmond, *A Woman of Texas,* 43.

61. Ogren, *The American State Normal School,* 162.

62. Knox, *Mrs. Percy V. Pennybacker,* 72.

63. W. S. Sutton to Percy V. Pennybacker, 1915, box 2M84, Pennybacker Papers.

64. Clippings in family scrapbook, 1877, box 2M74, Pennybacker Papers; newspaper clipping in family scrapbook, 1 September 1873, box 2M74, Pennybacker Papers.

65. Pennybacker, "My Experiences at the Sam Houston Normal Institute in 1879–80," Pennybacker Papers.

66. Sylvia Hunt, "'Throw Aside the Veil of Helplessness': A Southern Feminist at the 1893 World's Fair," *Southwestern Historical Quarterly* 99 (1996): 48–62.

CHAPTER 2

1. Pennybacker, "My Experiences at the Sam Houston Normal Institute in 1879–80," Pennybacker Papers.

2. Patricia A. Carter, *Everybody's Paid but the Teacher: The Teaching Profession and the Women's Movement* (New York: Columbia University Press, 2002), 12–13.

3. Ibid.

4. Ibid. The issue of women teachers was also discussed in at least one *Texas School Journal* article. See J. E. Dow, "Woman in School Work," *Texas School Journal* 1, no. 6 (1883): 102–8. Anna, herself, would draw on this assumption when she wrote her "Letters to a Young Teacher" series for the *Texas School Journal.* Her narrator reminds the young teacher that she passed her county exam (and likely obtained her position) due to the popularity of her "uncle, the state senator" and was in need of further training to take the state examination: "Your conscience testifies that you really didn't deserve the second grade you won." Anna J. H. Pennybacker, "Letters to a Young Lady No. 3," *Texas School Journal* 8, no. 4 (1890): 81–84.

5. Carter, *Everybody's Paid but the Teacher,* 101.

6. Frederick Eby, *The Development of Education in Texas* (New York: MacMillan, 1925).

7. B. M. Baker, "Editorial Department," *Texas School Journal* 4, no. 9 (1886): 231–32.

8. Ibid.

9. Percy V. Pennybacker, "Bryan Graded School. Annual Report of the Superintendent," [1881], newspaper clipping, box 2M74, Pennybacker Papers.

10. Ibid.

11. Ibid.

12. Ibid.

13. Ibid.

14. Tellingly, Percy does not provide statistics about the black students' progress in his second annual report. Percy V. Pennybacker, "Bryan Graded School. Annual Report," Pennybacker Papers.

15. "The Bryan Public Graded Schools," 1881, flyer in scrapbook, box 2M84, Pennybacker Papers.

16. Knox, *Mrs. Percy V. Pennybacker,* 50.

17. "Summer Normal Principals, 1886," *Texas School Journal* 4, no. 6 (1886): 218.

18. Anna J. H. Pennybacker, "Missouri Notes," [1882], newspaper clipping in scrapbook, box 2M84, Pennybacker Papers.

19. Ibid.

20. Ibid.

21. Ibid.

22. "Room 1 Gave Its Last Public Exercise," newspaper clipping in scrapbook, box 2M84, Pennybacker Papers.

23. "Last Friday Afternoon," newspaper clipping in scrapbook, box 2M84, Pennybacker Papers.

24. "Room 1 Gave Its Last Public Exercise," Pennybacker Papers.

25. Ibid.

26. "A Surprise," newspaper clipping in scrapbook, box 2M84, Pennybacker Papers.

27. Pennybacker, "Missouri Notes," Pennybacker Papers.

28. Ibid.

29. Anna J. H. Pennybacker, "Literary Department. Margaret Fuller," [*Carthage (MO) Press,* 1884], newspaper clipping, box 2M84, Pennybacker Papers.

30. Ibid.

31. Ibid.

32. Anna J. H. Pennybacker, "We take pleasure," [*Carthage (MO) Press,* 1884], newspaper clipping, box 2M84, Pennybacker Papers.

33. "Women in Germany," newspaper clipping in scrapbook, box 2M74, Pennybacker Papers.

34. "Development of the Sexes," newspaper clipping in scrapbook, box 2M74, Pennybacker Papers.

35. Knox, *Mrs. Percy V. Pennybacker,* 77; Anna J. H. Pennybacker, "Our Boys," *Texas School Journal* 7, no. 8 (1889): 208–10; Anna J. H. Pennybacker, "Another Talk About Our Boys," *Texas School Journal* 7, no. 9 (1889): 242–43; Anna J. H. Pennybacker, "What About Our Girls?" *Texas School Journal* 7, no. 10 (1889): 261–63.

36. "The Negro and His Future," newspaper clipping in scrapbook, box 2M74, Pennybacker Papers.

37. McArthur, *Creating the New Woman,* 144.

38. Knox, *Mrs. Percy V. Pennybacker,* 52, 139.

39. Jesse Lyman Hurlbut, *The Story of Chautauqua* (New York: G. P. Putnam and Sons, 1921), 134.

40. John C. Scott, "The Chautauqua Movement: Revolution in Popular Higher Education," *Journal of Higher Education* 70, no. 4 (1999): 396.

41. Anna J. Hardwicke Pennybacker, "The C.L.S.C.," clipping from unidentified newspaper [1883], in scrapbook, box 2M84, Pennybacker Papers.

42. Ibid.

43. "Carthage Literature: The Five Societies of the City Give Their Annual Entertainment to Their Friends: The Elite of the City Present," newspaper clipping in scrapbook, box 2M84, Pennybacker Papers.

44. "The Omega Society," newspaper clipping, in scrapbook, box 2M84, Pennybacker Papers.

45. "A Surprise," Pennybacker Papers.

46. "Notes of Travel," [*Carthage Press?*], newspaper clipping in scrapbook, box 2M84, Pennybacker Papers.

47. "Quite a Number of the Relatives," newspaper clipping in scrapbook, box 2M74, Pennybacker Papers.

48. Leila O. Thornton, "Editorial Department—Smith County," *Texas School Journal* 3, no. 4 (1885): 160.

49. "County Items," *Texas School Journal* 2, no. 12 (1884): 381.

50. "Married," newspaper clipping in scrapbook, box 2M84, Pennybacker Papers; "Rev. Dr. Hardwick Started Monday," newspaper clipping in scrapbook, box 2M84, Pennybacker Papers.

51. "Tyler is represented," *Carthage Press,* reprinted in *Tyler Democrat,* clippings in scrapbook, box 2M74, Pennybacker Papers; Knox, *Mrs. Percy V. Pennybacker.*

52. Carter, *Everybody's Paid but the Teacher,* 16.

53. Ibid.

54. Florence B. Cotnam to Helen Knox, 28 January 1915, box 2M84, Pennybacker Papers.

55. Ibid.

56. Knox, *Mrs. Percy V. Pennybacker.*

57. Leila O. Thornton, "Editorial Department—Smith County," *Texas School Journal* 3, no. 4 (1885): 160.

58. "County Items," *Texas School Journal* 1, no. 9 (1883): 195.

59. Leila O. Thornton, "Editorial Department—Smith County," *Texas School Journal* 3, no. 3 (1885): 126.

60. Leila O. Thornton, "Editorial Department—Smith County," *Texas School Journal* 3, no. 2 (1885): 82.

61. Leila O. Thornton, "Editorial Department—Smith County," *Texas School Journal* 3, no. 4 (1885): 160.

62. Anna J. Hardwicke Pennybacker, "Chips from the Tyler Work-Shops," *Texas School Journal* 4 (1886): 121–23.

63. Ibid.

64. Ibid., 123.

65. Percy V. Pennybacker to Honorable Board of Trustees, 4 January [1889], box 2M74, Pennybacker Papers.

66. "The Colored Baptist Church: Not So Wealthy as It Thought It Was," [1889], newspaper clipping, box 2M74, Pennybacker Papers.

67. Ibid.

68. Ibid.

69. "School Board Meeting," [1889], newspaper clipping, box 2M74, Pennybacker Papers.

70. Ibid.

71. Pennybacker, "To Honorable Board of Trustees."

72. John Kooken, "Unanimously Elected," in *Journey from Ignorant Ridge: Stories and Pictures of Texas Schools in the 1800s,* ed. Mary Ley and Mike Bryan 115–19 (Austin: Texas Congress of Parents and Teachers, 1976).

73. Kate E. White to Helen Knox, 28 January, box 2M84, Pennybacker Papers.

74. Pennybacker, "Chips from the Tyler Work-Shops," 122.

75. Ibid.

76. Barbara Finkelstein, *Governing the Young: Teacher Behavior in Popular Primary Schools in Nineteenth-Century United States* (New York: Falmer Press, 1989), 136.

77. Anna J. H. Pennybacker, "Letters to a Young Teacher No. 1," *Texas School Journal* 8, no. 2 (1890): 4–6.

78. White to Helen Knox, 28 January; Knox, *Mrs. Percy V. Pennybacker,* 53.

79. Pennybacker, "Letters to a Young Teacher No. 1," 39.

80. Pennybacker, "Chips from the Tyler Work-Shops," 123.

81. Dabney's argument is described in B. M. Baker, "Editorial Department," *Texas School Journal* 4, no. 9 (1886): 231–32.

82. Finkelstein, *Governing the Young,* 44–45.

83. "The Public Free Schools," [*Courier*], newspaper clipping in scrapbook, box 2M74, Pennybacker Papers; Anna Pennybacker's teaching also is described in her many articles for the *Texas School Journal.* For examples, see Anna J. H. Pennybacker, "Miss A's History Class," *Texas School Journal* 6, no. 10 (1888): 268–70; Anna J. H. Pennybacker, "Study of United States History," *Texas School Journal* 6, no. 8 (1888): 204–6; Anna J. H. Pennybacker, "Study of United States History," *Texas School Journal* 6, no. 11 (1888): 300–2.

84. "Texas Superintendents' Association," *Texas School Journal* 3, no. 2 (1885): 42–45.

85. Leila O. Thornton, "Correspondence," *Texas School Journal* 3, no. 3 (1885): 83.

86. Ibid.

87. Percy V. Pennybacker, "To Educators and Boards of Trustees," *Texas School Journal* 4, no. 2 (1886): 58–59.

88. "Editorial Department," *Texas School Journal* 4, no. 7 (1886): 223.

89. "News and Notes. S.H.N.I. Alumni," *Texas School Journal* 5, no. 8 (1887): 242.

90. Ibid.

91. "News and Notes. S.H.N.I. Alumni," *Texas School Journal* 5, no. 10 (1887): 238; "Report of the State Board of Examiners for Summer Normal Certificates," *Texas School Journal* 8, no. 9 (1890): 230–31; T. J. Witt, P. V. Pennybacker, W. S. Sutton, and J. E. Rodgers, "Report of the State Board of Examiners," *Texas School Journal* 7, no. 9 (1889): 252.

92. "State Teachers' Meeting," clipping in scrapbook, box 2M74, Pennybacker Papers.

93. "Proceedings of the State Teacher Association," *Texas School Journal* 7, no. 11 (1889): 287.

94. "News and Notes," *Texas School Journal* 8, no. 4 (1890): 96.

95. "News and Notes. The Galveston Meeting," *Texas School Journal* 13, no. 1 (1895): 11–21; Percy V. Pennybacker, "To Educators and Boards of Trustees," *Texas School Journal* 4, no. 2 (1886): 58–59.

96. Carter, *Everybody's Paid but the Teacher,* 10.

97. Anna J. H. Pennybacker, "Letters to a Young Lady No. 6," *Texas School Journal* 8, no. 7 (1890): 156–57; [Smith County Teachers Association], [1890], clipping in scrapbook, box 2M74, Pennybacker Papers.

98. Baker, "Editorial Department," 389.

99. "Texas State Teachers Association. Miss Annie Pennybacker," *Texas School Journal* 4, no. 3 (1886): 87.

100. "Texas State Teachers Association," *Texas School Journal* 9, no. 4 (1886): 97–99.

101. "Texas State Superintendents' Association and Texas State Teachers' Association," *Texas School Journal* 10, no. 5 (1892).

102. "Program Texas State Teachers' Association and Superintendents' and Principals' Association," *Texas School Journal* 16, no. 4 (1898): 124–29; "Program of the East Texas Teacher's Association," *Texas School Journal* 16, no. 4 (1898): 288.

103. "News and Notes. State Items," *Texas School Journal* 13, no. 4 (1895): 136.

104. "Sam Houston Normal Institute," *Texas School Journal* 17, no. 10 (1900): 787.

105. J. L. Long, T. G. Harris, Lillie Shaver, S. M. N. Mars, Mrs. Willie D. House, and Anna J. H. Pennybacker, "News and Notes. To the Teachers and School Trustees of Texas," *Texas School Journal* 13, no. 2 (1894): 66–67.

106. Mindy Spearman, "The Peripatetic Normal School," (PhD. diss., University of Texas at Austin, 2006).

107. "From San Marcos. Normal Institute Program—Kidnapping Case," Special Correspondence of the *Daily Express*, 11 August, 1881, clipping in scrapbook, box 2M84, Pennybacker Papers.

108. "Summer Normal Principals, 1886," 218; "The Summer Normals," *Texas School Journal* 4, no. [8] (1886): 272–73.

109. "The Summer Normals," 272–73.

110. "University Summer Normal School, Austin, Texas," *Texas School Journal* 5, no. 7 (1887): 200.

111. "News and Notes. Smith County," *Texas School Journal* 8, no. 6 (1887): 148.

112. Ogren, *The American State Normal School.*

113. Ibid., 21.

114. Ibid.

115. Pennybacker, "Letters to a Young Lady No. 3," 82.

116. Ibid.

117. Ibid., 81–84.

118. Anna J. H. Pennybacker, "Memorial Days I," *Texas School Journal* 4, no. 9 (1886): 278; Anna J. H. Pennybacker, "Memorial Days II," *Texas School Journal* 4, no. 10 (1886): 307–8; Anna J. H. Pennybacker, "Memorial Days III," *Texas School Journal* 4, no. 11 (1886): 339–40; Anna J. H. Pennybacker, "Memorial Days IV," *Texas School Journal* 4, no. 12 (1886): 373–74.

119. Pennybacker, "Letters to a Young Teacher. No. 1," 36–39.

120. Ibid.

121. Mindy Spearman, "Everything to Help, Nothing to Hinder: The Story of the Texas School Journal" (paper presented at the annual meeting of the Midwest History of Education Society, Chicago, 2006).

122. Pennybacker, "Letters to a Young Teacher. No. 1," 36–39.

123. Anna J. H. Pennybacker, "Letters to a Young Lady No. 5," *Texas School Journal* 8, no. 5 (1890): 129–30; Anna J. H. Pennybacker, "Letters to a Young Teacher No. 7," *Texas School Journal* 8, no. 8 (1890): 185–86.

124. Pennybacker, "Letters to a Young Teacher. No. 1," 36–39.

125. Ibid., 37.

126. Pennybacker, "Letters to a Young Lady No. 6," 156.

127. Ibid., 157.

128. Anna J. H. Pennybacker, "Letters to a Young Teacher [No. 2]," *Texas School Journal* 8, no. 3 (1890): 58–60.

129. Ibid.

130. "S.H.N.I. Alumni," *Texas School Journal* 4, no. 4 (1886): 11.

131. Anna J. H. Pennybacker to county clerk, Anderson County, 10 July 1925, box 2M15, Pennybacker Papers.

132. "Texas State Teachers' Association. Eighteenth Annual Meeting," *Texas School Journal* 15, no. 5 (1897): 195–99.

133. Richmond, *A Woman of Texas,* 100–10.

134. "$5.00 Reward," *Texas School Journal* 7, no. 7 (1890): 172; "Teachers Bureau Advertisement," *Texas School Journal* 10, no. 11 (1892): 753.

135. "State News and Notes," *Texas School Journal* 16, no. 4 (1897): 117–23.

136. "State News and Notes," *Texas School Journal* 17, no. 2 (1899): 459–64.

137. Richmond, A Woman of Texas, 73.

138. Knox, *Mrs. Percy V. Pennybacker;* Richmond, *A Woman of Texas.*

CHAPTER 3

1. Richmond, *A Woman of Texas.*

2. Ibid., 57–58.

3. E. E. Barker to Percy V. Pennybacker, 23 February 1895, box 2M17, Pennybacker Papers. Barker provides an extensive quotation from Wilson's American History, which explains the origin of the name Texas. Similar letters are available in the same folder.

4. Jno. E. Bishop to Anna J. H. Pennybacker, 13 August 1903, box 2M17, Pennybacker Papers. Bishop corrects Pennybacker's account of the Sibley Brigade in New Mexico. An officer in the brigade, Bishop offers detailed descriptions of the battle of Apache Canyon. Adina de Zavala to Anna J. H. Pennybacker, 20 January 1895, box 2M17, Pennybacker Papers.

5. Anna J. Hardwicke Pennybacker, *A New History of Texas for Schools* (Tyler, Tex.: Mr. and Mrs. Percy V. Pennybacker, 1888).

6. Ibid., vi.

7. Miles Myers, *Changing Our Minds: Negotiating English and Literacy* (Urbana, Ill.: National Council of Teachers of English, 1996).

8. Anna J. H. Pennybacker, Brief: Points Concerning a History of Texas by Anna J. H. Pennybacker, [October 1920 or later], box 2M83, Pennybacker Papers.

9. Pennybacker, *A New History of Texas for Schools,* 1.

10. Ibid., v.

11. Knox, *Mrs. Percy V. Pennybacker;* Richmond, *A Woman of Texas,* 65.

12. Robert I. Curtis, "Confederate Classical Textbooks: A Lost Cause?" *International Journal of the Classical Tradition* 3, no. 4 (1997): 433–68.

13. *Circular 2. Just Out! A New History of Texas for Schools.* [1888], box 2M17, Pennybacker Papers.

14. The 1895 and 1900 versions were essentially the same, with the exception of material between pages 313 and 319 added to the 1900 version.

15. John Barnes Pratt to Anna J. H. Pennybacker, 16 April 1903, box 2L520, Pennybacker Papers.

16. Anna J. H. Pennybacker, Brief: Points Concerning a History of Texas by Anna J. H. Pennybacker, [October 1920 or later], box 2M83, Pennybacker Papers.

17. W. H. Rushing, letter in support of Pennybacker's *A History of Texas,* 7 February 1901, box 2M83, Pennybacker Papers.

18. Wm. A. Bowen. "An Alleged History: Wonderful Powers of Invention Displayed in Narrative," *San Antonio Daily Express,* December 14, 1891, 2, col. 4.

19. Ibid.

20. Ibid.

21. Pennybacker, Brief: Points Concerning a History of Texas.

22. J. M. Glinn to Percy V. Pennybacker, 12 December 1894, box 2M17, Pennybacker Papers.

23. L. C. Libby to Anna J. H. Pennybacker, 13 December 1894, box 2M17, Pennybacker Papers; W. H. Russell to Anna J. H. Pennybacker, 12 December 1894, box 2M17, Pennybacker Papers.

24. H.F. Estill to Percy V. Pennybacker, 24 September 1894, box 2M17, Pennybacker Papers.

25. Ibid.

26. Pennybacker, *A New History of Texas for Schools* (1888), vi.

27. H. A. Ivy to Anna J. H. Pennybacker, 11 December 1894, box 2M17, Pennybacker Papers.

28. H. Glasgow to Anna J. H. Pennybacker, 11 December 1894, box 2M17, Pennybacker Papers.

29. This information is based on my examination of the 1900 version of the textbook and Pennybacker's correspondence about it.

30. Dorene Rawls to Anna J. H. Pennybacker, 13 December 1894, box 2M17, Pennybacker Papers; F. J. Wood to Anna J. H. Pennybacker, 10 December 1984, box 2M17, Pennybacker Papers.

31. J. C. Nagle to Anna J. H. Pennybacker, 1895, box 2M17, Pennybacker Papers.

32. Anna J. H. Pennybacker, *A New History of Texas for Schools* (Austin: Mrs. Percy V. Pennybacker, 1900).

33. Pennybacker, *A New History of Texas for Schools* (1888), 37.

34. Pennybacker, *A New History of Texas for Schools* (1900), 71–72.

35. T. V. Orr to Anna J. H. Pennybacker, 16 December 1894, box 2M17, Pennybacker Papers.

36. Curtis, "Confederate Classical Textbooks," 433–68; George Arthur Goethe, A Brief History of Textbook Laws in Texas (master's thesis, University of Texas, 1952).

37. Curtis, "Confederate Classical Textbooks," 433.

38. Ibid.

39. Goethe, *A Brief History of Textbook Laws in Texas,* 24.

40. Fred A. Bailey, "Free Speech and the 'Lost Cause' in Texas: A Study of Social Control in the New South," *Southwestern Historical Quarterly* 97, no. 3 (1994): 452–77.

41. Goethe, *A Brief History of Textbook Laws in Texas,* 24.

42. Bailey, "Free Speech and the 'Lost Cause' in Texas," 452–77.

43. Ibid., 463.

44. C. C. Cummings to H. G. Askew, 12 May 1913, box 2J88, United Confederate Veterans Texas Division Archive, 1862–1944, 1888–1917. Center for American History, University of Texas at Austin.

45. J. M. Carlisle, W. S. Sutton, T. J. Witt, E. F. Comegys, J. E. Rogers, and C. A. Bryant, Memorial presented to the House of Representatives, Twenty-first Legislature, by the Executive Committee of the Texas State Teachers' Association, 1888–89, box 2M17, Pennybacker Papers.

46. An Act to Create a State Text-Book Board. Texas State Senate, Twenty-fifth Legislature, box 2M17, Pennybacker Papers.

47. Bailey, "Free Speech and the 'Lost Cause' in Texas"; Cummings to H. G. Askew, 12 May 1913.

48. Percy V. Pennybacker. "The Text-book Question" (paper presented at the Texas State Superintendents Association, Galveston, June 24, 1890).

49. Bailey, "Free Speech and the "Lost Cause" in Texas."

50. United Daughters of the Confederacy, *Proceedings of the Thirteenth Annual Convention of the Texas United Daughters of the Confederacy* (n.p.: United Daughters of the Confederacy, 1908).

51. John Barnes Pratt to Anna J. H. Pennybacker, 8 January 1912, box 2L525, Pennybacker Papers.

52. Ibid.

53. Ibid.

54. John Barnes Pratt to Anna J. H. Pennybacker, 29 February 1912, box 2L525, Pennybacker Papers.

55. John Barnes Pratt to Anna J. H. Pennybacker, 29 February 1912 (second letter of this date), box 2L525, Pennybacker Papers.

56. Ibid.

57. Ibid.

58. Ibid.

59. Paulina to Anna J. H. Pennybacker, [12 March 1912?], box 2L525, Pennybacker Papers.

60. Mamie Sexton to My Dear Friend [Mrs. P. V. Pennybacker], 13 March 1912, box 2L525, Pennybacker Papers.

61. C. E. Evans to Anna J. H. Pennybacker, 21 March 1912, box 2L525, Pennybacker Papers.

62. Jessica Sayers to Anna J. H. Pennybacker, 13 March 1912, box 2L525, Pennybacker Papers.

63. W. F. Jourdan to Eugene C. Barker, 21 May 1912, box 2B93, Eugene C. Barker Papers, Center for American History, University of Texas at Austin (hereafter cited as Barker Papers).

64. Eugene C. Barker to My Dear Mr. Jourdan, 1912, box 2B93, Barker Papers.

65. Walter Connally to Anna J. H. Pennybacker, 19 March 1912, box 2L525, Pennybacker Papers.

66. E. Reid to Anna J. H. Pennybacker, 12 March 1912, box 2L525, Pennybacker Papers.

67. Anna J. H. Pennybacker, *A History of Texas Revised* (Austin: Mrs. Percy V. Pennybacker, 1908), 344–45.

68. Clara Sterzing to Anna J. H. Pennybacker, 16 February 1909, box 2L473, Pennybacker Papers; Mrs. Jos. B. Dibrell to Anna J. H. Pennybacker, 21 January 1909, box 2L473, Pennybacker Papers.

69. Mary Y. Terrell to Anna J. H. Pennybacker, January 1909, box 2L473, Pennybacker Papers.

70. Katie Daffan to Anna J. H. Pennybacker, 6 February 1912, box 2L525, Pennybacker Papers.

71. Eugene C. Barker to Mr. Peterson, 3 June 1912, box 2B93, Barker Papers.

72. Bailey, "Free Speech and the 'Lost Cause' in Texas," 469.

73. Pennybacker, *A New History of Texas for Schools* (1888), 134–35.

74. Eugene C. Barker, Charles S. Potts, and Charles W. Ramsdell, *A School History of Texas* (Chicago: Row, Peterson, & Company, 1912).

75. Ibid., 204.

76. Ibid., 206–7.

77. Eugene C. Barker to Mr. Peterson, 3 June 1912.

78. Eugene C. Barker to Row, Peterson, & Company, 4 April 1912, box 2B93, Barker Papers.

79. D. Wilmott to Anna J. H. Pennybacker, 18 October 1912, box 2L525, Pennybacker Papers.

80. McArthur, *Creating the New Woman.*

81. Pratt to Anna J. H. Pennybacker, 29 February 1912.

82. Anna J. H. Pennybacker to Helen Knox, 28 January 1919, box 2M13, Pennybacker Papers.

83. Helen Knox to Anna J. H. Pennybacker, 5 February 1919, box 2M13, Pennybacker Papers.

84. Helen Knox to Pennybacker, 16 September 1919, box 2M13, Pennybacker Papers.

85. Pennybacker, Brief: Points Concerning a History of Texas.

86. *Handbook of Texas Online,* ed. R. Tyler (Austin: Texas State Historical Association, 1999), s.v. "Dobie, James Frank," http://www.tshaonline.org/handbook/online/articles/DD/fdo2.html (accessed June 8, 2009)

87. John Graves, "The Old Guard: Dobie, Webb, and Bedicheck," in *The Texas Literary Tradition: Fiction, Folklore, History,* ed. Don Graham, James W. Lee, and William T. Pilkington, (Austin: College of Liberal Arts, University of Texas at Austin and Texas State Historical Association, 1983), 16–25.

CHAPTER 4

1. Knox, *Mrs. Percy V. Pennybacker,* 139.

2. Ibid., 52, 139.

3. John C. Scott, "The Chautauqua Movement: Revolution in Popular Higher Education," *Journal of Higher Education* 70, no. 4 (1999): 396.

4. Hurlbut, *The Story of Chautauqua,* 159.

5. Mary Y. Terrell. "Succinct History of the Woman's Club Movement," *Dallas Morning News,* November 22, 1903.

6. Knox, *Mrs. Percy V. Pennybacker,* 69.

7. Anna J. H. Pennybacker to Helen Winslow, 14 July 1913, box 2L480, Pennybacker Papers.

8. Knox, *Mrs. Percy V. Pennybacker,* 69.

9. "The Gay World of Fashion," *Dallas Morning News,* April 2, 1888, 3, col. 1.

10. "Tyler," *Dallas Morning News,* March 1, 1886, 3.

11. "Tyler," *Dallas Morning News,* January 31, 1887, 2.

12. "The Gay World of Fashion," *Dallas Morning News,* June 6, 1887, 2, col. 5.

13. "Tyler," *Dallas Morning News,* January 31, 1887, 2.

14. "Tyler," *Dallas Morning News,* March 1, 1886, 3.

15. "Tyler," *Dallas Morning News,* January 31, 1887, 2.

16. "Doings of the Beau Monde," *Dallas Morning News,* November 1, 1886, 6, col.1–5; "Tyler," *Dallas Morning News,* January 31, 1887, 2.

17. Knox, *Mrs. Percy V. Pennybacker.*

18. Carol Herrington, e-mail message to the author, January 4, 2005.

19. Knox, *Mrs. Percy V. Pennybacker,* 139.

20. Terrell, "Succinct History of the Woman's Club Movement;" Mary I. Wood, *The History of the General Federation of Women's Clubs for the First Twenty-Two Years of its Organization* (New York: History Department, General Federation of Women's Clubs, 1912).

21. Karen J. Blair, *The Clubwoman as Feminist* (New York: Holmes and Meier, 1980).

22. Sandra Harsanger, *Organized Womanhood,* 111.

23. Blair, *The Clubwoman as Feminist,* 95; Wood, *History of the General Federation of Women's Clubs,* 317.

24. Blair, *The Clubwoman as Feminist.*

25. McArthur, *Creating the New Woman,* notes, 155.

26. Schneider and Schneider, *American Women in the Progressive Era.*

27. Mary Jean Houde, *Reaching Out: A Story of the General Federation of Women's Clubs* (Chicago: Mobium Press, 1989), 81.

28. Wood, *History of the General Federation of Women's Clubs,* 310.

29. Dorothy Schneider and Carl J. Schneider, *American Women in the Progressive Era, 1900–1920* (New York: Facts on File, 1993), 98.

30. Wood, *History of the General Federation of Women's Clubs,* 310.

31. Grover Cleveland, "Woman's Mission and Woman's Clubs," *Ladies' Home Journal,* May 1905, 3–5.

32. Ibid.

33. Ibid.

34. Stella L. Christian, *The History of the Texas Federation of Women's Clubs* (Houston: Dealy-Ady-Elgin, copyrighted by the Texas Federation of Women's Clubs, 1919), 11.

35. Terrell, "Succinct History of the Woman's Club Movement."

36. Ted Ownby, *Subduing Satan: Religion, Recreation and Manhood in the Rural South, 1865–1920* (Chapel Hill: University of North Carolina Press, 1990), 11.

37. Ibid., 11.

38. Houde, *Reaching Out,* 84.

39. Richmond, *Woman of Texas,* 85; Christian, *History of the Texas Federation of Women's Clubs,* 5.

40. Christine Carter, "Indispensable Spinsters: Maiden Aunts in the Elite Families of Savannah and Charleston," in *Negotiating Boundaries of Southern Womanhood : Dealing with the Powers that Be,* ed. Janet L. Coryell (Columbia: University of Missouri Press, 2000) 251, 119.

41. Richmond, *Woman of Texas,* 86.

42. Christian, *History of the Texas Federation of Women's Clubs,* 6.

43. Richmond, *Woman of Texas,* 86.

44. Christian, *History of the Texas Federation of Women's Clubs,* 3.

45. Ibid., 11.

46. Christian, *History of the Texas Federation of Women's Clubs,* 11.

47. Terrell, "Succinct History of the Woman's Club Movement."

48. Christian, *History of the Texas Federation of Women's Clubs,* 52.

49. John C. Jurgensmeyer, "The Evolution of a Southern Lady: The Role of Anna J. Hardwicke Pennybacker in the Woman's Suffrage Movement, 1912–1920" (master's thesis, Baylor University, 2002).

50. Christian, *History of the Texas Federation of Women's Clubs,* 52–59.

51. "The Session Over," *Dallas Morning News,* May 4, 1901, 5.

52. Christian, *History of the Texas Federation of Women's Clubs.*

53. Terrell, "Succinct History of the Woman's Club Movement."

54. Mary Y. Terrell to Anna J. H. Pennybacker, 8 February 1901, box 2L471, Pennybacker Papers; Belle G. Smith to Anna J. H. Pennybacker, 23 March 1901, box 2L471, Pennybacker Papers.

55. A resolution adopted by the convention at which Pennybacker was elected TFWC president illustrated the clubwomen's attempts to remain apolitical. The resolution began, "Whereas, This organization should be non-political in its methods inasmuch as it is non-partisan in its aims," and continued to ban vote trading and "influence" in advance of open discussion or the selection of officers. Terrell, "Succinct History of the Woman's Club Movement."

56. Mary Y. Terrell to Anna J. H. Pennybacker, 7 February 1901, mss 32, box 3, Texas Federation of Women's Clubs Papers, Woman's Collection, Texas Woman's University (hereafter cited as TFWC Papers).

57. Richmond, *Woman of Texas,* 89.

58. Christian, *History of the Texas Federation of Women's Clubs,* 47.

59. Mary Y. Terrell to Anna J. H. Pennybacker, 7 February 1901, mss 32, box 3, TFWC Papers.

60. Ibid.

61. Ibid.

62. Christian, *History of the Texas Federation of Women's Clubs,* 62.

63. "They Vote Today," *Dallas Morning News,* May 3, 1901, 8.

64. "State Clubs Here," *Dallas Morning News,* May 2, 1901.

65. "The Session Over," *Dallas Morning News,* May 4, 1901, 5.

66. "Federation of Clubs: Mrs. Pennybacker of Austin Was Elected President," *Houston Post,* May 4, 1901, 8.

67. Ibid.

68. *Handbook of Texas Online,* ed. R. Tyler (Austin: Texas State Historical Association, 1999) s.v. "Brackenridge, Mary Eleanor," http://www.tshaonline.org/handbook/online/articles/view/BB/fbr4.html (accessed June 8, 2009).

69. Terrell to Pennybacker, 9 May 1901, box 2L471, Pennybacker Papers.

70. Mary Eleanor Brackenridge to Anna J. H. Pennybacker, October 1901, mss 32, box 3, TFWC Papers.

71. Ibid.

72. Judie Gammage, "Quest for Equality: An Historical Overview of Women's Rights Activism in Texas, 1890–1975" (PhD diss., North Texas State University, 1982), 42–43.

73. Texas Federation of Women's Clubs, *1900–1901 Year Book of the Texas Federation of Women's Clubs,* ([Austin?]: Texas Federation of Women's Clubs, 1900–1901), 3.

74. Christian, *History of the Texas Federation of Women's Clubs,* 55.

75. Mary Y. Terrell to Anna J. H. Pennybacker, 7 February 1901, mss 32, box 3, TFWC Papers.

76. Elizabeth L. Ring to Anna J. H. Pennybacker, 14 February 1902, mss 32, box 3, TFWC Papers.

77. Texas Federation of Women's Clubs, *1901–1902 Year Book of the Texas Federation of Women's Clubs* ([Austin?]: Texas Federation of Women's Clubs, 1901–1902).

78. Anna J. H. Pennybacker, "A Message from the Federated Women's Clubs to the Teachers of Texas," 1901, Pennybacker Papers; Terrell. "Succinct History of the Woman's Club Movement."

79. Christian, *History of the Texas Federation of Women's Clubs*, 73.

80. "They Vote Today," *Dallas Morning News*, May 3, 1901, 8.

81. W. Crossley to Anna J. H. Pennybacker, 12 November 1901, mss 32, box 1, TFWC Papers.

82. Terrell, "Succinct History of the Woman's Club Movement."

83. Christian, *History of the Texas Federation of Women's Clubs*.

84. Anna J. H. Pennybacker, "President's Greeting" in *Year Book of the Texas Federation of Women's Clubs* ([Austin?]: Texas Federation of Women's Clubs, 1902–1903), 8–9.

85. Christian, *History of the Texas Federation of Women's Clubs*.

86. Anna J. H. Pennybacker, "Report from Texas," 1902, box 2L471, Pennybacker Papers.

87. Birdie May Lewin to Anna J. H. Pennybacker, 4 April 1903, mss 32, box 2, TFWC Papers.

88. Knox, *Mrs. Percy V. Pennybacker*, 142.

89. William L. Prather to Anna J. H. Pennybacker, 17 August 1901, mss 32, box 3, TFWC Papers.

90. Printed sheet regarding Women's Dormitory, University of Texas, 1903, box 4Q165, University of Texas President's Office Records, Center for American History, University of Texas at Austin.

91. Wallace Buttrick to Anna J. H. Pennybacker, 19 July 1902, mss 32, box 1, TFWC Papers.

92. Kate Friend, "Texas," *Clubwoman* 9, no. 4 (1902): 161.

93. Anna J. H. Pennybacker, "To the Five Thousand Club Women of Texas," subject file, box 5, TFWC Papers.

94. Ibid.

95. Mary D. Bonner to Anna J. H. Pennybacker, 7 June 1902, mss. 32, box 1, TFWC Papers.

96. Arthur LeFevre to Anna J. H. Pennybacker, 6 June 1902, mss. 32, box 1, TFWC Papers.

97. Kate Perry Womack to Anna J. H. Pennybacker, 2 October 1902, subject file, box 5, TFWC Papers.

98. J. S. Waldrop to Anna J. H. Pennybacker, 2 August 1902, box 2L471, Pennybacker Papers.

99. Luther W. Clark to Anna J. H. Pennybacker, 8 June 1902, mss. 32, box 1, TFWC Papers.

100. Pennybacker, "President's Greeting."

101. Terrell, "Succinct History of the Woman's Club Movement."

102. H. N. Fitzgerald to Anna J. H. Pennybacker, 9 May 1901, box 2L471, Pennybacker Papers.

103. Kate Friend to Anna J. H. Pennybacker, 5 May 1901, mss. 32, box 1, TFWC Papers.

104. Jacquelyn M. McElhaney, *Pauline Periwinkle and Progressive Reform in Dallas* (College Station: Texas A&M University Press, 1998); *Handbook of Texas Online,* ed. R. Tyler (Austin: Texas State Historical Association, 1999) s.v. "Calloway, Sara Isadore Sutherland," http://www.tshaonline.org/handbook/online/articles/view/CC/fcaba.html (accessed June 8, 2009).

105. Mary D. Bonner to Anna J. H. Pennybacker, 1901, mss. 32, box 1, TFWC Papers.

106. Kate Friend, "Texas," *Clubwoman* 9, no. 4 (1902): 161.

107. McGerr argues that racial segregation was an important aspect of progressive thought. Many progressive whites justified their belief in white superiority using social Darwinism and "scientific" ideas about race. Segregation, they argued, allowed the black race to develop as a race free from competition from whites, which would certainly crush the weaker race. Segregation would "allow the process of reform to continue among African Americans as it did else where among whites." McGerr, *A Fierce Discontent,* 192–99.

108. Richmond, *Woman of Texas,* 93.

109. "The Sixth Biennial," *Club Woman: Woman's World,* June 1902, 321–43.

110. "Woman's Federation May Split on Social Equality; Two Distinct Organizations for North and South Which May Result from Color Question," Special to *New York Times,* May 28, 1902, 2.

111. "New Color Question More Trying Yet," *Los Angeles Daily Times,* May 1, 1902, 11.

112. Anna J. H. Pennybacker "My First Biennial," June 1924, box 2M17, Pennybacker Papers.

113. Ibid.

114. "Mrs. P. Q. Pennybacker of Texas: The Previous Question Delegate," *Los Angeles Daily Times,* [May 1?], 1902, quoted in Richmond, *A Woman of Texas, Mrs. Percy V. Pennybacker,* 94–95.

115. "Last Battle Fought on Color Lines," *Los Angeles Daily Times,* sec.1, May 7, 1902.

116. Anna J. H. Pennybacker, "My First Biennial."

117. Terrell, "Succinct History of the Woman's Club Movement."

118. "Biennial Presidency Practically Decided," *Los Angeles Times,* May 3, 1902, 5.

119. Ibid.

120. Blair, *The Clubwoman as Feminist,* 108–10; Corinna A. Buchholz, "The Ruffin Incident and Other Integration Battles in Women's Clubs, 1890–1902" (master's thesis, Sarah Lawrence College, 2000).

121. Christian, *History of the Texas Federation of Women's Clubs,* 99–101.

CHAPTER 5

1. "Boulder Chautauqua: Mrs. Pennybacker on Her Way to Assume Her Duties There," *Austin Statesman,* July 23, 1903, clipping in box 2L471, Pennybacker Papers.

2. Annie M. Moores to Anna J. H. Pennybacker, 5 September 1903, box 2L471, Pennybacker Papers; B. Tayler to Anna J. H. Pennybacker, June [1904], box 2L471, Pennybacker Papers.

3. Houde, *Reaching Out,* 109.

4. Wood, *History of the General Federation of Women's Clubs.*

5. Ibid., 190–91; Sarah S. Platt Decker to Anna J. H. Pennybacker, 8 April, box 2L471, Pennybacker Papers.

6. Anna J. H. Pennybacker and Mary I. Wood, report recommending a bureau of information, 27 December 1904, box 2L471, Pennybacker Papers.

7. Houde, *Reaching Out,* 116.

8. Ibid.

9. Sarah S. Platt Decker to Anna J. H. Pennybacker, 25 November 1904, box 2L471, Pennybacker Papers.

10. Wood, *History of the General Federation of Women's Clubs,* 205.

11. Ibid.

12. Ibid., 206.

13. Mary M. Abbott to Anna J. H. Pennybacker, 29 January 1906, box 2L472, Pennybacker Papers.

14. Houde, *Reaching Out,* 111.

15. Richmond, *A Woman of Texas,* 117.

16. Ibid.

17. Ibid., 122–23.

18. Pennybacker to Decker, 21 May 1912, box 2L508, Pennybacker Papers.

19. Decker to Pennybacker, 22 January 1906, box 2L472, Pennybacker Papers.

20. Richmond, *A Woman of Texas,* 128.

21. Pennybacker to Decker, 21 May 1912.

22. Ibid.

23. McArthur, *Creating the New Woman,* 28–29.

24. Hazel Pedlar, "Bomb is Cast into Convention," 1912, newspaper clipping, box 2M73, Pennybacker Papers.

25. "Mrs. Pennybacker and Mrs. Carpenter Placed in Nomination by Committee," 1912, newspaper clipping, box 2M73, Pennybacker Papers.

26. Richmond, *A Woman of Texas,* 138.

27. Pennybacker to Decker, 21 May 1912.

28. For a description of how Pennybacker ran her campaign to give the impression that she was above politics, see McArthur, *Creating the New Woman,* 26–29.

29. McArthur, *Creating the New Woman,* 29.

30. Mary Y. Terrell to Anna J. H. Pennybacker, 23 July 1912, box 2M508, Pennybacker Papers.

31. Ibid.

32. Houde, *Reaching Out,* 113.

33. Ibid.

34. Grace Julian Clarke to Anna J. H. Pennybacker, 1 June 1913, box 2L480, Pennybacker Papers.

35. Houde, *Reaching Out;* Agnes Squire Potter, "Official Report of the Twelfth Biennial Convention of the General Federation of Women's Clubs" (paper presented at the Twelfth Biennial Convention of the General Federation of Women's Clubs, New York, June 9–19, 1914).

36. *Thirteenth Biennial Convention,* ed. Mrs. Harry L. Keefe (New York: General Federation of Women's Clubs, 1916), 173.

37. Anna J. H. Pennybacker, Draft of the President's address for the 1914 GFWC Biennial, 1914, box 2M80, Pennybacker Papers.

38. Lawrence Cremin, *American Education: The Metropolitan Experience, 1876–1980* (New York: Harper & Row), 1988.

39. Mrs. C. H. McMahon to Anna J. H. Pennybacker, 18 August 1912, box 2L475, Pennybacker Papers.

40. Anna Hertzberg to Anna J. H. Pennybacker, 20 August 1912, box 2L475, Pennybacker Papers.

41. Wood, *History of the General Federation of Women's Clubs.*

42. Mrs. C. H. McMahon, "Press Committee," *General Federation Bulletin,* August 1912, 402–3.

43. John Barnes Pratt to Anna J. H. Pennybacker, 29 February 1912, box 2L525, Pennybacker Papers.

44. Helen Varick Boswell to Anna J. H. Pennybacker, 9 October 1912, box 2L476, Pennybacker Papers.

45. Harriet Bishop Waters to Mrs. Blankenburg, 11 February 1913, box 2L478, Pennybacker Papers.

46. "Announcement!" *General Federation Magazine,* January 1913, 1.

47. Pennybacker to Waters, 10 February 1913 box 2L479, Pennybacker Papers.

48. Pennybacker to Mrs. Blankenburg, 9 June 1913, box 2L480, Pennybacker Papers.

49. Anna J. H. Pennybacker to Julia Gould Sibert, 31 January 1920, box 2L512, Pennybacker Papers.

50. Eva Perry Moore to Alice Stone Blackwell, 18 March 1913, box 2L479, Pennybacker Papers.

51. Clarke to Pennybacker, 1912, box 2L476, Pennybacker Papers.

52. Edith Rickert, Outline for Club Department in the Journal, 9 September 1912, box 2L475, Pennybacker Papers.

53. Ibid.

54. Mary I. Wood to Anna J. H. Pennybacker, 1 October 1912, box 2L476, Pennybacker Papers.

55. Wood to Pennybacker, 5 October 1912, box 2L476, Pennybacker Papers.

56. Wood, undated letter fragment, 1912, box 2L476, Pennybacker Papers.

57. Waters to Pennybacker, [October?] 1912, box 2L476, Pennybacker Papers.

58. Eva Perry Moore in "Official Report of the Biennial," *General Federation Bulletin,* July 1912, 262–65.

59. For detailed accounts of race-based anti-suffrage arguments, see Marjorie Spruill Wheeler, *New Women of the New South: The Leaders of the Woman Suffrage Movement in the Southern States* (New York: Oxford University Press, 1993); and Elna C. Green, *Southern Strategies: Southern Women and the Woman Suffrage Question* (Chapel Hill: University of North Carolina Press, 1997).

60. McArthur, *Creating the New Woman,* 146.

61. "Mrs. Pennybacker and Mrs. Carpenter Placed in Nomination by Committee," 1912, clipping from unidentified newspaper, box 2M73, Pennybacker Papers.

62. "Suffrage Wins and Loses in Biennial: President Favors Cause, Kills Resolution," 1912, newspaper clipping, box 2M73, Pennybacker Papers.

63. Pennybacker quoted in Florence Dancy, "Texas Bulletin," *General Federation Bulletin,* September 1912, 453–54. The phrase "timid women" was a GFWC euphemism for conservative women who did not support suffrage. See, for example, Moore's comments: "Citizenship is the greatest thing coming to women, there is no doubt of it. But in this organization you have a very decided minority, whether it is here or whether it has stayed at home. Your majority vote at any time in support of suffrage would be your weakest argument, because it takes out from this organization the minority we want with us—the timid, conservative women from all over the United States, whom we are to educate toward citizenship," in "Suffrage Wins and Loses in Biennial: President Favors Cause, Kills Resolution."

64. Grace Julian Clarke, "The Washington Council," *General Federation Magazine,* May 1913, 3.

65. Anna J. H. Pennybacker, "The President's Message," *General Federation Bulletin,* August 1912.

66. "The New President," *General Federation Bulletin,* September 1912, 420.

67. Ibid.

68. Ibid.

69. Grace Julian Clarke, "Meeting of the Board of Directors," *General Federation Bulletin,* September 1912, 416–19.

70. Clarke, "The Washington Council."

71. Anna J. H. Pennybacker, "Individual Education," *Ladies' Home Journal,* November 1914, 2.

72. Anna J. H. Pennybacker, "The President's Message," *General Federation Bulletin,* August 1912, 392.

73. Madeline McD. Breckinridge, "A Mother's 'Sphere,'" *General Federation Bulletin,* August 1912, 404–5.

74. Ibid.

75. Ibid.

76. Anna J. H. Pennybacker, "The Business of Saving Time," *Ladies' Home Journal* [date unknown], 2.

77. Ibid.

78. Anna J. H. Pennybacker, "Individual Education," 2.

79. Karl Edwin Harriman to Anna J. H. Pennybacker, 20 February 1913, box 2L479, Pennybacker Papers.

80. Anna J. H. Pennybacker, unidentified article, 1914, box 2M80, Pennybacker Papers.

81. Blair, *Clubwoman as Feminist,* 108; McArthur, *Creating the New Woman,* 108.

82. Blair, *Clubwoman as Feminist,* 113.

83. McArthur, *Creating the New Woman,* 23.

84. Ibid.

85. Blair, *Clubwoman as Feminist.*

86. Clarke to Pennybacker, 6 March 1913, box 2L479, Pennybacker Papers.

87. Helen Varick Boswell to Mrs. Blankenburg, 9 September 1913, box 2L481, Pennybacker Papers; Boswell to Anna J. H. Pennybacker, 13 September 1913, box 2L481, Pennybacker Papers.

88. Clarke to Pennybacker, 17 May 1914, box 2L485, Pennybacker Papers.

89. Anna J. H. Pennybacker to Mrs. Francis D. Everett, 9 March 1914, box 2L484, Pennybacker Papers.

90. Mrs. Everett to Pennybacker, 5 March 1914, box 2L484, Pennybacker Papers.

91. Mrs. Everett to Dear President [Pennybacker], 20 November 1914, box 2L493, Pennybacker Papers.

92. Mrs. W. H. Felton to Anna J. H. Pennybacker, 6 August 1915, box 2L492, Pennybacker Papers.

93. Anna J. H. Pennybacker to Mary A. Aiken, 31 July 1914, box 2L486, Pennybacker Papers.

94. Letter to Mrs. Josiah Evans Cowles, [1916], box 2M13, Pennybacker Papers.

95. "Appreciation for Austin Clubwoman," 1913, clipping from *Austin Daily Statesman,* 13 February 1913, in scrapbook, box 2L479, Pennybacker Papers.

96. Anna J. H. Pennybacker to Harriet Gillespie, 19 January 1914, box 2L483, Pennybacker Papers.

97. Harriet C. Towner to Anna J. H. Pennybacker, 6 April 1913, box 2L480, Pennybacker Papers.

98. Jane Bernard Powers, *The Girl Question in Education: Vocational Education for Young Women in the Progressive Era* (London: Falmer Press, 1992), 51.

99. Helen Varick Boswell to Anna J. H. Pennybacker, 14 February 1916, box 2L494, Pennybacker Papers.

100. Powers, *The Girl Question in Education,* 69.

101. Ibid., 66.

102. Anna J. H. Pennybacker, "What About Our Girls?" *Texas School Journal* 7, no. 10 (1889): 261–63.

103. Anna J. H. Pennybacker to Edward Bok, 6 January 1915, box 2L488, Pennybacker Papers.

104. Pennybacker, "The Business of Saving Time."

105. Anna J. H. Pennybacker to My Dear Madam President, 23 January 1915, box 2L489, Pennybacker Papers; Mary Barry to the *Dallas News,* 18 January 1915, box 2L489, Pennybacker Papers.

106. Houde, *Reaching Out.*

107. [Anna J. H. Pennybacker] to My Dear Friend, 15 March 1913, box 2L479, Pennybacker Papers.

108. Anna J. H. Pennybacker to Mary Jennings Bryan, 18 March 1913, box 2L479, Pennybacker Papers.

109. *Baby Saving Campaigns* (Washington, D.C.: U.S. Department of Labor, Children's Bureau, 1913).

110. Anna J. H. Pennybacker to Joseph T. Johnson, 6 April 1914, box 2L485, Pennybacker Papers; Florence Kelley to Anna J. H. Pennybacker, 3 April 1914, box 2L485, Pennybacker Papers; Harriet C. Towner to Anna J. H. Pennybacker, 16 April 1914, box 2L485, Pennybacker Papers.

111. Julia C. Lathrop to Anna J. H. Pennybacker, 18 October 1915, box 2L493, Pennybacker Papers.

112. Etta R. Goodwin to Anna J. H. Pennybacker, 25 October 1915, box 2L493, Pennybacker Papers.

113. Mary I. Wood to Mrs. Dixon Williams, 25 October 1916, box 2L494, Pennybacker Papers.

114. Ibid.

115. *Nation-Wide Baby Week, March 4–11, 1916* (Washington, D.C.: U.S. Department of Labor, Children's Bureau, 1916).

116. Anna J. H. Pennybacker. "Address to the Twelfth Biennial Convention of the General Federation of Women's Clubs" (paper presented at the Twelfth Biennial Convention of the General Federation of Women's Clubs, New York, June 9–19, 1914).

117. Mary W. Barry to Anna J. H. Pennybacker, [June] 1913, box 2L480, Pennybacker Papers; Mary Barnum to Anna J. H. Pennybacker, 5 June 1913, box 2L480, Pennybacker Papers.

118. Barnum to Anna J. H. Pennybacker, 5 June 1913.

119. Anna J. H. Pennybacker to Mrs. Rudolf Blankenburg, 12 March 1913, box 2L479, Pennybacker Papers.

120. Manley O. Hudson to Anna J. H. Pennybacker, 13 April 1913, box 2L479, Pennybacker Papers.

121. "Hurrying the Hatch," 1 May 1913, clipping from unidentified newspaper, box 2L480, Pennybacker Papers.

122. Anna J. H. Pennybacker to My Dear Board Member, 5 January 1915, box 2L488, Pennybacker Papers.

123. *Press Bulletin, No. 27. Clubwomen and Peace* (General Federation of Women's Clubs, 1915).

124. Ibid.

125. Anna J. H. Pennybacker, untitled draft, [1915–1916], box 2M17, Pennybacker Papers.

126. Ione V. H. Cowles, *Program of Work of the Peace Committee of the* GFWC (General Federation of Women's Clubs, 1914–1916).

127. Anna J. H. Pennybacker to My Dear Friend, 2 April 1915, box 2L490, Pennybacker Papers.

128. McGerr, *A Fierce Discontent,* treats the World War and progressivism. For a discussion of how women activists, including those involved in the peace and suffrage movements responded to the war, see Maureen Flanagan, *America Reformed: Progressives and Progressivisms, 1890s–1920s* (Oxford: Oxford University Press, 2007).

129. Anna J. H. Pennybacker to Mrs. Frank White, 2 March 1915, box 2L490, Pennybacker Papers.

130. Mrs. Frank White to Anna J. H. Pennybacker, 14 March 1914, box 2L484, Pennybacker Papers.

131. Mary I. Wood to Anna J. H. Pennybacker, 25 March 1914, box 2L484, Pennybacker Papers; Grace Julian Clarke to Anna J. H. Pennybacker, 29 February 1916, box 2L494, Pennybacker Papers.

CHAPTER 6

1. Richmond, *A Woman of Texas,* 198–200.

2. Helen Knox to Mrs. J. A. Hodges, 20 August 1917, box 2M13, Pennybacker Papers.

3. Anna J. H. Pennybacker to Helen Knox, 28 January 1919, box 2M13, Pennybacker Papers; Anna J. H. Pennybacker to Mrs. G. R. Scott, 30 April 1919, box 2L496, Pennybacker Papers.

4. Anna J. H. Pennybacker to Mrs. Noah Yount, 14 February 1919, box 2L496, Pennybacker Papers.

5. Jurgensmeyer, "The Evolution of a Southern Lady," 54.

6. Sara Hunter Graham, *Woman Suffrage and the New Democracy* (New Haven: Yale University Press, 1996), 21.

7. Ibid., 33.

8. Ibid., 21, 15. For a more thorough discussion of the anti-suffragists, see Eleanor Flexnor, *Century of Struggle: The Woman's Rights Movement in the United States* (New York: Atheneum, 1970).

9. Elna C. Green, *Southern Strategies: Southern Women and the Woman Suffrage Question* (Chapel Hill: University of North Carolina Press, 1997), 83.

10. Graham, *Woman Suffrage and the New Democracy*, 35.

11. Ibid., 33–34.

12. Ibid., 33.

13. Ibid., 38.

14. See Graham, *Woman Suffrage,* 66–67, for more on suffrage leaders using federated club structures to introduce suffrage issues.

15. Ibid., 73.

16. Ibid.

17. Eleanor Flexnor, *Century of Struggle,* 275.

18. Ibid., 274; Graham, *Woman Suffrage,* 81.

19. Graham, *Woman Suffrage,* 86.

20. Anna J. H. Pennybacker to Carrie Chapman Catt, 22 April 1918, box 2M12, Pennybacker Papers.

21. Leslie Woman Suffrage Commission, *Minutes of the First Meeting of Incorporators, Leslie Suffrage Commission* (New York: Leslie Woman Suffrage Commission, 1917).

22. Leslie Woman Suffrage Commission, *Minutes of a Special Meeting of Members of the Leslie Woman Suffrage Commission* (New York: Leslie Woman Suffrage Commission, 1917).

23. Carrie Chapman Catt to Anna J. H. Pennybacker, 31 March 1917, box 2M12, Pennybacker Papers.

24. Leslie Woman Suffrage Commission, *By-Laws of the Leslie Woman Suffrage Commission* (New York: Leslie Woman Suffrage Commission, 1917).

25. Leslie Woman Suffrage Commission, *Minutes of the Meeting of the Executive Committee of the Leslie Woman Suffrage Commission, Inc. April 23, 1917* (New York: Leslie Woman Suffrage Commission, 1917); Gracia Goller to Anna J. H. Pennybacker, 31 May 1917, box 2M12, Pennybacker Papers.

26. Graham, *Woman Suffrage,* 93–95.

27. Carrie Chapman Catt to Anna J. H. Pennybacker, 31 March 1917.

28. Leslie Woman Suffrage Commission Inc., *Minutes of the Annual Meeting of the Members of the Leslie Woman Suffrage Commission, Inc.* (New York: Leslie Woman Suffrage Commission, 1917).

29. Jennifer Baugh Hancock, "Society Suffragists: Women's Struggle for the Ballot in Rural East Texas" (master's thesis, Stephen F. Austin University, 1999), 66–67.

30. Gammage, "Quest for Equality," 43.

31. Ibid.

32. Potter, too, had had disputes with Pennybacker in the past. A member of one of Tyler's most prominent families, in 1902 Potter had excoriated Pennybacker for assisting a woman seeking a teaching position in the town, reminding Pennybacker that the Herndon family had been instrumental in placing the

Pennybackers in the Tyler schools in the late 1800s. Elizabeth Herndon Potter to Anna J. H. Pennybacker, 6 June 1902, mss 32, box 3, TFWC Papers.

33. Hancock, "Society Suffragists," 67; Gammage, "Quest for Equality," 43.

34. Janet G. Humphrey, *A Texas Suffragist. Diaries and Writings of Jane Y. McCallum* (Austin: Ellen C. Temple, 1988), 65.

35. Ibid., 69.

36. Ibid., 71.

37. Graham, *Woman Suffrage and the New Democracy*, 124. For a thorough discussion of the southern strategy for gaining women's suffrage, see Marjorie Spruill Wheeler, *New Women of the New South: The Leaders of the Woman Suffrage Movement in the Southern States* (New York: Oxford University Press, 1993).

38. Wheeler, *New Women of the New South*, 142–45.

39. Anna J. H. Pennybacker "As a Southerner and a Democrat," 1919, box 2M12, Pennybacker Papers.

40. Gammage, "Quest for Equality"; Graham, *Woman Suffrage and the New Democracy;* Wheeler, *New Women of the New South*, 102–12. Wheeler, in particular, documents widespread belief among white southern suffragists that blacks were unfit for the vote.

41. Graham, *Woman Suffrage and the New Democracy*, 97–98.

42. Graham, *Woman Suffrage and the New Democracy;* Gammage, "Quest for Equality," 74.

43. Graham, *Woman Suffrage and the New Democracy*, 105.

44. McArthur, *Creating the New Woman*, 121.

45. Helen Knox to Mrs. Gary Connally, 11 October 1917, box 2M13, Pennybacker Papers.

46. McArthur, *Creating the New Woman*, 122.

47. Judith N. McArthur and Harold L. Smith, *Minnie Fisher Cunningham: A Suffragist's Life in Politics* (New York: Oxford University Press, 2003), 56.

48. Judith McArthur, *Creating the New Woman*, 128.

49. Ibid.

50. H. S. Braucher to Anna J. H. Pennybacker, 16 September 1918, box 2M87, Pennybacker Papers.

51. Ibid.

52. Anna J. H. Pennybacker to Mrs. M. B. Terrell, 16 October 1918, box 2M87, Pennybacker Papers; United War Work Campaign, *Report of the Executive Secretary, Women's Work in Texas, September 1918* (United War Work Campaign, 1918).

53. Knox, *Mrs. Percy V. Pennybacker*, 215.

54. Bertha E. Tomlinson to Anna J. H. Pennybacker, 14 February 1918, box 2M11, Pennybacker Papers.

55. Tomlinson to Pennybacker, 18 March 1918, box 2M11, Pennybacker Papers.

56. William H. Short, Report of the League to Enforce Peace to the National Committee of Patriotic Societies, 24 April 1918, box 2M11, Pennybacker Papers.

57. Anna J. H. Pennybacker to Mrs. John Sparger, 31 July 1918, box 2M87, Pennybacker Papers.

58. Richmond, *A Woman of Texas,* 212.

59. Ibid., 213.

60. Ibid.

61. Lewis L. Gould, *Progressives and Prohibitionists: Texas Democrats in the Wilson Era* (Austin: University of Texas Press, 1973), 81.

62. Minnie Fisher Cunningham to Anna J. H. Pennybacker, 13 July 1917, box 2L496, Pennybacker Papers.

63. Anna J. H. Pennybacker to Mrs. Eltweed Pomeroy, 13 July 1917, box 2M12, Pennybacker Papers.

64. Ibid.

65. Ida C. Saunders to Anna J. H. Pennybacker, 5 January 1919, box 2M87, Pennybacker Papers.

66. Cunningham to Anna J. H. Pennybacker, 13 July 1917.

67. Ibid.

68. Cunningham to Pennybacker, 5 July 1917, box 2M12, Pennybacker Papers.

69. Anna J. H. Pennybacker to Edith Hinkle League, 1 July 1918, box 2M12, Pennybacker Papers.

70. Delphine Dodge Ashbaugh to State and Local Clubwomen, 11 March 1918, box 2L496, Pennybacker Papers.

71. Texas State Federation of Women's Clubs War Work Council, "Press Release for Sunday, March 3, 1918," 3 March 1918, box 2L496, Pennybacker Papers.

72. Helen Knox to Mrs. Gary Connally, 11 October 1917, box 2M13, Pennybacker Papers.

73. Knox to Mary Cain Thompson, 19 November 1917, box 2M13, Pennybacker Papers.

74. Knox to Anna J. H. Pennybacker, 12 October 1917, box 2M13, Pennybacker Papers.

75. Knox to Mrs. J. A. Hodges, 20 August 1917.

76. McArthur, *Creating the New Woman,* 136.

77. Cunningham to Pennybacker, 5 July 1917.

78. Knox to Pennybacker, 24 July 1917, box 2M13, Pennybacker Papers.

79. Ibid.

80. Ibid.

81. Ibid.

82. Cunningham to Pennybacker, 5 July 1917, box 2M12, Pennybacker Papers.

83. *The Battle Lost—And Won*, Texas State Library & Archives Commission, November 2, 2005 [cited July 3, 2006], available from http://www.tsl.state.tx.us/exhibits/suffrage/victory/page1.html.

84. Gammage, "Quest for Equality," 73.

85. Dora H. Fleming to Anna J. H. Pennybacker, 22 September 1917, box 2L496, Pennybacker Papers.

86. Gammage, "Quest for Equality," 73.

87. Graham, *Woman Suffrage and the New Democracy*, 132.

88. Carrie Chapman Catt to Anna J. H. Pennybacker, 4 January 1918, box 2M12, Pennybacker Papers.

89. Graham, *Woman Suffrage and the New Democracy*, 97.

90. Anna J. Hardwicke Pennybacker to R. B. Cousins, 8 January 1918, box 2M12, Pennybacker Papers; Anna J. H. Pennybacker to H. F. Estill, 9 January 1918, box 2M12, Pennybacker Papers.

91. Mary D. Woodson to Anna J. H. Pennybacker, 1 January 1918, box 2M12, Pennybacker Papers.

92. Ibid.

93. Cunningham to Pennybacker, 18 January 1918, box 2M12, Pennybacker Papers.

94. Jurgensmeyer, "The Evolution of a Southern Lady," 61.

95. Gammage, "Quest for Equality," 74–75.

96. Elizabeth M. Speer to Anna J. H. Pennybacker, 8 January 1918, box 2M12, Pennybacker Papers.

97. Cunningham to Pennybacker, 7 January 1918, box 2M12, Pennybacker Papers.

98. Jane Y. McCallum to Anna J. H. Pennybacker, 31 March 1919, box 2M12, Pennybacker Papers.

99. Anna J. H. Pennybacker, "An Interview," [31 March] [1919], box 2M12, Pennybacker Papers.

100. Gammage, "Quest for Equality," 75.

101. Ibid., 77.

102. McArthur and Smith, *Minnie Fisher Cunningham*, 61.

103. Anna J. H. Pennybacker to Carrie Chapman Catt, 13 June 1918, box 2M12, Pennybacker Papers; Leslie Woman Suffrage Commission, *Minutes of Special Meeting of the Executive Board of the Leslie Woman Suffrage Commission, Inc.* (Washington, D.C.: Leslie Woman Suffrage Commission, 1918).

104. Elizabeth Bass to Anna J. H. Pennybacker, 15 February 1918, box 2M87, Pennybacker Papers.

105. Ibid.

106. McArthur and Smith, *Minnie Fisher Cunningham*, 90.

107. Ibid.

108. Bass to Pennybacker, 15 February 1918.

109. Anna J. H. Pennybacker, "A Historical Event," 1919, box 2M12, Pennybacker Papers, 1.

110. Ibid., 2.

111. Ibid.

112. Ibid.

113. Ibid.

114. Ibid.

115. Ibid.

116. Ibid., 3.

117. Anna J. H. Pennybacker to O. S. Carlton, 3 June 1919, box 2M12, Pennybacker Papers.

118. "Democratic Leaders Call Party to Colors; Palmer is Optimistic," *Chicago Herald Examiner,* May 30, 1919, 4.

119. Anna J. H. Pennybacker, "A Historical Event," 3.

120. "The Woman's Department," 30 May 1919, clipping from unidentified newspaper, box 2M87, Pennybacker Papers.

121. Ibid.

122. Ibid.

123. Pennybacker to Bass, 9 March 1918, box 2M87, Pennybacker Papers.

124. Pennybacker to Bass, 1918, box 2M87, Pennybacker Papers.

125. Bass to Pennybacker, 24 June 1918, box 2M87, Pennybacker Papers.

126. Antoinette Funk to Mrs. F. T. Blesh, 26 June 1919, box 2M87, Pennybacker Papers.

127. Anna J. H. Pennybacker to Antoinette Funk, 26 June 1919, box 2M87, Pennybacker Papers.

128. Anna J. H. Pennybacker to Rose Young, 18 August 1919, box 2M12, Pennybacker Papers.

129. Cunningham to Pennybacker, 18 January 1918.

130. McArthur and Smith, *Minnie Fisher Cunningham,* 75.

131. Ibid.

132. Gammage, "Quest for Equality," 82.

133. Anna J. H. Pennybacker to Mrs. Ellis Meredith, 11 April 1919, box 2M12, Pennybacker Papers.

134. Ibid.

135. Pennybacker, "An Interview."

136. Ibid.

137. Gammage, "Quest for Equality," 87–88.

138. Anna J. H. Pennybacker to Margery Shuler, 6 September 1918, box 2M12, Pennybacker Papers.

139. Carrie Chapman Catt to Anna J. H. Pennybacker, 25 August 1919, box 2M12, Pennybacker Papers.

140. Pennybacker to Carrie Chapman Catt and Mrs. Frank Shuler, 10 November 1919, box 2M12, Pennybacker Papers.

141. McArthur and Smith, *Minnie Fisher Cunningham,* 86.

142. Carrie Chapman Catt to Dear Friends, "Press Release, of the National American Woman Suffrage Association, Press Department, Rose Young, Chairman," 14 November 1918, box 2M12, Pennybacker Papers.

143. Anna J. H. Pennybacker to President Woodrow Wilson, 19 November 1918, box 2M12, Pennybacker Papers.

144. "Sees Third Run for Wilson if League Fails," *New York Times*, May 28, 1919, 1.

145. "Ratify the Treaty, Say 250 Leaders In American Life," *New York Times*, September 15, 1919, 1.

146. W. R. Boyd Jr. to Anna J. H. Pennybacker, 19 September 1918, box 2M11, Pennybacker Papers.

147. Wendy B. Sharer, *Vote and Voice: Women's Organizations and Political Literacy, 1915–1930* (Carbondale: Southern Illinois University, 2004), 95.

148. Anna J. H. Pennybacker to Carrie Chapman Catt, 7 July 1919, box 2M12, Pennybacker Papers.

149. Carrie Chapman Catt to Anna J. H. Pennybacker, 12 May 1919, box 2M12, Pennybacker Papers.

150. Ibid.

151. Catt to Anna J. H. Pennybacker, 12 May 1919.

152. [Carrie Chapman Catt] to Anna J. H. Pennybacker, 29 April 1919, box 2M12, Pennybacker Papers.

153. Gertrude F. Brown to Anna J. H. Pennybacker, 5 August 1919, box 2M12, Pennybacker Papers.

154. Gertrude F. Brown to Anna J. H. Pennybacker, 1 July 1919, box 2M87, Pennybacker Papers.

155. Anna J. H. Pennybacker to Mrs. C. V. Williams, 14 November 1919, box 2M87, Pennybacker Papers.

156. Anna J. Hardwicke Pennybacker to Florence Kelley, 31 January 1920, box 2M12, Pennybacker Papers.

157. "Minutes of Meeting of Temporary Committee for Consideration of a Plan of Organization of a National Cooperative Committee on Legislation for the Welfare of Women and Children, at the Congress Hotel, Chicago," 12 February 1920, box 2M12, Pennybacker Papers.

158. "Summary of Pennybacker's Activities for January and February 1920," box 2L512, Pennybacker Papers.

159. Wenona Osbourn Pinkham to Anna J. H. Pennybacker, 26 February 1920, box 2L531, Pennybacker Papers.

160. Anna J. Hardwicke Pennybacker to Maude Wood Park, 1 March 1920, box 2M12, Pennybacker Papers.

161. Edna Fischel Gelhorn to Anna J. H. Pennybacker, 27 May 1920, box 2M87, Pennybacker Papers.

162. Anna J. Hardwicke Pennybacker to S. P. Brooks, 10 May 1920, box 2L531, Pennybacker Papers.

163. Hancock, "Society Suffragists: Women's Struggle for the Ballot in Rural East Texas," 30.

CHAPTER 7

1. Michael E. McGerr, *A Fierce Discontent: The Rise and Fall of the Progressive Movement in America* (New York: Free Press, 2003), 304–5.

2. Maureen A. Flangan, *America Reformed: Progressives and Progressivisms 1890s–1920s* (New York: Oxford University Press, 2007), 237.

3. Ibid., 240.

4. Ibid., 261. See also McGerr, *A Fierce Discontent*, 279–313.

5. Anna J. H. Pennybacker to Julia Gould Sibert, 31 January 1920, box 2L512, Pennybacker Papers.

6. "Honor the Memory of Col. Roosevelt; Leaders in All Walks of Life among the 2,000 at the Meeting in Carnegie Hall," *New York Times,* January 6, 1920, 13.

7. Ibid.

8. Ibid.

9. "Manning Assails American 'Reds,'" *New York Times,* January 5, 1920, 10.

10. "Dinner to Become Presidency Forum," *New York Times,* January 7, 1920, 1.

11. Thomas A. Bailey, "Woodrow Wilson Wouldn't Yield," *American Heritage Magazine,* 8, no. 4 (1957).

12. "Summary of Pennybacker's Activities for January and February 1921," [1920], box 2L512, Pennybacker Papers.

13. Anna J. H. Pennybacker to Mrs. George Gelhorn, 12 March 1920, box 2L531, Pennybacker Papers.

14. Richmond, *A Woman of Texas,* 240.

15. Anna J. H. Pennybacker to My Dear Officer, 4 October 1920, box 2L496, Pennybacker Papers.

16. Ibid.

17. Ibid.

18. Pennybacker charged a $100 fee for speaking and put the money toward the $750 she pledged to help the GFWC purchase its headquarters in Washington, D.C. Anna J. H. Pennybacker to Mrs. Maurice A. Quinn, 23 November 1920, box 2L496, Pennybacker Papers.

19. Unidentified newspaper clipping from Sioux Falls, South Dakota, 23 February 1921, Pennybacker Papers; Mrs. George C. Boyd to Anna J. H. Pennybacker, 23 February 1921, box 2L496, Pennybacker Papers.

20. Kristi Andersen, *Women in Partisan and Electoral Politics before the New Deal,* American Politics and Political Economy, ed. Benjamin I. Page (Chicago: University of Chicago Press, 1996), 27; Sharer, *Vote and Voice,* 17.

21. Anna J. H. Pennybacker to Mrs. John Henry Hammonds, 15 March 1920, box 2L531, Pennybacker Papers.

22. Richmond, *A Woman of Texas,* 241.

23. Sharer, *Vote and Voice,* 131.

24. Pennybacker to Catt, 17 March 1920, box 2L531, Pennybacker Papers; Pennybacker to Mrs. Emmet Finley, 29 July 1921, box 2L533, Pennybacker Papers.

25. Anna J. H. Pennybacker to Miss Willie Abbey, 29 July 1920, box 2L531, Pennybacker Papers.

26. Pennybacker to Mrs. George Gelhorn, 12 March 1920, box 2L531, Pennybacker Papers.

27. Richmond, *A Woman of Texas,* 234.

28. Pennybacker to Mrs. George Gelhorn, 12 March 1920.

29. Richmond, *A Woman of Texas,* 230.

30. Pennybacker to Mrs. Emmet Finley, 29 July 1921.

31. Andersen, *Women in Partisan and Electoral Politics,* 33–34; Sharer, *Vote and Voice.*

32. Katherine Ludington to Anna J. H. Pennybacker, 2 May 1921, box 2L533, Pennybacker Papers.

33. Andersen, *Women in Partisan and Electoral Politics,* 38.

34. Ibid., 37.

35. Ibid., 46.

36. Anna J. H. Pennybacker to Rose Young, 23 March 1920, box 2L531, Pennybacker Papers.

37. Anna J. H. Pennybacker to Louise Wallace Hackery, 3 December 1923, box 2L500, Pennybacker Papers.

38. General Federation of Women's Clubs, *Departments of Work* (Washington, D.C.: General Federation of Women's Clubs, 1922).

39. Anna J. H. Pennybacker to Mrs. Read, 11 July 1922, box 2L498, Pennybacker Papers.

40. Ibid.

41. Lydia Hafford to Mrs. Frank Gibson, 1 April 1921, box 4L296, Pennybacker Papers.

42. General Federation of Women's Clubs, *Departments of Work* (Washington, D.C.: General Federation of Women's Clubs, 1920).

43. Lydia Hafford to Miss Josie Golden, 28 July 1921, box 4L296, Pennybacker Papers.

44. Anna J. H. Pennybacker to presidents of all colleges and universities in Texas, 1 December 1920, box 2L496, Pennybacker Papers.

45. Mrs. D. H. Foresman, "Department of American Citizenship," with letter of 30 October 1922, box 2L498, Pennybacker Papers.

46. Nancy F. Cott, *The Grounding of Modern Feminism* (New Haven: Yale University Press, 1987), 102–5.

47. Anna J. H. Pennybacker, untitled draft of speech proposing a celebration for young men casting their first vote, 1906, Pennybacker Papers.

48. Ibid.

49. General Federation of Women's Clubs, *Departments of Work* (Washington, D.C.: General Federation of Women's Clubs, 1920).

50. General Federation of Women's Clubs, *Citizenship Day Program,* (Washington, D.C.: General Federation of Women's Clubs, 1920–22), 2–3.

51. Anna J. Hardwicke Pennybacker to Anna Steese Richardson, 29 April 1921, box 4L296, Pennybacker Papers.

52. Pennybacker to Richardson, 10 February 1922, box 2L497, Pennybacker Papers.

53. "Favors Citizenship Day," *New York Times,* February 25, 1922, 24.

54. Ibid.

55. Anna J. Hardwicke Pennybacker to Mrs. Thomas G. Winter, 18 January 1922, box 2L497, Pennybacker Papers.

56. Anna J. H. Pennybacker to Mrs. Adelaide P. Smith, 7 June 1923, box 2L500, Pennybacker Papers.

57. Anna J. H. Pennybacker to Mrs. F. J. Macnish, 7 February 1923, box 2L497, Pennybacker Papers.

58. Richmond, *A Woman of Texas,* 244.

59. General Federation of Women's Clubs, *Americanization Programs: Suggestions for Working Methods* (Division on Americanization, General Federation of Women's Clubs, 1919–1920): 3.

60. General Federation of Women's Clubs, *Americans All* (Division on Americanization, General Federation of Women's Clubs, 1922–1924).

61. McGerr, *A Fierce Discontent,* 279–313.

62. Gayle Gullett, "Women Progressives and the Politics of Americanization in California, 1915–1920," *Pacific Historical Review* 64, no. 1 (1995): 74–75. See also the discussion of Jane Addams's conception of the subjective necessity and Lillian Wald's ideal of settlements as "mutual learning" in Flanagan, *America Reformed,* 35–39, and Kathryn Kish Sklar, *Florence Kelley and the Nation's Work: The Rise of Women's Political Culture, 1830–1900* (New Haven: Yale University Press, 1995).

63. Gullett, "Women Progressives," 74–75.

64. Franklin K. Lane, quoted in General Federation of Women's Clubs, *Americanization Programs.*

65. Ibid., 3; Gullett, "Women Progressives," 87.

66. General Federation of Women's Clubs, *Americans All.*

67. General Federation of Women's Clubs, *Americans All,* 4.

68. General Federation of Women's Clubs, *Americans All;* General Federation of Women's Clubs, *Ninety Days of Opportunity* (Division on Americanization, General Federation of Women's Clubs, 1922–1924).

69. Mrs. E. B. Page to Anna J. H. Pennybacker, 15 April 1923, box 2L500, Pennybacker Papers.

70. Unidentified newspaper clipping from Sioux Falls, South Dakota, 23 February 1921, box 2L496, Pennybacker Papers.

71. For critiques of clubwomen's Americanization efforts, see Gullett, "Women Progressives."

72. Anna J. H. Pennybacker to Garland Powell, 31 May 1923, box 2L500, Pennybacker Papers.

73. [Mrs. George W. Plummer?], *Bulletin 4,* (Chicago: Department of American Citizenship, General Federation of Women's Clubs, 1923).

74. Mrs. M. L. Carpenter, "General Federation of Women's Clubs Committee on Friendly Co-operation with Ex-Service Men Plan of Work," 1922, box 2L497, Pennybacker Papers.

75. McGerr, *A Fierce Discontent,* 298; David A. Moss, *Socializing Security: Progressive Era Economists and the Origins of American Social Policy* (Cambridge, Mass.: Harvard University Press, 1995), 158.

76. [Mrs. George W. Plummer?], *Bulletin 10,* (Chicago: Committee for Friendly Cooperation with the Ex-Service Man, General Federation of Women's Clubs, 1923).

77. Mrs. Plummer to Anna J. H. Pennybacker, 2 June 1923, box 2L500, Pennybacker Papers.

78. Frank E. Robbins to Anna J. H. Pennybacker, 2 March 1922, box 2L497, Pennybacker Papers.

79. Anna J. H. Pennybacker to Senator Morris Sheppard, 17 April 1922, box 2L498, Pennybacker Papers; Anna J. H. Pennybacker to Senator Charles A. Culberson, 17 April 1922, box 2L498, Pennybacker Papers.

80. [Mrs. Woodallen Chapman?], "Committee on Motion Pictures," [March 1921], box 2L496, Pennybacker Papers.

81. John Whiteclay Chambers II, *The Tyranny of Change: America in the Progressive Era, 1900–1917* (New York: St. Martins Press), 1980, 95–99; McGerr, *A Fierce Discontent,* 270–71.

82. Katherine Scott Finn to Anna J. H. Pennybacker, 18 May 1922, box 2L498, Pennybacker Papers.

83. Ibid.

84. Anna J. H. Pennybacker to Mrs. Woodallen Chapman, 2 December 1921, box 2L497, Pennybacker Papers.

85. Anna J. H. Pennybacker to L. K. Lewis, 5 April 1922, box 2L497, Pennybacker Papers.

86. Will Hays, Address before the General Federation of Women's Clubs, Chautauqua, New York, box 2L498, Pennybacker Papers.

87. General Federation of Women's Clubs, Departments of Work.

88. Marie E. Finnegan to Anna J. H. Pennybacker, 1923, box 2L500, Pennybacker Papers.

89. Pennybacker to Finnegan, 16 August 1923, box 2L500, Pennybacker Papers.

90. H. E. Hollister to Anna J. H. Pennybacker, 9 August 1923, box 2L498, Pennybacker Papers.

91. Woodallen Chapman to Anna J. H. Pennybacker, 22 August 1922, box 2L498, Pennybacker Papers.

92. General Federation of Women's Clubs, Departments of Work.

93. Ibid.

94. Chapman to Anna J. H. Pennybacker, 22 August 1922.

CHAPTER 8

1. George W. Wickersham to Anna J. H. Pennybacker, 23 May 1922, box 2M11, Pennybacker Papers.

2. Rev. Alfred Williams Anthony to Anna J. H. Pennybacker, 6 May 1920, box 2L531, Pennybacker Papers; E. Dana Calkins to Pennybacker, 9 May 1922, box 2L513, Pennybacker Papers.

3. "Urges One Budget for Jewish Funds," *New York Times,* May 14, 1923, 18.

4. Anna J. H. Pennybacker to Carl Kelsey, 13 January 1921, box 2L533, Pennybacker Papers.

5. [Mrs. Quentin Quinn?] to Anna J. H. Pennybacker, 14 July 1922, box 2L513, Pennybacker Papers.

6. Richmond, *A Woman of Texas.*

7. Ibid.

8. Anna J. H. Pennybacker to Laura Wendt, 1 December 1925, box 2M15, Pennybacker Papers; Anna J. H. Pennybacker to Mrs. Wallis Tenner, 1 December 1925, box 2M15, Pennybacker Papers.

9. Anna J. H. Pennybacker to James B. Buchanan, 4 December 1920, box 2L496, Pennybacker Papers; Anna J. H. Pennybacker to Mrs. Henry Redmond, 20 February 1920, box 2L496, Pennybacker Papers.

10. Pennybacker to Mrs. Redmond, 20 February 1920.

11. [Decca Lamar West], "Campaign Committee for Mrs. Florence C. Floore," 1921, box 2L497, Pennybacker Papers.

12. Florence C. Floore to W. P. Hobby, 31 December 1920, box 2L496, Pennybacker Papers.

13. Ibid.

14. Lily Joseph to Mrs. E. D. Criddle, 10 May 1922, box 2L498, Pennybacker Papers.

15. Richmond, *A Woman of Texas,* 236.

16. Ibid., 236

17. Anna J. H. Pennybacker to Senator Wit, Representative Davis, and Dr. C. W. Smith, 5 March 1921, box 4L296, Pennybacker Papers.

18. Anna J. H. Pennybacker to James B. Buchanan, 4 December 1920; John A. Chappell, "The Whole is Greater than the Sum of Its Parts—At Least, Now It Can Be—Accomplishments of Disability Activists," *American Rehabilitation* (1994).

19. Molly Ladd-Taylor, "Sheppard-Towner Maternity and Infancy Protection Act," in *Reader's Companion to Women's History,* ed. Wilma Mankiller et. al. (Boston: Houghton Mifflin, 1998).

20. For a discussion of how support for the Sheppard-Towner bill was used to portray progressive women as covert socialists, see Cott, *Grounding of Modern Feminism,* 249–50.

21. Alice Ames Winter to Anna J. H. Pennybacker, 20 February 1922, box 2L497, Pennybacker Papers; Lida Hafford to Anna J. H. Pennybacker, 28 March 1922, box 2L497, Pennybacker Papers.

22. Pennybacker to Winter, 28 March 1925, box 2L497, Pennybacker Papers.

23. "Appoints Sponsors for Near East Work," *New York Times,* October 23, 1922, 12; Charles Vickrey to Anna J. H. Pennybacker, 16 February 1923, box 2M10, Pennybacker Papers.

24. "1,500 Eat 4-Cent Meals," *New York Times,* September 26, 1924, 21.

25. Florence Spencer Duryea to Anna J. H. Pennybacker, 3 January 1923, box 2M10, Pennybacker Papers.

26. Lillian M. Ascough to Anna J. H. Pennybacker, April 1923, box 2M10, Pennybacker Papers.

27. Charles Vickrey to Anna J. H. Pennybacker, 6 November 1923, box 2M10, Pennybacker Papers.

28. Vickrey to Pennybacker, 14 March 1924, box 2M10, Pennybacker Papers.

29. Jeannette Emrich to Carrie Chapman Catt, 10 January 1924, box 2M10, Pennybacker Papers.

30. Florence Spencer Duryea to Anna J. H. Pennybacker, 3 January 1923.

31. Duryea to Pennybacker, 2 January 1924, box 2L501, Pennybacker Papers.

32. Anna J. H. Pennybacker to Carrie Chapman Catt, 18 May 1928, box 2M13, Pennybacker Papers.

33. Ibid.; Rose Young, *The Record of the Leslie Woman Suffrage Commission, Inc. 1917–1929* (New York: Leslie Woman Suffrage Commission, 1929).

34. Cott, *Grounding of Modern Feminism,* 247.

35. Ibid., 248.

36. Ibid., 242.

37. R. M. Whitney, *Reds in America* (New York: Beckwith Press, 1924), 188; for a discussion of Whitney's ties to the FBI, see Regin Schmidt, *Red Scare: FBI and the Origins of Anti-Communism in the United States, 1919–1943* (Copenhagen: Museum Tusculanum Press, 2000), 103. For Catt's views on Whitney's book and the connection to Pennybacker, see Carrie Chapman Catt to Alice Ames Winter, 13 May 1926, box 2M11, Pennybacker Papers.

38. Cott, *Grounding of Modern Feminism,* 249.

39. Ibid., 255–56.

40. Irma Backer to Anna J. H. Pennybacker, 18 February 1925, box 2M10, Pennybacker Papers.

41. Anna J. H. Pennybacker, "Report of Mrs. Percy V. Pennybacker on Citizenship, to the National Council of Women," 1925, box 2M10, Pennybacker Papers.

42. Ibid.

43. Harland H. Lund to Anna J. H. Pennybacker, 4 April 1924, box 2M11, Pennybacker Papers.

44. Anna J. H. Pennybacker to Clara Guthrie D'Arcis, 5 May 1925.

45. Ibid.

46. Cott, *Grounding of Modern Feminism,* 256.

47. Ibid., 257.

48. Anna J. H. Pennybacker to Edward M. House, 25 May 1925, box 2M10, Pennybacker Papers.

49. Alice Lakey to Anna J. H. Pennybacker, 9 April 1925, box 2M10, Pennybacker Papers.

50. Anna J. H. Pennybacker to Lord and Lady Aberdeen, 30 December 1925, box 2M10, Pennybacker Papers.

51. Eva Perry Moore to Anna J. H. Pennybacker, 25 August 1925, box 2M10, Pennybacker Papers.

52. "Many Republicans Stand for League," *New York Times,* December 16, 1922, 10.

53. Anna J. H. Pennybacker to Sara Robinson, 7 February 1924, box 2M11, Pennybacker Papers.

54. Anna J. H. Pennybacker to Mrs. John B. Pratt, 28 March 1924, box 2L501, Pennybacker Papers.

55. Carrie Chapman Catt to Mrs. Thomas Winter, 8 May 1924, box 2M11, Pennybacker Papers.

56. Anna J. H. Pennybacker to My Dear Friends, 26 September 1924, box 2M11, Pennybacker Papers.

57. Anna J. H. Pennybacker to Frau Ender, 29 January 1926, box 2M10, Pennybacker Papers; Anna J. H. Pennybacker to Mrs. W. H. Alexander, 26 August 1925, box 2M10, Pennybacker Papers.

58. Anna J. H. Pennybacker to Arthur Sweetser, 1 July [1925], box 2M10, Pennybacker Papers.

59. Anna J. H. Pennybacker to Clara Bryant Heywood, 26 August 1925, box 2M15, Pennybacker Papers.

60. Virginia Roderick to Anna J. H. Pennybacker, 7 April 1926, box 2L511, Pennybacker Papers; Arthur Bestor, "Address" (paper presented at a tribute to Mrs. Percy V. Pennybacker, Chautauqua, New York, 1939).

61. Anna J. H. Pennybacker to May E. Spillar, 28 April 1924, box 2M11, Pennybacker Papers; Spillar to Pennybacker, 19 April 1921, box 2L511, Pennybacker Papers.

62. Blanche Weisen Cook, *Eleanor Roosevelt: Volume 2, The Defining Years, 1933–1938* (New York: Penguin Books, 2000).

63. Eleanor Roosevelt to Anna J. H. Pennybacker, 2 April 1927, box 2M13, Pennybacker Papers.

64. Eleanor Roosevelt to Pennybacker, 23 March 1928, box 2M13, Pennybacker Papers.

65. Pennybacker to Eleanor Roosevelt, 26 November 1928, box 2M13, Pennybacker Papers.

66. Eleanor Roosevelt to Pennybacker, 23 March 1928.

67. Anna J. H. Pennybacker to Mr. Chas. Bauer, 25 January 1930, box 2M11, Pennybacker Papers.

68. Anna J. H. Pennybacker to Eleanor Roosevelt, 22 February 1930, box 2M13, Pennybacker Papers; Pennybacker to Eleanor Roosevelt (second letter of this date), 22 February 1930, box 2M13, Pennybacker Papers.

69. Eleanor Roosevelt to Pennybacker, 18 March 1930, box 2M13, Pennybacker Papers.

70. Anna J. H. Pennybacker, "Introduction of Eleanor Roosevelt at Sam Houston State Teachers College," [1931], box 2M13, Pennybacker Papers.

71. "The Chautauqua Woman's Club is Entertained by Mrs. Franklin D. Roosevelt," *Chautauquan Weekly,* January 29, 1931.

72. Pennybacker to Eleanor Roosevelt, 22 January 1931, box 2M13, Pennybacker Papers.

73. Pennybacker to Eleanor Roosevelt, 11 January 1932, box 2M13, Pennybacker Papers.

74. Pennybacker to Eleanor Roosevelt (second letter of this date), 11 January 1932, box 2M13, Pennybacker Papers.

75. Pennybacker to Eleanor Roosevelt (third letter of this date), 11 January 1932, box 2M13, Pennybacker Papers.

76. Eleanor Roosevelt to Pennybacker, 5 April 1932, box 2M13, Pennybacker Papers.

77. Pennybacker to Eleanor Roosevelt, 28 January 1933, box 2M13, Pennybacker Papers.

78. Pennybacker to Eleanor Roosevelt, 11 January 1932, box 2M13, Pennybacker Papers.

79. Pennybacker to Eleanor Roosevelt, 29 August 1934, box 2M13, Pennybacker Papers.

80. Pennybacker to Eleanor Roosevelt (second letter of this date), 29 August 1934, box 2M13, Pennybacker Papers.

81. Eleanor Roosevelt to Pennybacker, 7 July 1936, box 2M13, Pennybacker Papers.

82. Pennybacker to Eleanor Roosevelt, 22 December 1936, box 2M13, Pennybacker Papers.

83. Anna J. H. Pennybacker to Belle Sherman, 2 March 1930, box 2M13, Pennybacker Papers.

84. Clipping from the *Bryan Eagle,* 11 January 1932, TFWC scrapbook, box 3L420, Pennybacker Papers.

85. Mollie Connor Cook, "Mrs. Pennybacker Honored on 70th Anniversary," May 1931, photocopy of an article from *Texas Federation News,* President's Papers, Women's History and Research Collection, GFWC, 4.

86. Ibid., 4.

87. J. C. Nagle, "An Appreciation of One of the 'First Citizens' of Texas, Mrs. Percy V. Pennybacker," photocopy in President's Papers, Women's History and Research Collection, GFWC.

88. Cook, " Mrs. Pennybacker Honored on 70th Anniversary."

89. Ibid., 4.

90. Ibid., 5.

91. Clipping from *Dallas Morning News,* 13 November 1935, TFWC scrapbook, box 3L420, Pennybacker Papers.

92. Alice Ames Winter, "A Gallant Leader Passes," May 1938, photocopy in President's Papers, Women's History and Research Collection, GFWC; [Pennybacker dies], 5 February 1938, clipping from the *Star-Telegraph* in bio file, TFWC Papers.

93. "Mrs. Pennybacker, Club Leader Dead," *New York Times,* February 5, 1928, 15.

94. Arthur Bestor, "Address," paper presented at a tribute to Mrs. Percy V. Pennybacker, Chautauqua, New York, 1939.

EPILOGUE

1. Norman K. Denzin, *Interpretive Biography,* Sage University Paper Series on Qualitative Research Methods (Beverly Hills: Sage Publications, 1989), 61.

2. Richmond, *A Woman of Texas,* 320.

3. Barbara Finkelstein, "Revealing Human Agency: The Uses of Biography," in *Writing Educational Biography: Explorations in Qualitative Research,* ed. Craig Alan Kridel (New York: Garland Publishing, 1988), 46.

4. Patricia Carter, *Everybody's Paid but the Teacher: The Teaching Profession and the Women's Movement* (New York: Columbia University Press, 2002).

5. John Dewey, *Democracy and Education* (Mineola, N.Y: Dover Publications, 2004).

6. Christine A. Ogren, *The American State Normal School: An Instrument of Great Good* (New York: Palgrave Macmillan, 2005); Carter, *Everybody's Paid but the Teacher.*

7. Richmond, *A Woman of* Texas, 236.

8. Jackie M. Bount, "Turning out the Ladies: Elected Women Superintendents and the Push for the Appointive System, 1900–1935," in *Sacred Dreams: Women and the Superintendency,* ed. C. Chryss Brunner (Albany: SUNY Press, 1999), 9–28.

9. Grace Julian Clarke to Mrs. Otto Jay Deeds, 23 November 1913, box 2L482, Pennybacker Papers.

10. Carter, *Everybody's Paid but the Teacher.*

11. Nancy F. Cott, *The Grounding of Modern Feminism* (New Haven: Yale University Press, 1987), 102–5. Cott notes that male participation was similarly low.

12. Gullett, "Women Progressives and the Politics of Americanization," 90.

13. Kim Tolley, *The Science Education of American Girls: A Historical Perspective* (New York: RutledgeFalmer, 2003).

14. Gullet, "Women Progressives and the Politics of Americanization."

15. Maureen A. Flanagan, *America Reformed: Progressivism, 1890s–1920s* (New York: Oxford University Press, 2007), vii.

16. Michael E. McGerr, *A Fierce Discontent: The Rise and Fall of the Progressive Movement in America* (New York: Free Press, 2003), xv.

17. Flanagan, *America Reformed,* 285.

18. Sylvia Hunt, "'Throw Aside the Veil of Helplessness': A Southern Feminist at the 1893 World's Fair," *Southwestern Historical Quarterly* 99 (1996): 61.

19. Knox, *Mrs. Percy V. Pennybacker,* 77.

20. Margaret Smith Crocco and O. L. Davis Jr., eds., *Bending the Future to Their Will: Civic Women, Social Education, and Democracy* (Lanham, Md.: Rowman and Littlefield, 1999).

21. Andrea Makler, "Courage, Conviction, and Social Education," in *Bending the Future to Their Will: Civic Women, Social Education, and Democracy,* ed. Margaret Smith Crocco and O. L. Davis Jr. (Lanham, Md.: Rowman and Littlefield, 1999), 253–76.

22. Richmond, *A Woman of Texas,* 315.

BIBLIOGRAPHY

ARCHIVES

Eugene C. Barker Collection. Center for American History, University of Texas at Austin.

Mrs. Percy V. Pennybacker Papers, 1878–1938. Center for American History, University of Texas at Austin.

Presidents Papers. Women's History and Research Collection. General Federation of Women's Clubs, Washington, D.C.

Texas Federation of Women's Clubs Papers. The Woman's Collection, Texas Woman's University.

United Confederate Veterans Texas Division Archive, 1862–1944, 1888–1917. Center for American History, University of Texas at Austin.

University of Texas President's Office Records. Center for American History, University of Texas at Austin.

BOOKS, ARTICLES, AND ELECTRONIC SOURCES

Andersen, Kristi. *Women in Partisan and Electoral Politics before the New Deal.* American Politics and Political Economy, ed. B. I. Page. Chicago and London: University of Chicago Press, 1996.

Baby Saving Campaigns. Washington, D.C.: U. S. Department of Labor, Children's Bureau, 1913.

Bailey, Fred A. "Free Speech and the 'Lost Cause' in Texas: A Study of Social Control in the New South," *Southwestern Historical Quarterly* 97, no. 3 (1994): 452–77.

Bailey, Thomas A. "Woodrow Wilson Wouldn't Yield," *American Heritage Magazine* 8, no. 4 (1957).

The Baptist Encyclopaedia: A Dictionary of the Doctrines, Ordinances, Usages, Confessions of Faith, Sufferings, Labors, and Successes and the General History of the Baptist Denomination in All Lands. ed. W. Cathcart. Philadelphia: Louis H. Everts, 1883.

Barker, Eugene C., Charles S. Potts, and Charles W. Ramsdell. *A School History of Texas.* Chicago: Row, Peterson, & Company, 1912.

The Battle Lost—And Won, Texas State Library & Archives Commission, November 2, 2005. Available from http://www.tsl.state.tx.us/exhibits/suffrage/victory/page1.html.

Blair, Karen J. *The Clubwoman as Feminist.* New York: Holmes and Meier, 1980.

Blount, Jackie M. "Turning Out the Ladies: Elected Women Superintendents and the Push for the Appointive System, 1900–1935," in *Sacred Dreams: Women and the Superintendency,* edited by C. Cryss Brunner. Albany: SUNY Press, 1999, 9–28.

Boswell, Angela. "Indispensable Spinsters: Maiden Aunts in the Elite Families of Savannah and Charleston." In *Negotiating Boundaries of Southern Womanhood: Dealing with the Powers that Be,* edited by J. L. Coryell. Columbia, MO: University of Missouri Press, 2000.

Carlisle, J. M., W. S. Sutton, T. J. Witt, E. F. Comegys, J. E. Rogers, and C. A. Bryant. *Memorial Presented to the House of Representatives, Twenty-first Legislature, by the Executive Committee of the Texas State Teachers' Association.* Texas State Teachers' Association, 1888–89.

Carter, Patricia A. *Everybody's Paid but the Teacher: The Teaching Profession and the Women's Movement.* New York: Columbia University Press, 2002.

Catt, Carrie Chapman, and Nettie Rogers Schuler, *Woman Suffrage and Politics: The Inner Story of the Suffrage Movement.* Seattle: University of Washington Press, 1926.

Chambers, John Whiteclay, II. *The Tyranny of Change: America in the Progressive Era, 1900–1917.* New York: St. Martins Press, 1980.

Chappell, John A. "The Whole is Greater than the Sum of Its Parts—At Least, Now It Can Be—Accomplishments of Disability Activists," *American Rehabilitation,* (1994).

Christian, Stella L. *The History of the Texas Federation of Women's Clubs.* Houston, TX: Dealy-Ady-Elgin Co., copyrighted by the Texas Federation of Women's Clubs, 1919.

Cook, Blanche Weisen. *Eleanor Roosevelt: Volume 2, The Defining Years, 1933–1938.* New York: Penguin Books, 2000.

Cott, Nancy F. *The Grounding of Modern Feminism.* New Haven: Yale University Press, 1987.

Cowles, Ione V. H. *Program of Work of the Peace Committee of the GFWC.* General Federation of Women's Clubs, 1914–1916.

Cremin, Lawrence. *American Education: The Metropolitan Experience, 1876–1980,* Vol. 2. New York: Harper & Row, 1988.

Crocco, Margaret Smith, and O. L. Davis Jr., eds. *Bending the Future to their Will: Civic Women, Social Education, and Democracy.* Lanham, Md.: Rowman and Littlefield, 1999.

Cuban, Larry. *How Teachers Taught: Constancy and Change in American Classrooms 1880–1990.* New York: Teachers College Press, 1993.

Curtis, Robert I. "Confederate Classical Textbooks: A Lost Cause?" *International Journal of the Classical Tradition,* 3, no. 4 (1997): 433–68.

Denzin, Norman K., and Yvonna S. Lincoln, eds. *Handbook of Qualitative Research.* Thousand Oaks: Sage Publications, 2000.

Dewey, John. *Democracy and Education.* Minneola, N.Y: Dover Publications, 2004.

Eby, Frederick. *The Development of Education in Texas.* New York: MacMillan, 1925.

Finkelstein, Barbara. *Governing the Young: Teacher Behavior in Popular Primary Schools in Nineteenth-Century United States.* New York: Falmer Press, 1989.

———. "Revealing Human Agency: The Uses of Biography." In *Writing Educational Biography: Explorations in Qualitative Research,* edited by Craig Alan Kridel, 45–60. New York: Garland Publishing, 1988.

Flanagan, Maureen A. *America Reformed: Progressives and Progressivisms 1890s-1920s.* New York: Oxford University Press, 2007.

Flexnor, Eleanor. *Century of Struggle: The Woman's Rights Movement in the United States.* New York: Atheneum, 1970.

Gould, Lewis L. *Progressives and Prohibitionists. Texas Democrats in the Wilson Era.* Austin: University of Texas Press, 1973.

Graham, Sara Hunter. *Woman Suffrage and the New Democracy.* New Haven: Yale University Press, 1996.

Graves, John. "The Old Guard: Dobie, Webb, and Bedicheck." In *The Texas Literary Tradition: Fiction, Folklore, History,* edited by Don Graham, James W. Lee, and William T. Pilkington, 16–25. Austin: College of Liberal Arts, University of Texas at Austin and The Texas State Historical Association, 1983.

Green, Elna C. *Southern Strategies: Southern Women and the Woman Suffrage Question.* Chapel Hill: University of North Carolina Press, 1997.

Gubrium Jaber F., and James A. Holstein. "Analyzing Interpretive Practice." In *Handbook of Qualitative Research,* edited by N. K. Denzin and Y. S. Lincoln, 487–508. Thousand Oaks: Sage Publications, 2000.

Gullett, Gayle. "Women Progressives and the Politics of Americanization in California, 1915–1920," *Pacific Historical Review* 64, no. 1 (1995).

Harlan, Judith. *Feminism: A Reference Handbook.* Contemporary World Issues. Santa Barbara: ABC-CLIO, 1998.

Harsanger, Sandra. *Organized Womanhood: Cultural Politics in the Pacific Northwest, 1840–1920.* Norman: University of Oklahoma Press, 1997.

Hoffman, Nancy. *Woman's "True" Profession: Voices from the History of Teaching.* New York: Feminist Press and McGraw Hill, 1981.

Houde, Mary Jean. *Reaching Out: A Story of the General Federation of Women's Clubs.* Chicago: Mobium Press, 1989.

Humphrey, Janet G. *A Texas Suffragist. Diaries and Writings of Jane Y. McCallum.* Austin: Ellen C. Temple, 1988.

Hunt, Sylvia. "'Throw Aside the Veil of Helplessness': A Southern Feminist at the 1893 World's Fair." *Southwestern Historical Quarterly* 99 (1996): 48–62.

Hurlbut, Jesse Lyman. *The Story of Chautauqua.* New York: G. P. Putnam and Sons, 1921.

Janney, Caroline E. "To Honor Her Noble Sons. The Ladies Memorial Association of Petersburg, 1866–1912." In *Virginia's Civil War,* edited by P. Wallenstein and B. Wyatt-Brown, 256–69. Charlottesville: University of Virginia Press, 2005.

Keefe, M. H. L., ed. *Thirteenth Biennial Convention.* New York: General Federation of Women's Clubs, 1916.

Kerber, Linda K. *Toward an Intellectual History of Women.* Chapel Hill: University of North Carolina Press, 1997.

Knupfer, Ann Mies. "If You Can't Push, Pull; If You Can't Pull, Please Get Out of the Way: The Phyllis Wheatley Club and Home in Chicago, 1896 to 1920." *Journal of Negro History* 82, no. 2 (1997): 221–31.

Ladd-Taylor, Molly. "Sheppard-Towner Maternity and Infancy Protection Act." In *Reader's Companion to Women's History,* edited by Wilma Mankiller, et al. Boston: Houghton Mifflin, 1998.

Ley, Mary, and Mike Bryan, eds. *Journey from Ignorant Ridge: Stories and Pictures of Texas Schools in the 1800s.* Austin: Texas Congress of Parents and Teachers, 1976.

Leslie Woman Suffrage Commission. *Minutes of the Meeting of the Annual Meeting of the Members of the Leslie Woman Suffrage Commission, Inc.* New York: Leslie Woman Suffrage Commission, 1917.

———. *Minutes of the Meeting of the Executive Committee of the Leslie Woman Suffrage Commission, Inc., April 23, 1917.* New York: Leslie Woman Suffrage Commission, 1917.

Kingseed, Cole C. *The American Civil War.* Greenwood Guides to Historic Events 1500–1900, ed. L. S. Frey and M. L. Frey. Westport, Ct.: Greenwood Press, 2004.

Knox, Helen. *Mrs. Percy V. Pennybacker: An Appreciation.* New York: Fleming H. Revell, 1916.

Kooken, John. "Unanimously Elected." In *Journey from Ignorant Ridge: Stories and Pictures of Texas Schools in the 1800s,* edited by M. Ley and M. Bryan, 115–19. Austin: Texas Congress of Parents and Teachers, 1976.

Kridel, Craig Alan, ed. *Writing Educational Biography: Explorations in Qualitative Research.* New York: Garland Publishing, 1988.

Makler, Andrea. "Courage, Conviction, and Social Education." In *Bending the Future to their Will: Civic Women, Social Education, and Democracy,* edited by Margaret Smith Crocco and O. L. Davis Jr., 253–76. Lanham, Md.: Rowman and Littlefield, 1999.

McArthur, Judith N. *Creating the New Woman: The Rise of Southern Women's Progressive Culture in Texas, 1893–1918.* Urbana: University of Illinois Press, 1998.
McArthur Judith N., and Harold L. Smith, *Minnie Fisher Cunningham: A Suffragist's Life in Politics.* New York: Oxford University Press, 2003.
McElhaney, Jacquelyn M. *Pauline Periwinkle and Progressive Reform in Dallas.* College Station: Texas A& M University Press, 1998.
McGerr, Michael E. *A Fierce Discontent: The Rise and Fall of the Progressive Movement in America.* New York: Free Press, 2003.
Moss, David A. *Socializing Security: Progressive Era Economists and the Origins of American Social Policy.* Cambridge, Mass.: Harvard University Press, 1995.
Myers, Miles. *Changing Our Minds: Negotiating English and Literacy.* Urbana, Ill.: National Council of Teachers of English, 1996.
Nation-Wide Baby Week, March 4–11, 1916. Washington, D.C.: U.S. Department of Labor, Children's Bureau, 1916.
Newman, Louise Michelle. *White Women's Rights: The Racial Origins of Feminism in the United States.* New York: Oxford University Press, 1999.
Nielsen, Kim E. *Un-American Womanhood. Antiradicalism, Antifeminism, and the First Red Scare.* Columbus: Ohio State University Press, 2001.
Ogren, Christine A. *The American State Normal School: An Instrument of Great Good.* New York: Palgrave Macmillan, 2005.
Olesen, Virginia L. "Feminisms and Qualititative Research at and into the Millennium." In *Handbook of Qualitative Research,* edited by N. K. Denzin and Y. S. Lincoln, 215–56. Thousand Oaks: Sage Publications, 2000.
Ownby, Ted. *Subduing Satan: Religion, Recreation and Manhood in the Rural South, 1865–1920.* Chapel Hill: University of North Carolina Press, 1990.
Pennybacker, Anna J. Hardwicke. *A History of Texas Revised.* Austin, Tex.: Mrs. Percy V. Pennybacker, 1908.
———. *A New History of Texas for Schools.* Tyler, Tex.: Mr. and Mrs. Percy V. Pennybacker, 1888.
———. *A New History of Texas for Schools.* Austin, Tex.: Mrs. Percy V. Pennybacker, 1900.
———. "President's Greeting." In *Year Book of the Texas Federation of Women's Clubs1902–1903,* 8–9.
Pennybacker, Percy V. "The Text-book Question." Paper presented at the Texas State Superintendents Association, Galveston, June 24, 1890.
Powers, Jane Bernard. *The Girl Question in Education: Vocational Education for Young Women in the Progressive Era.* Studies in Curriculum History, ed. I. Goodson. London: Falmer Press, 1992.
Richmond, Rebecca. *A Woman of Texas: Mrs. Percy V. Pennybacker.* San Antonio: Naylor, 1941.
Robertson, James I. *Civil War Virginia: Battleground for a Nation.* Charlottesville: University Press of Virginia, 1991.

Ryan, Barbara. *The Women's Movement: References and Resources.* Reference Publications on American Social Movements, edited by I.T. Sander. New York: G. K. Hall, 1996.

Schmidt, Regin. *Red Scare: FBI and the Origins of Anti-Communism in the United States, 1919–1943.* Copenhagen: Museum Tusculanum Press, 2000.

Schneider Dorothy, and Carl J. Schneider, *American Women in the Progressive Era, 1900–1920.* New York: Facts on File, 1993.

Schwandt, Thomas A. *Dictionary of Qualitative Inquiry,* 2nd ed. Thousand Oaks: Sage Publications, 2001.

———. "Three Epistemological Stances for Qualitative Inquiry: Interpretivism, Hermeneutics, and Social Constructionism." In *Handbook of Qualitative Research,* edited by N. K. Denzin and Y. S. Lincoln. Thousand Oaks: Sage Publications, 2000.

Scott, John C. "The Chautauqua Movement: Revolution in Popular Higher Education." *Journal of Higher Education* 70, no. 4 (1999): 389–412.

Sharer, Wendy B. *Vote and Voice: Women's Organizations and Political Literacy, 1915–1930.* Carbondale: Southern Illinois University Press, 2004.

Sklar, Kathryn Kish. *Florence Kelley and the Nation's Work: The Rise of Women's Political Culture, 1830–1900.* New Haven: Yale University Press, 1995.

Spearman, Mindy. "Everything to Help, Nothing to Hinder: The Story of the Texas School Journal." Paper presented at the Texas Midwest History of Education Society Annual Conference, Chicago, Illinois, 2006.

Texas Federation of Women's Clubs. *1901–1902 Year Book of the Texas Federation of Women's Clubs.* 1901–1902.

Texas State Senate. An Act to Create a State Text-Book Board. Twenty-fifth Legislature, 258.

Tolley, Kim. *The Science Education of American Girls: A Historical Perspective.* New York: RutledgeFalmer, 2003.

Tyler, R., ed. *Handbook of Texas Online* ed. R. Tyler. Austin: Texas State Historical Association. 1999.

Ulrich, Laurel Thatcher, *Well-Behaved Women Seldom Make History.* New York: Random House, 2007.

United Daughters of the Confederacy J. E. B. Stuart Chapter. *War Days in Fayetteville, North Carolina: Reminiscences of 1861 to 1865.* Judge Printing Company, March 28, 2005. Available from "Documenting the American South," University Library, University of North Carolina, http://docsouth.unc.edu/fpn/chapter/chapter.html.

Wagner-Martin, Linda. *Telling Women's Lives.* New Brunswick, N.J.: Rutgers University Press, 1994.

Welch, June. *The Colleges of Texas.* Dallas: GLA Press, 1981.

Wheeler, Marjorie Spruill. *New Women of the New South: The Leaders of the Woman Suffrage Movement in the Southern States.* New York: Oxford University Press, 1993.

Whitney, R. M. *Reds in America.* New York: Beckwith Press, 1924.

Wood, Mary I. *The History of the General Federation of Women's Clubs for the First Twenty-Two Years of its Organization.* New York: History Department, General Federation of Women's Clubs, 1912.

Young, Rose. *The Record of the Leslie Woman Suffrage Commission, Inc. 1917–1929.* New York: Leslie Woman Suffrage Commission, 1929.

THESES AND DISSERTATIONS

Bohan, Chara Haeussler. "Go to the Sources: Lucy Maynard Salmon and the Teaching of History." PhD diss., University of Texas, Austin, 1999.

Buchholz, Corinna A. "The Ruffin Incident and Other Integration Battles in Women's Clubs, 1890–1902." Master's thesis, Women's History, Sarah Lawrence College, 2000.

Gammage, Judie "Quest for Equality: An Historical Overview of Women's Rights Activism in Texas, 1890–1975." North Texas State University, 1982.

Goethe, George Arthur. "A Brief History of Textbook Laws in Texas." Master's thesis, University of Texas, 1952.

Hancock, Jennifer Baugh. "Society Suffragists: Women's Struggle for the Ballot in Rural East Texas." Master's thesis, Stephen F. Austin University, 1999.

Jurgensmeyer, John C. "The Evolution of a Southern Lady: The Role of Anna J. Hardwicke Pennybacker in the Woman's Suffrage Movement, 1912–1920." Master's thesis, Baylor University, 2002.

Spearman, Mindy. "The Peripatetic Normal School." PhD diss., University of Texas, Austin, 2006.

INDEX

Note: The initials AP indicate Anna Pennybacker; PVP indicate Percy Pennybacker.

ISBN-13: 978-1-60344-185-8
ISBN-10: 1-60344-185-9

53995

9 781603 441858